Cover Photos

Group photo: Standing (l to r): Antonnette Haughton, author, Abijah, Alicia Roskind, Julia Roskind, Red, Panner, Errol Chambers, Bell, Scram. Sitting (l to r): Hyacinth Morgan, Denroy Morgan, Mortimo Planno, Luciano, unknown.

Single photo: Luciano, Antonnette Haughton and Red, Denroy Morgan, Abijah.

Reviews from readers of our accompanying book

Rasta Heart: A Journey Into One Love

"I finished your book about two weeks ago and it is so hard to put into words how it has changed me. I have been waiting my whole life to read these words. It is like I knew all the things about the food and God but when I read the book it made those concepts the truth. It was like I had found my tribe. Love, **Tamara**"

"I would like to express gratitude to you for writing such a beautiful book. The book was written with Love and is about Love. The book has touched me in many ways. To you and the God inside you that connects us all in love, I give thanks. **Robert Meyerhoff**"

"As I keep close tabs on the events of this world, my heart sometimes grows too heavy to even carry with the weight of the sadness the human race fills me with. But you, Robert, and your family and your associates blow a gentle wind on the flame of my soul and help its fire glow bright again. It gives me hope that my time here on this planet can at least in some small measure or even for some short time coincide with an evolutionary step towards a higher plane by and for all humans. Peace, brother, One Love, **Steve Gilberto**"

"I'd like to thank you for writing *Rasta Heart*. I'm 15 now and I used to be violent and have a short temper but with your book I've changed my life. I cut out all violence from my life and changed my ways and reached a higher high for my spirit. I have also been doing good deeds for people and showing love to every one. Thank you, one love, **Chris**"

"Visiting a friend of mine last week, he insisted that I borrow and read your book. I loved your book. Your narrative is heartfelt and heartical. I am the consultant to the original House of Blues (Cambridge, MA) 'Reggae Greats' series, now about to begin our sixth year. You are to be congratulated. **Kevin J. Aylmer**, Jamaica Plain, MA"

"It was truly inspiring! I read your speech at the **Gathering of the Healers**. Reading the speech gave me total inspiration. I give thanks that there is an alignment of spirit power in the universe. I publish a small reggae magazine called Reggae Runnins. Peace and love, **Polly Riddims**"

"Thanks for the update. Enjoyed the book very much. Actually read it twice and will probably read it again! Your doing some very nice work here! Respect, **Joe Bonomi**"

"I was sent a copy of your reasoning at **The Gathering of Healers.** Thank you for what you said and what you are doing. We only need to begin the healing process and move forward in Love. Peace and One Love, **Asher**"

"Hi, I keep reading of the righteous moves you are doing and I had to send respect from Australia. I grew up in Jamaica and am an artist in the Australian outback now. However the bonfires around Jamaica caught my soul and I just had to make contact to send my support. Keep up the movement. One Love, **Glenn Woodley**"

"I just wanted to say thank you for your book, ***Rasta Heart***. I just finished your book, (about to read it again!) and it reminded me so much of my own journeys in Jamaica. I think it also served to calm me and get me back on track. One Love, **Goldilocks**"

"I am 1/2 way through ***Rasta Heart*** and loving it. It is incredibly informative and insightful. It really inspires some deep thought and soul searching. I can't wait to finish it but at the same time I will be sad to turn the last page. Thanks, **Bree**"

"I sent one of the books to someone on the Negril.com website who visits Negril often. He was going thru a divorce and dealing with a strange blood disease. He read the book and said I was an Angel to send it to him. I knew I made the right move. Much peace to you and your family. **Susan**"

―――――――――――

"Your book has lead me to experience the beginnings of hope that there is in fact one love and that maybe my sacrifice has been more self inflicted. I am so amazed by this Rasta way, this spirituality. It is very much inside of me. And so I want to continue this education of their ways. One Love, **Jessamyn**"

―――――――――――

"I have been affected by your book and the message that the elders in Jamaica are saying and you are saying and publishing. You have got it right teaching all people about One Love. I am seeing a surge from youths who are my peers. I am 25 years of age. Many people in this generation are about love and dealing with love towards all people and it's beautiful and warms my heart just thinking of it. I am hopeful for the future that JAH will cause the world to dwell in peace and love. Many thanks. **Ras Joshua Jeresek**"

―――――――――――

"I purchased your *Rasta Heart* book shortly before I went to Jamaica and began reading it there. I've enjoyed reading it so very, very much!!! Thank you for your inspiration into the heart of becoming Rasta! **Phyllis, (AKA Reggae Girl)**"

―――――――――――

"Greetings. I'm a 17 year-old boy from Portugal (yes, you have reached Portugal) and let me tell you that I have the uttermost respect for you and your work. I really enjoy your book *Rasta Heart*. It has given me strength for the low tides. **Carlos Netto**"

―――――――――――――――――――――

"Greetings, and thanks for sending me, *Rasta Heart*. It's too good to put down, one of the most informative books about Rasta I have read so far. And thanks for all your work. One love, **Lioness**"

The Gathering of the Healers:
The Healing of the Nation

by

Robert A. Roskind

One Love Press
P.O. Box 2142
Blowing Rock, North Carolina 28605
(828) 295-4610 Fax: (828) 295-6901
e-mail: onelovepress@hotmail.com
Website: www.onelovepress.com

Sweet Peace to You Both, One Love, Julia

Other Books By Robert Roskind

In This Rasta Series

Rasta Heart: A Journey Into One Love

The Fires of Forgiveness: The Healing of the Nations

Books on Unconditional Love

Memoirs of an Ex-Hippie: Seven Years in the Counterculture

In the Spirit of Marriage

In the Spirit of Business

How-To Books

Building Your Own House

Before You Build

The Complete Disaster Home Preparation Guide

View at: www.onelovepress.com

I-dication

This book is I-dicated to the Jamaican healers everywhere and especially to the seven teachers of love who joined with my family at The Bob Marley Museum in Kingston, Jamaica on February 4, 2002 to send out a vibration of One Love to the world:

Abijah
Thomas Anderson (Scram)
Dr. Dennis Forsythe
Antonnette Haughton
Luciano
Denroy Morgan
Mortimo Planno

Acknowledgements

To my wife, **Julia**, for her love, support, help and humor—always;

To my daughter, **Alicia**, who grew into every
situation she encountered;

To my editor, **Jeannie Parker**, who always understood exactly where
I was going and helped me get there;

To **JD Dooley**, for a great layout and an easy-going disposition;

To **Trevor Grouch**, for the wonderful photos of the conference:

To **Jonathan Gullery**, for yet another beautiful cover;

And to everyone in the book who shared this journey with me.

Artists we suggest listening to while reading this book

(as their message is the same as ours):

Morgan Heritage	Beres Hammond
Luciano	Tony Rebel
Abijah	Kymani Marley
Bushman	Burning Spear
Don Carlos	Marcia Griffiths

"Peace between countries must rest on the solid foundation of love between individuals."

—Mahatma Gandhi

Chapter 1
December 21, 2001

We Return

This book is the second in a series written about a spiritual journey that my family began in October 2000. At that time, we went on a family vacation to Jamaica that turned out to be much more. Our first book, *Rasta Heart: A Journey Into One Love*, chronicles the events that occurred over a 10 month period (October 2000 to July 2001) when I, often along with my wife, Julia, and daughters, Alicia and Julie, took several trips to Jamaica to meet with the elder Rastas, the few that really knew and taught One Love, unconditional love for all. That book, along with chronicling our journey, also offers information regarding the history and way of life of the Rastafarians, the life story of Bob Marley, the history of slavery in Jamaica.

This book takes up our journey from where *Rasta Heart* left off. However, more importantly, where *Rasta Heart* is a guide book for exercising One Love in our personal relationships, this book, and the one I am soon to begin, *The Fires of Forgiveness: The Healing of the Nations*, are guides for exercising this love on a national and societal level. I had no idea that this would be the way these books would evolve but looking back it is clear to me that a Higher Power planned it that

1

Gathering of the Healers

way.

On December 21, 2001, I returned to Jamaica to introduce and promote *Rasta Heart* and begin this book. My plan was to do a media launch of *Rasta Heart* in Jamaica during Bob Marley's birthday week beginning February 6. More importantly, while Julia and I were working on *Rasta Heart*, we decided during the launch we would invite all Jamaicans to join us in making One Love and Bob's songs real. We would do this by encouraging everyone to forgive, as much as they were able, anyone they were holding bitterly in their hearts. Our vision is to see if Jamaica can be the first society in history to heal itself with love. It is this message I was hoping the Jamaican press would carry forward for us. After all, billboards all over the island featured a large picture of Bob Marley with the message, "One Love-Jamaica's Message to the World," so why not make it real? As with all my trips to the island, this one turned out to be like nothing I had imagined.

I arrived in Montego Bay mid-day with Alicia, then fourteen. I planned to stay on the island for two months, until mid-February, and Alicia was going to stay over the Christmas break and then return again for the book launch in February with Julia. Julia remained behind in our home in Blowing Rock, North Carolina, a small village in the Blue Ridge Mountains. She had just returned from Jamaica three months earlier after spending three weeks living in a tent in the remote Blue Mountains near Moore Town. This small village is the ancestral home of the Windward Maroons, the descendents of escaped slaves who fled to the area in the 1600s and 1700s. After 80 years of unsuccessful warfare, the English gave the Maroons their freedom in 1738, one hundred years before the island's general emancipation.

While working on *Rasta Heart*, Julia had an inspiration to build geodesic domes out of bamboo and thatch to demonstrate inexpensive, organic and life-nurturing structures and her goal was to build one in Moore Town. While there, Julia had "gone native"—working the land, eating the local produce, drinking the sweet water from the springs. For years she had longed to live simply as millions of indigenous people do all over the world. She had loved it. Taking nothing for distraction but a CD player, she had planted gardens, built paths and steps, cooked over

Gathering of the Healers

an open fire and interacted with the locals, most of whom were amazed to see a white woman on her own far away from the tourist areas. Unfortunately, the heavy rains of the fall and the events around 9/11 cut her planned four month trip short.

Alicia had also been profoundly and positively changed by her trips to the island. They had broken the spell created by the American media. Our visits and contacts with the Rastas and other Jamaicans had showed her a much deeper side of life. Already mature beyond her years, Jamaica had called to her and she had answered.

For Julia and I, our changes had also been profound and welcome. Becoming vegetarians after our encounter with Bongo Roach, a Rasta featured in *Rasta Heart*, we had both lost considerable weight and were feeling physically much better and more energetic. My blood pressure, high for decades, was almost normal, and my other minor body problems had cleared up. Also, we were taking long hikes daily in the mountains near our home, finding exercising in nature a great improvement over exercising indoors. Living on the oldest mountain on the planet, Grandfather Mountain, we were spending more time in JAH's world (JAH is the Rasta name for God taken from Psalm 68) world and less time in man-made and machine-made environments.

Most importantly, all of us were becoming increasingly aware that our lives had taken on a new direction. A subtle, yet powerful, undercurrent was now guiding us, complete with many frequent and seemingly inexplicable coincidences ("JAH-incidences" as Julia came to call them). These seemingly random yet magical events happen in everyone lives, like when you think of someone and they call or when a "minor" incident leads to a major life change. However, as we walked more knowingly on the "Beauty Path," as a Cherokee Indian chief once called it, the number and power of these JAH-incidences greatly increased.

After clearing customs, Ralph from Chalis Car Rentals picked Alicia and I up at the airport. We had met Ralph and his wife Andrene on our earlier trips and always rented from them because of their open hearts and reasonable prices. In Jamaica, even the car rental people become friends. We packed up our car and headed toward Port Antonio, our "Jamaican home." Our five-hour drive along the coast went quickly, as

3

Gathering of the Healers

we listened to reggae artists Luciano, Bob Marley, Morgan Heritage and Bushman along the way. Alicia loved coming back and staying at her favorite hotel, the San San Tropez, where she was close friends with the owners and always made new friends with the guests.

Shortly before dark we drove through Port Maria, a small coastal village along our route. It was the Friday before Christmas and the traditional market day so it was bumper-to-bumper traffic and we had slowed to a crawl. Soon our car was surrounded by people. It was a typical Jamaican village scene—people everywhere were laughing, shopping, singing, jiving with each other, sometimes arguing (a favorite Jamaican pastime). The work week was over, the Christmas holidays were beginning and it was time to party (*the* favorite Jamaican pastime). Sidewalk stalls were selling everything from jerk chicken to Christmas gifts. As I looked over at Alicia, tears had welled up in her eyes.

"What's the matter, sweetheart?" I asked, wondering if she was scared.

"I just love it, Dad," she said holding back her sobs and looking at the animated crowd. "It so easy for people to be together here. This is how I want to live."

We arrived in Port Antonio and stopped to see Scram (his birth name is Thomas Anderson), our Rasta friend featured in *Rasta Heart*. Like most of the Rastas in the book he was low on the economic ladder, even by Jamaican standards, but high on the spiritual ladder. He had been a Rasta for over 30 years. He earned money by cleaning the marketplace every night from midnight to dawn for US $10 per day. He also had a small shop where he sold a few staples and lived upstairs. He had lived in the area all his life and had gone from being another youth in the community to be scorned and rejected as a young Rasta and now, finally, somewhat respected as a Rasta and a man. He greeted us in the front yard of his small shop with big hugs and laughter. Irman, his thirty-something son, and Scram's friend, Bell, were also there and gave us equally enthusiastic welcomes. We were all glad to be back together. Having anticipated our arrival, Scram had prepared an Ital meal of vegetable stew and fresh-squeezed sorreal juice made from a plant native to Jamaica that only blooms around Christmas.

4

Gathering of the Healers

I had been looking forward to showing everyone *Rasta Heart*. Scram was the main character in the book and Irman and Bell were also included. We had just gotten our copies from the printer a month earlier and I was excited about giving them theirs. I handed them their books and was surprised when they told me they had already seen it.

It seems Glen Gilpin, a Jamaican living in Brooklyn, had showed Scram his copy a few weeks earlier. How Glen got one of our first copies was another one of our many JAH-incidences. The previous June we had met a Maroon, Bookson, who told us he would be in New York in a month to play drums at an African Festival, on a weekend we planned to be in New York. We made plans to meet Bookson, thinking it was ironic to meet him first in the mountains of Jamaica and then a month later amid the mountains of New York City.

Glen was the African Festival organizer and the contact person in New York. When we arrived, we called Glen only to find out that Bookson wasn't coming. However, Glen came over to our hotel and we became instant friends. Before Alicia and I returned to Jamaica, I had sent Glen one of the first copies of *Rasta Heart*. After receiving it, he flew to Jamaica arriving a week before us, found Scram and showed him the book.

After our welcome back dinner with Scram, Irman and Bell, Alicia and I headed over to the San San Tropez, a quaint seven-room hotel in nearby San San Beach. The hotel is run by two Italians, Nino and Fabio, and features one of the best Italian restaurants on the island. It has a warm, family-like atmosphere and you instantly feel right at home with the staff and guests, all who congregate in the restaurant, poolside or on the patio. Often there are more locals there than tourists. Staying there is truly a "Jamaican experience."

Many musicians stay at the San San Tropez because it is near Geejam Studios, a small recording studio built by Jon Baker, an entrepreneur from England. There are often jam sessions by the pool with some pretty talented musicians. Everyone there was glad to see us and we instantly felt like we had never left.

"We plan to introduce *Rasta Heart* during Bob Marley's birthday week in February," I told Fabio, as we all sat by the pool catching up on

5

Gathering of the Healers

each other's lives, "In fact, before I left the U.S., I sent Peter Shukkat several copies of the book to give to Bob Marley's children. Peter is the Marley family lawyer in New York and a good friend of my cousin Bobby. I especially wanted Kymani Marley to get a copy because I think he really carries the spirit of his father's message."

"Kymani will be staying here next week," Fabio said, "so you can give him a book yourself."

"No way!" Alicia said in disbelief.

"I'm not kidding," Fabio said equally amazed. "There's this band staying here, Adelante. Kymani is singing some songs on their new CD. And he's coming here to record at Geejam Studios next door to us."

Before coming, I had decided while I was on the island planning the book launch I would start my next book, this book, about the "ridge Rastas." These were Rastas I had heard about who are living along the mountain ridges from one end of the island to the other. Unlike the "waterfront Rastas," they have little to no contact with "Babylon." Babylon is the Rasta term for the commercialized world of government, business, and bureaucracies— a world they believe leads people astray and takes them away from God. Many ridge Rastas were supposedly living a very Ital life (the Rasta word for organic, ethical living). Many were eating nothing but organic fruits and vegetables, living very close to nature, praising God and sending out One Love vibrations to the planet. They live alone, in families or in small groups often centered around an elder.

I figured in the six weeks between when Alicia left and the launch of *Rasta Heart* during Bob Marley's birthday week, I would see if my Rasta friends throughout the island would take me to meet some of these people. However, not wanting to leave Alicia too much on her own, I decided that for the next 10 days I would just vacation with her and stay around Port Antonio.

The days drifted by at a leisurely pace. Scram and I would go around and visit some of the other people featured in *Rasta Heart* to give them

Gathering of the Healers

their copies. We gave several copies to the local libraries and town leaders like the police chief, mayor, head of the tourist board and hotel owners to let them know that the book was out and that hopefully it would benefit the area. We also gave copies to many interested individuals throughout the community, knowing that the US$15 cover price would be all but impossible for most rural Jamaicans.

During the week, I would go over to Scram's small shop and hang out with him and Bell, sometimes reading out loud to them from the book. That week I was asked to speak to a gathering of local college kids as well as the hotel association, where Scram joined me in talking to the local hotel owners. I knew for Scram this was a big lift. He had lived in or around Port Antonio all his life. Like most Rastas, in his younger days he had been scorned and harassed by everyone from the locals to the police. For eight years he stayed aloof, wearing only a turban and shorts, doing whatever he could to feed and clothe his wife and children (now all in the States). Many people had thought he was crazy and steered a wide path around him.

Alicia soon made a new friend at the San San. Kim, a thirty-something computer programmer from Minneapolis, became her constant companion. Also she had become friends with the members Adelante. Adelante was the brainstorm of Mikele Vicino, a well-known Italian singer, songwriter and producer, who we had met the summer before when he was staying at the hotel. His concept for Adelante was to blend reggae and Latin music so he assembled a group of musicians from Jamaica, Italy and Latin America to come together and cut a CD. The group includes: Kymani Marley; Italians, Alberto D'ascola, Alessandro, and Miguel El Flaco; New Yorker Tkae Mendez; Karu Ramirez and Carlos Bess from the Dominican Republic and Farenheit from Jamaica.

They had been on the island for several months creating songs and were staying at the hotel. I gave everyone in the band a book and left one for Kymani, who was soon to arrive.

The week went by slowly, gently. Christmas eve Alicia and I took Scram and his granddaughter from New Jersey out to eat at a local restaurant and invited Irman, Kim and Bell to join us. It meant a lot to Scram and we had a good time, except for a few minutes when Alicia,

Gathering of the Healers

not knowing that Jamaican hot sauce is *really* hot, sprinkled too much on her food and it set her mouth on fire and brought her to tears.

I had expected Christmas eve to be a quiet family-oriented night. Not in Jamaica! Downtown Port Antonio was packed with thousands of people. In rural Jamaica, Christmas eve and night and New Year's eve are community, almost tribal, holidays. Everyone gathers in the town square, dances, sings, cooks jerk chicken, gossips, and just enjoys the camaraderie of long-standing friends, relatives, and neighbors.

I have found Jamaicans to be amazing people. Quick to anger but quicker yet to forgive and laugh, they are hard-working, helpful, humorous, volatile, intelligent, informed and relaxed within themselves and their environment. Though a small minority can be sullen, cantankerous and confrontational, the average Jamaican is so open-hearted that you feel you have made an immediate close friend.

Jamaica is an island of extremes and bold contrasts. Jamaicans are proud, passionate people who believe there is no greater place on earth than Jamaica and no finer people anywhere. They love their country but for the most part are extremely frustrated with its political and business institutions and its decades-long slide downward, as they have every right to be.

When we asked many Jamaicans we met living in the small towns and the countryside how they liked their lives, their immediate and enthusiastic response was usually, "I love it, mon! I love it!" Those who have chosen not to frustrate themselves always wanting more money have relaxed into a peaceful life—full of lifelong friends and adventures in a tropical paradise. After all, what can be sweeter than watching the sunset from a cliff overlooking the ocean or by a pristine waterfall with people you enjoy? Many Jamaicans do this everyday. Many tourists pay thousands of dollars to do this one week a year.

However, I do not wish to give the impression that all Jamaicans have been able to rise above grinding poverty and enjoy their lives. Gandhi once said, "Poverty is the worst form of violence." *The Jamaica Observer* reported in August 2002 that "500,000 Jamaicans (one out of five) are living with mental and behavioral disorders...that contributed to mortality directly by suicide, as well through abuse, violence and its influence on the development of many chronic diseases...41 percent of the men and 52 percent of the women reported feeling depressed." Though many Jamaicans have made healthy mental and emotional adjustments to their poverty, it is a daily struggle for others.

Jamaica, with its African heritage, is still very much a tribal culture. Often in the cities, villages and countryside people still live in "yards," a collection of small homes built around a common yard often including a "yard pot" for communal cooking.

Everything about their culture (at least away from Kingston) draws them together, just as everything about modern city life draws us apart. With few TVs, movie theatres, air conditioners, large homes, money to shop, or individually-owned cars, the average Jamaican spends much of their time relating with friends, neighbors and relatives, often outside in nature—a world where everything is free. In more affluent countries we are spending more and more of our time in front of TV sets or computers, in our cars or shopping and less and less time with each other. Many people in the First World are spending most of their lives in man-made environments and are seldom out in nature except to walk from the driveway to the house. Something is lost from our lives when we are always surrounded by sheetrock, metal, glass and carpeting.

Outside of the few unban areas, the country is set up for people with little money. Unlike the U.S., you don't really need a car to get around. To get a ride, just step out on the road and put your hand out and for a small price you quickly get picked up by a legal or maverick taxi or a public bus. The taxis and buses are packed with people, giving everyone a chance to share stories and information. Julia used this system during her three week stay in Moore Town. Catching a taxi on the dirt road near her tent spot, she would squeeze in on top of someone's lap, often to find as many 12 children and adults stuffed into a hot Toyota sedan station wagon. The conversations were many, loud and animated, often punctuated by the soft chirps of baby chicks being transported to market. As are many things in Jamaica, the public transportation system is chaotic, functional, colorful, and often illegal.

If it starts to rain, you just pick a huge leaf from a thatch palm to use as an umbrella. If you're hungry, organic fruits are dripping off the trees.

Gathering of the Healers

Instead of fast-food restaurants, there are thousands of small shops selling bananas, breadfruit, pineapples, peanuts, star fruit, mangoes, watermelon, and coconuts ("jellies" as they are called)—all cheap and healthy. Every shop has its own social sphere, almost like someone's living room.

There are no set prices at this level of "informal commerce," which represents approximately 30 to 40 percent of the Jamaican economy. People everywhere, even small children, are involved in the gathering, selling, buying and bartering of everything from fruits and vegetables to shoes and sunglasses. It's a common sight to see someone walking or riding a bike with a string of freshly-caught fish for sale. Everything is open to bargaining ("higgling"), which most Jamaicans do vigorously. To the outsider it almost looks like angry yelling but to them it is only the normal process of negotiating.

Even housing in the country is set up for the poor. All over the island, citizens "squat" on government, and occasionally private, land. People everywhere build their homes on this "captured" land, often being able to purchase it from the government for a small price. Squatter communities exist all over Jamaica, reminding everyone that the government only has limited control of its citizens.

The *Jamaica Observer* reported in February, 2002 that former housing minister, Easton Douglas, believed that "some 600,000 or a quarter of the island's population are squatters." The *Jamaica Gleaner* uses a conservative estimate of 500,000, which does not include inner-city squatters and the homeless who live in the streets and bushes. When these are included, the proportion of squatters and homeless could be in the region of one third of the nation's population! The government is trying to turn the tide on illegal squatting. In August, 2002, Water and Housing Minister Donald Buchanan condemned squatting and said the full weight of the law would be brought to bear on anyone caught engaged in the practice.

In the slums of Kingston thousands of people live along the "gully banks," with no garbage collection, no water, no sanitary convenience, no waste disposal except the gully courses from where it is washed to the sea. Sections of Montego Bay and Ocho Rios are no better. Some

Gathering of the Healers

slum dwellers who have light or water do not pay for those commodities as rate collectors are afraid to go in their areas. Though these slums are breeding grounds for crime, the majority of slum dwellers are not violent people but, like poor people everywhere, are often politically voiceless.

Given that so few Jamaicans were raised in traditional families but rather often reared by neighbors, relatives, aunties, and grandparents, in many ways it is a nation of orphans—still seeking the love an attention they never received as children. They talk loudly, forcefully and always over each other, each person wanting to be heard. However, in many ways, especially in the countryside and smaller towns and villages, you feel you are in one huge, crazy, dysfunctional—but basically loving—extended family. In a poor country people are always needing help, which tends to keep their hearts open to each other. In affluent countries, people are more and more independent and know and care little about the needs of their neighbors or even family and friends.

After our Christmas dinner, Scram, Alicia and I sat out by the pool at the San San and chatted. Scram started talking about his childhood in Bellvue, a small village in the Blue Mountains. Scram was born there in 1944 when the village of 3,000 had no roads, electricity, phones, radios or TVs. He had to walk three miles to the road to catch a bus to Port Antonio. Over the last year he had told me many stories about his early life in Bellevue and I always loved to hear them.

It had been a very happy childhood. He was raised by his mother along with several siblings. He never really knew his father who moved away when Scram was an infant. The villagers were self-sustaining. They grew their own food, built their own houses, created their own entertainment and took care of each other like tribal villages everywhere. Though everyone was poor financially, it was an incredibly wholesome and nurturing environment.

"When de radio came," Scram said, "when I was still a young child,

11

Gathering of the Healers

it was not so bad. But when de TV came everyt'ing started to go down-hill, especially now becuz dey put t'ings on de TV dat we did not even know about. We never saw dese t'ings. We may hear about it but when we hear about it you hear like it is a million miles away. De kids dey see all dese t'ings an' it 'as a corruptin' influence on dem. Like it is a devil. An' when Rasta say, 'Away wit' all dese t'ings!' dey want to fight back. Dey want to class Rastafari as de lowest but de lowest is de ground an' de ground is de foundation," he said and we both busted out laughing.

Like most Jamaicans, English is Scram's second language. Most Jamaicans speak patois (PA-twah) which is a type of Creole English with Spanish, Portuguese, African and Rastafarian terms mixed in to create a musical, lyrical dialect that sounds like a "child's ball gently bouncing down the stairs." When speaking either language, Jamaicans speak loudly and emphatically, often taking soft-spoken foreigners by surprise. When English is spoken, the "h" is usually dropped ("his" becomes "'is," "those" becomes "dos," "that" becomes "dat," etc.) and patois syntax is peppered in ("What is this road?" becomes "What road dis?").

"But I would 'ave to speak of myself most time," Scram continued, "becuz dere are still many tall hair people (people with dreadlocks) who know de beauty of Rastafari an' still doan't 'ave de heart. It is a small group dat is livin' dis righteous livity in movement wit' de people, wit' de masses. Dey are earth wide. But we 'ave a shield. When we say 'JAH Rastafari, de Almighty!' it 'as a lot of power." ("Livity" is the Rasta word for the fullness of life—joy created by being in tune with the Creator and nature.)

"What is the function of these small groups?" I asked.

"You are a part of one of dos small groups. Dat is your administra-tion. Dat's de work dat you an' Miss Julia are doing since you started it. You's a true leader fe dis administration an' you are supposed to prevail an' go ahead wit' dis t'ing fe life. It's simple like dat," he said, laughing loudly and slapping his palm in mine.

"And where do you think our administration is going?" I asked.

"Well, now. I t'ink dat it is 'eading to de four corners of de earth an' dat all de people cayn realize what dis true love means to your neigh-

Gathering of the Healers

bor, de next mon over dere. You wake up in de mornin' an' you know what time he gonna wake an' you call an' you doan't see 'im, so you give 'im a buzz to find out if he woke up. You pass it on just like dat an' you find just a strange livity rise up in de atmosphere an' dere is a healing of de mind of de people," he said, touching his fingertips to his temple.

"And what do you see happening when this change starts to come about?" I asked.

"When it reach to de masses, you're gonna find dat de whole earth change, mon, becuz dat is de clothes dat de earth want to wear," he said and cracked up laughing. "Forever. Care about each ot'er."

"You think we're going to hit that point soon?" I asked.

"Yeah. Yeah, mon. We 'it dat point. We 'it dat point from de day de Berlin Wall fell. It is comin' true."

"So what your saying," I said, "is that the Berlin Wall was the symbolic end of communism, even though it took several more years for that to be obvious. And Julia and I have been thinking that the collapse of the World Trade Centers, the symbol of world capitalism, represents the beginning of the end of capitalism as we know it, even though it may not be obvious for some time. Communism was built on the idea that the individual had to work entirely for the state, for the whole. It fell because it crushed individual incentive. There was no personal motivation built into the system. Capitalism may fall because it is *mostly* personal incentive, which can turn into greed. There is little working toward the whole society built into the system. It is this part of capitalism, this exploitation of the masses, that may cause us to redesign the system as well."

"When a person say 'love' and when de hear de 'eads of government call to dis One Love now," Scram said, "we goin' get evert'ing under one shield. An' den we're not goin' to fight again one to anot'er any more. I want to see dat point an' dat point got to come up. An' it was said from de beginning, it comin' under a God power. An' I hear Bush and Blair start to talk about dis love. An we 'ave to get de rest of de guys to change up an' to let us live like bredren an' sistren an den we cayn know what love is."

13

"If ya gwanna win de revolution, you must win it with Rasta (One Love). Ya caynnot win no o'ter way. Becuz if ya win anot'er way, ya gwan fight again. When ya Rasta, dere's no more war."
—Bob Marley

Chapter 2
January 1, 2002

A New Year

The rest of the week went by quickly. On New Year's morning, Alicia and I headed out to Montego Bay to catch her flight home. Alicia slept a good part of the trip. She had been up most of the night celebrating the New Year with Kim and her friends in Adelante. They had started at a restaurant overlooking the famous Blue Lagoon, a beautiful, jade lagoon over 200 feet deep and about a 100 yards across, surrounded by lush jungle vegetation. After that, everyone in her group went into downtown to celebrate with the locals at The Roc, a small private night club that had just opened overlooking the town square.

Like almost every holiday in Jamaica, New Year's eve is celebrated rather uniquely. Most Jamaicans believe it is important where you are when the clock strikes twelve on New Year's eve—that it in some way affects your year. So almost everyone is in church at that time (Jamaica is over 90 percent Christian with the highest number of churches per capita in the world and the highest number of bars). Minutes after midnight, church doors are thrown open and everyone pours out and an islandwide party begins and continues full force until dawn. In Port Antonio, thousands of people flood into the downtown square where a stage is built and local reggae, gospel, rap and other artists perform until daylight. The locals talk, laugh, drink, smoke ganja (marijuana), eat,

14

Gathering of the Healers

dance and otherwise have a great time, as Alicia did. Not much for loud parties, I sat by the pool enjoying the solitude and contemplating the weeks ahead.

As we approached Mobay Alicia woke up and we started talking about the last ten days. Once again her trip had been moving and if she could have stayed another month, maybe forever, she would have. Like her previous trips, she had enjoyed every minute on the island, taking to the people and culture like a native. She was sad to be leaving and I was sad to see her go. We travel well together and I knew I would miss her. After lunch at the Hip Strip in Mobay, I took her to the airport and waited with her until her flight left.

I felt a little disoriented. I would be on my own staying in hotel rooms for the next six weeks. It would be my longest time alone since Julia and I met 21 years earlier. Also my vision as to what to do next was a little murky.

Though I had planned to seek out the ridge Rastas living in the mountains, Scram said he really didn't know any so I was on my own. Also, I wasn't really feeling drawn to spend weeks hiking through the hills. But then what would I do over the next month? The idea of hanging out at various hotels didn't sound appealing. The truth was I had no clear vision of my next step and I found that very disconcerting.

"Bye, Dad," she said giving me a big hug. "That was great. I wish I could stay with you the next two months. I'm going miss you and Jamaica."

"I wish you could, too," I said. "But you might see me sooner than you think. I'm not sure I'll stay the next two months. I may just meet with the press this week and come back in a week or two."

"Don't you dare, Dad!" she said so strongly it took me aback. "Don't come back a day early. You've got everything set up: the rental car, the hotels, Mom and I are set up to handle everything at home. Don't you dare come home early. This is where you are supposed to be now!"

"Thank you, sweetheart. I needed to hear that—and from you!" Such wisdom from one so young.

As I drove toward Kingston, after putting Alicia on her flight, I felt a little depressed still but Alicia's words rang in my ears. By midway to

Gathering of the Healers

Kingston I started to feel a little better. As I drove along listening to Bob Marley, I passed one of the many "One Love—Jamaica's Message to the World!" billboards that dot the island, with his picture on it. To many it would seem ridiculous that the country with the highest per capita murder rate in the world could make such a claim but I knew the problem was mostly in the Kingston slums where a mixture of politics, guns and cocaine had blended into a deadly soup. It did not reflect the true nature of the island or its people—the most loving I had ever met. I knew the message in our book, the same message of One Love that Bob Marley was bringing forward, fell on fertile ground here but I wasn't sure how to get our message out. I was unknown on the island and would have a hard time getting a "listening ear."

As I traveled through the rural countryside I had an epiphany, one as strong as I had 15 months earlier when I decided to write *Rasta Heart* after floating down the Rio Grande River near Port Antonio. I realized that though I didn't have a voice on the island, if I could find well-known Jamaican teachers of love to join me in asking the entire island to heal itself with love, it would be very powerful. We could hold a press conference at Bob's home, The Bob Marley Museum, in Kingston and invite all Jamaicans to not just listen to his songs but to live them by healing their personal relationships through forgiveness.

I would call it, "The Gathering of the Elders: The Healing of the Nation." (Elders are those who teach love to the tribe. Thanks to Jaime Delgado, the owner of the Bob Marley Experience in Mobay, who strongly felt the term "elders" would be misconstrued, I later changed the name to "The Gathering of the Healers: The Healing of the Nation"). I could ask everyday Jamaicans to tell me who the "healers" were in their country; who were the national figures who taught love and forgiveness. I could also invite Prime Minister Patterson and Opposition Leader Edward Seaga to come as "chiefs" to listen to their healers, something that is done in many tribal cultures. They were soon to be locked in an intense election. Violence was already escalating on the island and it was feared that there would be a repeat of the election in 1981 when over 800 people were killed, mostly due to political turmoil.

As I drove toward Kingston contemplating this idea, I realized why it

16

Gathering of the Healers

just might be Jamaica that could heal itself with love. Why Jamaica to lead the world into this One Love vibration? Why this small island? It was clear this vibration was not emanating strongly from the world capitals of Washington, Moscow or London or even from the religious capitals of Jerusalem, Rome or Mecca. But why Jamaica?

There were some reasons. Few, if any, countries in the world have known the suffering of Jamaica. For over 500 years, since Columbus first set foot at Discovery Bay, foreign powers, have dominated Jamaican life and never with concern for the happiness and well-being of its people. Within two decades of Columbus' arrival, all 60,000 indigenous Taino Indians (until recently thought to be Arawak Indians) were dead. Then began over 300 years of the most brutal slavery imaginable. The average slave worked 18 hours a day and was dead after seven years. After Emancipation in 1838 and up to today, the Jamaican people have continued to be exploited by both local and foreign powers. If Jamaica, with its great "sufferation," as the Rastas would call it, could heal itself through love and forgiveness, after all it has been through, it would have the moral authority to look to the world and say, "You, too, can heal your nation with the love of your people."

The island's suffering seemed to be the essential part of its destiny. Just as pressure on a piece of coal makes a diamond, so had the pressure of this suffering created a diamond here—the Jamaican people in general and the heart Rastas in particular. Many people here, especially many Rastas, have made a very enlightened, philosophical adjustment when confronted with their poverty. When you take away from people the chance to enjoy the material comforts of life, the clearest thinking of the tribe will say, "Where can I find happiness and peace?" And many have found their joy, their "livity," in what God has given everyone for free: His love, the love of others and nature.

However, the pressure of the suffering had also brought out the negative in people which is why Jamaica has so many problems with crime, broken families, drugs, and AIDS. Once again, Jamaica is a country of extremes and contrasts—a virtual "garden of good and evil."

It also explains why so many of the reggae artists from Jamaica are like global tribal drummers, sending out this message of One Love. No

Gathering of the Healers

other society is producing this musical vibration of love. Superstars like Madonna, Emenim, Britney Spears, and Michael Jackson are not singing elevating songs as do reggae stars like Bob Marley, Luciano, Bushman, Morgan Heritage, Tony Rebel, Beres Hammond, Dennis Brown, Burning Spear, Marcia Griffiths, Don Carlos and Abijah. And almost every well-known reggae artist *is* Jamaican and Rasta. Of course it had to be Jamaica! As Scram had told me so many times, "Jamaica is de 'eadquarters. It is de 'eadquarters fe dis One Love!"

The more I thought about the idea of asking others to join me at Bob Marley's home, the more excited I became. Though this was a total change in my plans, I knew that God shows me my path by what is calling most to my heart ("Follow your bliss," as writer/philosopher Joseph Campbell would say). I was willing to change the course of my next month and this book if I maintained this enthusiasm.

Arriving in Kingston later in the day, I checked in my hotel figuring I'd spend a few days there meeting with various people including Mike Henry, the owner of LMH Publishing, who had agreed to distribute *Rasta Heart* in the Caribbean. The next morning I met with Mike in his offices near my hotel. Mike is in his mid-seventies but like so many Jamaicans, looks much younger. I was pleased to learn that he had co-written *Bob Marley and Me* with Don Taylor, Bob's manager. He was also the first to publish the English version of the *Kebra Negast*, the Ethiopian Bible studied by many Rastas. His personal and corporate goal was to distribute and publish books that were about his people and would help educate and uplift them. I discussed my concept of the "Gathering of the Healers" with him and he seemed guarded but encouraging.

After leaving Mike's I drove over to the Bob Marley Museum on Hope Road near my hotel. I thought if I could get permission to hold our press conference there during Bob's birthday week, it would send the right message to the island. The home, an old "great house" that Bob bought from Chris Blackwell, owner of Island Records and the man credited for getting Marley's music out worldwide, was set directly on Hope Road, one of the busiest thoroughfares in Kingston. The home, a two-story red brick house, is attractive without being opulent, large by

Gathering of the Healers

Jamaican standards but average size and quality by U.S. standards. The grounds are now full with gift shops: the Queen of Sheba Restaurant, a replica of Bob's original record shop (Wail'm Soul'm), offices, a theatre and exhibit hall and a pleasant back courtyard complete with a large waterfall fountain. "The Journey of Bob Marley Superstar," six murals depicting Bob's life painted by Rasta artist Ras Witter Dread, are painted on the inside of the front wall and in the back courtyard.

An Ethiopian flag greets you as you pull in and in the center of the front courtyard is a statue of Bob with his guitar, a soccer ball and a picture of former Ethiopian Emporer Haile Selassie I at his feet (his three loves). I paid my US$10 and joined a tour with 10 or 12 other tourists. After showing us the bullet holes that ripped through the rear wall of the house during an assassination attempt on Bob's life in 1976, we all went inside. Except for his bedroom and upstairs small kitchen, which are pretty much the way he left them, personal effects and all, the other rooms are showcases with gold and platinum records, newspaper and magazine articles, awards (including his Order of Merit presented by the Jamaican government) and photos on the walls of bare rooms. There is a research library and a museum manager's office upstairs.

After the tour I asked to see the museum manager, Barrington Laing. He was out but I left a book for him and word I would get up with him later. As I was walking out of the front door, I noticed a group of Rastas hanging out and talking. As I looked closely I realized one of them was Bob's son and recording artist, Julian. I was surprised to see him there, so accessible though unnoticed by the steady stream of tourists.

Born in 1975 in London, where he lived most of his life, the son of Bob and Lucy Ponder, Julian is a electrifying performer and a skillful, self-taught musician, mastering the bass, drums, and keyboards. In 1989 he released his first album titled *Uprising*, also the name of his new band. He moved to Jamaica in 1992 and began to work with such reggae veterans as Aston "Family Man" Barrett, Earl "Wire" Lindo, Tyrone Downie and Earl "Chinna" Smith.

His music, much of which he writes himself, is known for its conscious vibrations. "I was born in Rasta and music," he told one interviewer. "This is what I've penetrated from creation." Julian is tall, well-

Gathering of the Healers

built and clean shaven, with long dreadlocks, similar to his father's. Marshalling up all the chutzpah I could, I went over to talk with him. From what I could tell of the group, these men were friends, hanging around the museum on a regular basis. Though they spoke in Patois, from what I could make out, they were "railing against Babylon."

Waiting for a break in their conversation, I handed Julian a book and told him what I planned and asked if I could use his father's home for the press conference. When I finished, an elderly Rasta, Tartar V. Ford, one of the regulars, sitting in a wheelchair with his legs amputated at the knees, started shouting at me, "You know! You know! You do dis t'ing, mon! You do dis t'ing!" over and over again with a look of glee on his face—endorsement from an unexpected source.

"Well, now," Julian finally said, looking at me askance, "I wouldn't want any of those politicians coming here." He looked disinterested.

"Patterson and Seaga would be coming here to listen to the wisdom of others," I countered, "not to speak as a teacher of love. I think your father would like this. He got Seaga and Michael Manley to join hands together when they were running against each other in the seventies and the island was in crises. This just continues his idea." Julian offered no response and just looked off like I wasn't there but then I was one of many strangers he would encounter that day.

As I was pulling out of the parking lot, a Rasta that looked to be in his thirties approached my car. I had noticed him earlier listening to my talk with Julian.

"Yeah, mon," he said. "I heard what you are planning. Dis is a good t'ing and it should happen here. Bob would like dis t'ing."

"That's what I think but I'm not so sure I'm going to get the approval of the family."

"I am dere cousin," he said. "Bob's mother, Mama B, dere grandmother, is my aunt too. I t'ink if you go to see her, she will want you to use dis place."

"I thought she lived in Miami," I said.

"Some of de year she is dere. But now she is on de island in her home at Nine Mile. Here is her phone number. Tell her you talked to me. My name is Ras Barrett. Call her and tell her what you are planning."

20

Gathering of the Healers

Feeling somewhat encouraged by Ras Barrett's advice and the thought of meeting Bob Marley's mother, I went to meet with Lemuel Lindo, known as Colonel Lindo. Colonel Lindo is the program coordinator for the government's Social and Economic Support Program Unit and a personal friend of Prime Minister Patterson. Before coming to the island, I had been given his name and number by Glen Gilpin, the man from New York who showed Scram the book before I arrived. He suggested I contact Colonel Lindo as an approach to the Prime Minister.

I had called Colonel Lindo earlier in the day and he was very cordial, saying Glen had told him about me and agreed to meet me after I visited the Bob Marley Museum. Leaving the museum, I drove around the corner to Jamaica House, the seat of the national government. Colonel Lindo, a well-built, middle-aged man, serious but friendly, greeted me warmly in his office, which I found comforting given that I am not use to traveling in these circles. I gave him a copy of my book and told him of my concept and my desire to invite the Prime Minister to join us.

He seemed genuinely enthusiastic and I could sense he was a high-minded man with the interest of his people at heart. He asked me to put my concept and invitation in writing and he would personally take it to Prime Minister Patterson. When I told him that may take a few days as I didn't have access to a computer in Kingston, he invited me to take over his desk and use his computer. I wrote the following letter:

> Dear Prime Minister Patterson:
> I am an American author who has just released the enclosed book, *Rasta Heart: A Journey into One Love*. During Bob Markley's birthday week in February, I plan to launch the book here in Jamaica. To do this I am planning a press conference (hopefully at the Bob Marley Museum) called the "Gathering of the Healers: The Healing of the Nation." At this press conference I plan to ask well-known Jamaican "healers" (teachers of love) to join me in asking all Jamaicans to join us in not just singing and listening to Bob Marley's songs but living his words by forgiving, as much as they can, anyone they

Gathering of the Healers

hold bitterly in their hearts.

We are inviting you and Opposition Leader Seaga to attend this gathering, not as healers but as a "chiefs" to listen to the healers. Please understand that the goal of the healers is to "big up" the chiefs and the Jamaican people to claim their destiny to teach One Love to the world (just as your billboards say). If a political healing can occur that would reduce the violence, the legacies of both you and Mr. Seaga would be that you *together* led your country into this healing and by doing so set an example for all politicians of placing their people first.

Please let me know if you or your representative plan to attend. As head of state, I would welcome any words you would like to offer to the press and the country. If no one will be attending, please let me know in writing why so that I do not misinterpret your reason to the press.

We hope you will be joining us,

One Love,

Robert Roskind

I gave the letter and a copy of *Rasta Heart* to Colonel Lindo and he promised to deliver it to the Prime Minister later in the week. I was pleased and somewhat surprised by his enthusiastic assistance. Months later, Glen told me he saw *Rasta Heart* on Colonel Lindo's bookshelf and when he asked him if he had read it, Colonel Lindo said, "Yes. What this man is presenting is nothing less than a revolution without guns." When I asked Glen if he said that in a positive way or as if he was threatened by this concept, Glen said, "Oh, no. He said it in a positive way."

Feeling more encouraged after my meeting with Colonel Lindo, I drove a few blocks away to Mutabaruka's bookstore, Books About Us. I had heard Muta's name many times since I began coming to the island and knew that if I could get him to join us it could make a big difference. Every Wednesday night, Muta, a world-famous African poet, reggae producer, emcee, actor, performer, social critic and singer, hosts his

Gathering of the Healers

very popular radio show, "The Cutting Edge," on IRIE!FM, the big reggae station. The show, which runs from 11 pm to 2 am (not considered late by Jamaican standards) is a combination of music, his poetry, interviews, news and information—all with a Rasta/African/Jamaican/Black consciousness orientation. Most talk show hosts on the island have a rather Establishment or religious view. Not Muta. He's an "in-your-face" renegade, a revolutionary, a noble warrior. Muta is an incredibly powerful figure and his presence and voice in Jamaica has a huge impact on molding Jamaican consciousness, especially at the grassroots level.

"The Cutting Edge" is hugely popular on the island. Jamaicans love talk radio and TV. They listen to local pundits and talk shows incessantly. Much more so than their American neighbors to the north, the average Jamaican has a thorough and thoughtful grasp on both national and international affairs. At the slightest provocation they will drop into a deeply philosophical discussion on anything from love to the Mideast crisis; from the government's performance to how the Reggae Boyz, the national soccer team, is doing. However, most Jamaicans, especially the men, are much better talkers than listeners.

Born Allan Hope in 1952 in Rae Town, Jamaica, Muta was trained in electronics, working for the telephone company. Raised as a Roman Catholic, he rejected his traditional religious roots." In the 1960s and 1970s, when Black Awareness was growing in Jamaica and the U.S., he was drawn into the movement, seeing himself as a young revolutionary. However, over time he moved toward Rastafari, which he views as part of a universal quest which may also be pursued by other routes, such as Hinduism, Buddhism or Christianity. Soon he stopped combing his hair, started growing locks, altered his diet, and declared himself Rastafarian. A number of his friends thought he was going mad. Today, in deference to his African roots, he goes everywhere barefoot, even when traveling by plane into cold climates.

In a 1998 interview with Carter Van Pelt, Muta shared some of his worldview. Real reggae music is "...a combination of the human touch and the human spirit. Because the (newer) music is no longer of the spirit again. It's more of the physical...When the music was in the spirit,

Gathering of the Healers

there was musicians playing it, what was being said was spiritual. Now we all see the trend moving and we can see everything change to mechanical...And now that the human spirit is there no more. They get frustrated and they find something else to listen to...My song, 'What About The Land' is really keeping within the context of my evaluation of what is taking place right now amongst indigenous people. We've been to Australia for the first time, and when we look on what is taking place in Australia amongst the Aborigines, we feel that as a spoken word person, it was my duty to express something about it and link it with the indigenous people of America, which we have been speaking about for years. Since the first time we came to America, we have been writing poems about that. Plus the Africans, plus the Amazon people. So that poem is combination of feelings and attitude that we pick up over the years with all these indigenous things that is taking place. We just get the music to suit it."

Marley historian, Roger Steffens, captured Muta's spirit when he said, "Just above his forehead, poet Mutabaruka has a strip of white hair that bisects his jet black locks. That is the only white thing about this revolutionary writer whose 'Every Time I hear Dis Sound' burst through the mellow reggae of the early '80s like a bullet from an AK-47. Performing sans shoes and shirt, Muta's deep-voiced uncompromising rants make his a unique, almost fearsome, figure whose melding of poetry and dub music make him seem akin to an Old Testament prophet saying, 'Listen—or else!' "

Muta's bookstore is one block off the main street in downtown New Kingston, in a small strip center set behind a high concrete block wall. I parked in front and walked in. The front room was small and filled with African clothes and artwork. The larger windowless back room offers Black/African-oriented books and music. A tall Rasta, Ras Isa, was behind the counter reading a magazine. I introduced myself and he warmly reciprocated with a big smile which put me instantly at ease. I asked for Muta and he said he was in his office directly behind me. Walking into his office, I was greeted by Muta's daughter at her desk and then noticed Muta sitting directly to my right. Muta is a large, well-built and strikingly handsome man. Dressed in a traditional African robe

Gathering of the Healers

and turban, he rose, his six-foot plus frame towering over my five feet seven inches. I introduced myself and he looked at me rather quizzically, perhaps a little interested, perhaps a little irritated at the intrusion.

I gave him a copy of *Rasta Heart* and immediately explained what I was doing with the "Gathering of the Healers" and as he listened I began to sense he really didn't want to hear it. When I was finished, I invited him to join us. He looked at me and said nothing. I sensed what he was thinking.

"Muta, look, JAH sent white," trying to address his unspoken concern. "I don't know why JAH sent me but He did. It feels as strange for me to be here talking to you as it must for you to be listening. Think about what I've said and if you feel in your heart you'd like to join us, do. I'll call you when I'm back in Kingston."

"I will think about it," he said and walked out of the store.

"Well. I guess that didn't go too well," I said to Ras Isa as I walked back into his good vibes.

"No, mon," he said. "I liked what you said and I know Muta will t'ink about it too. I been looking t'ru your book an' I like what I see. Cayn I get a copy?"

I signed a copy for him and left feeling a little better but by now emotionally spent. I knew that if I could get Muta to join me in encouraging One Love and forgiveness, it could make a big difference. However, I also knew it wouldn't be an easy sell. Muta was more known for his message of standing up for your rights. Though the messages of One Love and standing up for your rights are *not* contradictory, they are often perceived this way. Standing up for your rights from love rather than anger and bitterness, as demonstrated by leaders such as Gandhi, King and Mandela, brings a healing quality to the struggle and serves to lessen and weaken any counterattacks.

Perhaps one of the best examples of merging love and forgiveness with standing up for your rights and righting past injustices is the Commission of Truth and Reconciliation (TRC) formed in South Africa immediately after apartheid fell and Nelson Mandela was elected president. This endeavor is historic in that it demonstrates a new way to deal with great injustice without bitterness or revenge.

25

Gathering of the Healers

The South African Truth and Reconciliation Commission was set up by the Government of National Unity to help deal with what happened under apartheid. The conflict during this period resulted in violence and human rights abuses from all sides. No section of society escaped these abuses. As stated by Mr. Dullah Omar, former Minister of Justice, "... a commission is a necessary exercise to enable South Africans to come to terms with their past on a morally accepted basis and to advance the cause of reconciliation."

What follows is the Commission's opening address by Archbishop Desmond Tutu, chair person of the Commission, in his remarks in 1995:

> Absolutely central to our concern in the work of our Commission is helping our land and people to achieve genuine, real and not cheap and spurious reconciliation. Some view the Commission with considerable misgiving and indeed suspicion and even hostility because they have convinced themselves that the Commission is going to degenerate into an Inquisition, a witch-hunt hell-bent on bringing miscreants to book and the assumption is that it would be miscreants from one side only.
>
> We must scotch that rumor or suspicion from the outset. We are meant to be a part of the process of the healing of our nation, of our people, all of us, since every South African has to some extent or other been traumatized. We are a wounded people because of the conflict of the past, no matter on which side we stood. We all stand in need of healing. We on the Commission are no superhuman exceptions. We too need forgiving and to forgive. I hope that our churches, mosques, synagogues and temples will be able to provide liturgies for corporate confession and absolution.
>
> We are privileged to be on this Commission to assist our land, our people to come to terms with our dark past once and for all. They say that those who suffer from

Gathering of the Healers

amnesia, those who forget the past, are doomed to repeat it. It is not dealing with the past to say facilely, let bygones be bygones, for then they won't be bygones. Our country, our society would be doomed to the instability of uncertainty—the uncertainty engendered by not knowing when yet another scandal of the past would hit the headlines, when another skeleton would be dragged out of the cupboard.

We will be engaging in what should be a corporate nationwide process of healing through contrition, confession and forgiveness. To be able to forgive one needs to know whom one is forgiving and why. That is why the truth is so central to this whole exercise.

But we will be engaging in something that is ultimately deeply spiritual, deeply personal. That is why I have been appealing to all our people—this is not something just for the Commission alone. We are in it, all of us together, black and white, colored and Indian, we this rainbow people of God. That is why I have appealed to our different communities of faith, Christian, Muslim, Jewish, Hindu, etc., to uphold the Commission in fervent prayer and intercession that we may be showered with the divine blessings of wisdom, courage and discernment.

We have seen a miracle unfold before our very eyes and the world has marveled as South Africans, all South Africans, have won this spectacular victory over injustice, oppression and evil. The miracle must endure. Freedom and justice must become realities for all our people and we have the privilege of helping to heal the hurts of the past, to transcend the alienations and the hostilities of that past so that we can close the door on that past and concentrate in the present and our glorious future.

We have it in us as South Africans to become a scintillating success. God bless us in our high calling.

My first day of trying to put my vision together had not gone particularly well. Julian and Muta had given me a chilly reception and only Colonel Lindo had warmed to the idea. I would have thought it would be the other way around, with Colonel Lindo being the least receptive and Bob Marley's son the most receptive. I headed back to the hotel to reassess things.

I was again confronting my fear that I was not up to the task or that the vision was just a self-induced, ego-oriented fantasy. After all, who was I to think I could be a catalyst of One Love on the island? I had no great track record that would indicate I could do this. My two previous books on unconditional love, *In the Spirit of Marriage* and *In the Spirit of Business,* had been out for several years and only sold small numbers (though Oprah Winfrey had bought 150 copies of my business book and made it mandatory reading for her entire staff on their annual retreat). I had organized others to work together in a common goal before but only on a modest level, including founding a school, the Owner Builder Center, in California and re-energizing several small institutions some years later.

Feeling overwhelmed, I called Julia and Alicia for support, the first of many such calls I would make in the next two weeks.

"I don't know," I said to Julia, "I'm starting to feel this vision strongly but I'm not sure I'm the right person. I'm white, a middle-class American, no great credentials, no real contacts. Whose going to listen to me? What if I just make a fool of myself and realize it was all from ego?"

"You've still got an ego. I can testify to that," she said, laughing, "but that's not why you're doing this. We've spent our lives trying to get out a message of love. We've both wanted to do this for as long as we can remember, since we were kids. This is just the next step. You can't make a fool of yourself even if nobody listens. You're offering a message of One Love, pure and simple."

Gathering of the Healers

"You're right," I said, already feeling much better. "And if there are ordinary people who envision themselves doing massive destruction, like the World Trade Center terrorists, then there must be ordinary people like us who envision ourselves doing massive healing."

Before I fell asleep, I picked up a copy of *Rasta Heart* that was lying on the bed and randomly opened it to the beginning of chapter 17 and read a quote from Nelson Mandela: "We ask ourselves, who am I to be brilliant, gorgeous, talented and fabulous? Actually, who are you not to be? You are a child of God. You're playing small doesn't help the world. There's nothing enlightening about shrinking down so someone won't feel insecure around you. We were born to make man into the glory of God that is within us. It's not just in some of us, it's in everyone."

Falling asleep, I felt the support of my companions, near and far, on my journey.

By the next morning I was feeling reinvigorated, trusting once again in the concept shared with me in *Rasta Heart* by Ras Thomas. Ras Thomas was our guide when I took the family the previous summer on a tour of Mayfield Falls in the hills between Mobay and Negril. He shared with me how 12 years earlier, when he was 18 and a "baldhead," he had a vision in which a Rasta dressed in a white rob appeared to him and told him he was to "teach Rastafari to the world." When I asked him if he had any idea how he was to do that given that he was living in a very remote area of the island, he said simply, "No. But JAH gave me de vision so I knew JAH would show me de way." Seven years later a local woman developed Mayfield Falls, an area Ras Thomas had played in all his life, as a tourist attraction. Ras Thomas has been a guide there ever since—teaching Rastafari to the world.

I went down to the restaurant to have breakfast with Dr. Dennis Forsythe, one of the Rastas featured in *Rasta Heart*. A well-known attorney, ex-university professor, PhD, and author of *Rastafari: For the Healing of the Nations*, Dennis had become a heart friend. Years earlier, Dennis had become an outcast in the upper echelons of Jamaican society when he, as one of the country's brightest and best, left the

Gathering of the Healers

straight and narrow and publicly became a Rasta. Seeking chastisement for what they viewed as his corrupted and misguided course, the Jamaican court system lashed out at him. In a custody battle with the mother of his young son, he was arrested for one spliff (marijuana cigarette) and labeled an "unrepentant drug addict" and thereby denied access and custody of his child. The blow was devastating to him and he was still fighting it in court. Even at a great personal cost, Dennis refused to bow to the powers-that-be and continued to write about the repressive ganja laws and call for their repeal.

After a warm greeting, Dennis and I settled at our table overlooking the pool. I noticed that Dennis was limping and asked him what had happened. He said he had been jailed the week before as part of his custody fight and had hurt his foot in jail.

"I was in custody for four days," he said. "I was there innocently but I was put in a cell with sex offenders, murderers, other violent criminals. I was taken away from the section they call Pegasus, named after this very hotel, and in that section you have foreigners and other middle-class criminals—criminals in quotation marks. There are traffic offenders and many innocent offenders that are treated to the same degradation. I learned so much in that week. I was first out in the Pegasus section but then they said I didn't appreciate the tribulation I was causing the policemen and judges so they said they were going to teach me a lesson. So they took me away from Pegasus to the extreme section for hardened criminals."

"What was that like?" I asked, amazed that they would treat a respectable practicing attorney like that.

"It was dark. It was gloomy," Dennis answered. "I told them about my heart problem and they laughed at me but many things transpired there. JAH sent an Inspector of Police who discovered that I was inside and when he came he saw me sweating profusely and he took me back out and said that this was no place for me and he put me back down in Pegasus. But when he was off-duty, I had to go back into the extreme section of the cell. There it was hard to breathe. It was overcrowded and it was in that section that I fell and splintered a bone in my heel. It is the most cruel and inhumane thing I have ever come across. It is the first

Gathering of the Healers

time I have been exposed to the reality of prison life. They degrade you. You have to watch people defecate in plastic buckets. They don't provide any means of disposing of feces or urine."

"You mean the bucket just sits there?" I asked.

"Yes. And many of the policemen came to beg money from me," Dennis said.

"Why would they be begging money?" I asked.

"Well, they are underpaid and when they need money they often go to lawyers," Dennis continued. "One of the policemen there I had given money to not long ago. Several of them would take me out and put me back in Pegasus but one policeman kept putting me back downstairs because he had instructions from the higher-ups to teach me a lesson. He put me in a cell where one of the inmates had a knife and they mixed up my identity with a man who was molesting his son and I was in danger of being attacked. There was kind of a trial inside there and they discovered that I was not this man."

"If they had found you guilty would they have stabbed you?" I asked.

"Yes. They would have," he continued. "It was a conspiracy. Imagine I'm fighting for my son, for pure love, and they're mixing me up with a sexual pervert and putting me in a place where I can be stabbed or killed. It shows how vicious the system is. It's almost too big to fight. There was much more conflict in my cell before I went there and eventually there was much more harmony with the six of us in the cell. In fact I'm going over there to bail one of my cellmates out tomorrow because I promised some to assist them because they can't afford a lawyer. You have desperate souls in there and I have become very close to that category of people. Some are innocent and a lot of the guilty are suffering more than they should. The system is trying to destroy them. I have gone to visit prisoners who I represented but it is different when you are locked in there. The prison system needs to be drastically reformed. Prisons don't heal prisoners or society. It's a joke. It's a kind of social revenge."

"Why were you in jail for the four days?" I asked.

"Because I took my son to the hospital for treatment of scabies and I was late bringing him back to the mother. But the boy is subject to these

31

conditions because his mother doesn't give him a place where there is running water or a refrigerator. I give her money but the court will not give me my son and she wants to keep him so she can keep getting money from me. The judge who put me in jail was a classmate of mine. He didn't even want to hear my side. In spite of our independence in 1962, the same historically structured system remains intact. In spite of my being a lawyer and all the glaring evidence against the mother, the system cannot remand the child to the black man. This is a continuation of the slave mentality of undermining the place of the black man within his own family. This is the significance of the struggle for custody of my child. The system conspires with the mother of the child against the father. For six years they have denied me reasonable custody of my child. Mostly this is due to the power of the judiciary branch, the judges. Their power is more than the power of the political and economic leaders. That fact hasn't been brought out in social analysis of any country. Judges are not critically evaluated as are the politicians. They have tenure. They are the backbone of the power elite. But the fact that we can now criticize them shows that we are getting somewhere."

(In the summer of 2002, after a continuing struggle in the press and finally coming in front of a fair-minded judge, Dennis was finally given half custody of his son.)

We talked for over two hours and before we parted I explained my concept to Dennis and he enthusiastically agreed to join me, as I knew he would.

"The reason I think God guided you to be part of this," I said, "is because you represent the very personal pain that governments create especially around the issue of ganja. To take a man's son away from him for smoking a spliff is wrong."

"And that is part of the systematic technique of Babylon," he said. "But what would you say to people who say that Jamaica already has more churches per capita than anywhere else and the violence continues?"

"I would tell them that we are just asking Christians to do more of what Jesus told us to do," I answered, "when he said 'love our enemies, do good to those that hate you, to pray for those that mistreat you.' This is not a Rasta thing but a One Love thing. And love is at the core of all religions."

"Well, even though the Christians espouse love," he continued, "they do not often practice it. They do not see love in a biological way like a Rasta does, as an expression of a wholesome self, a holistic self, healed in mind, body and spirit."

"Dennis," I replied, "you know if every one wus to do," I answered, "when he said 'love our enemies, do good to those that hate you, to pray for those that mistreat you.' This is not a Rasta thing *but* a One Love thing. And love is at the core of all religions."

"Well, even though the Christians espouse love," he continued, "they do not often practice it. They do not see love in a biological way like a Rasta does, as an expression of a wholesome self, a holistic self, healed in mind, body and spirit."

"Dennis," I replied, "you know if every one who wore dreads and everyone who wore a cross practiced the love their faith espouses, we wouldn't be even having this discussion. Rastas and Christians both forget who they are. However, after a year studying Rastafari, I've concluded there are three things Rastas are stressing that the other religions are not."

"What things are those?" Dennis asked.

"The Rastas understand the integration of body, mind and spirit," I answered. "They understand the importance of taking care of your structure, your body. That's why Rastas emphasize not eating meat or fish or shrimp anything that involves killing for food, only fruits, vegetables, grains and nuts. And only organic foods with no pesticides, or fertilizers or hormones. Rastas like yourself understand that if we are going to kill innocent animals and devour their flesh, it will affect us negatively physically, mentally and spiritually. It creates karma. Almost all humans are naturally repulsed by killing and butchering animals. That tells me if we are repulsed by the way we get our food, we shouldn't be doing it that way. No one is repulsed by picking a fruit or a vegetable. Secondly, Rastas remind us of the importance of getting away from the man-made world and out in to nature, the JAH-made world. Lastly, they remind us of the importance to keep checking ourselves to see where we have adopted values of possessing, vanity, pleasuring, and power."

"Yes. Rasta says you must love yourself," Dennis said. "Rasta is a renaissance movement and it corroborates a lot of the teachings of Christ."

"And many religions say we are sinners, even from birth, and we must beg forgiveness from a punitive, judgmental God," I replied. "This concept just perpetuates a cycle of low self-esteem and it encourages believers to be judgmental and punitive themselves. It does not encourage them to forgive unless others beg their forgiveness as they believe they must beg God's. But I know that if people begin to forgive just a little bit, even without the other asking to be forgiven, it will feel so good in their hearts that they'll do it more and more and more because that feeling of love is what we're all looking for."

"Yes. That is true," Dennis said, "because I wrote an article called, *Trodding the Road to Zion* and the point was once I started trodding I didn't know where each step would take me but I looked forward to the next step because it brought so much illumination, energy, vitality—the fruits of love—so to speak. You never stop trodding on that pathway."

"Exactly," I agreed, "and as the love spreads, things will change. The employer will be more generous to their employees. The police will treat people with more respect. The politicians will be more concerned with the people. The husband will treat the wife better and visa versa. We don't have to be attached to where the path goes or to the results. Maybe it will just be you and me and Julia and Scram at the press conference. Maybe no one else will join us but it doesn't matter. Gandhi said 'Don't be attached to success or fear failure.' It's the effort that matters—not the results. Jesus 'failed' in getting everyone to embrace love but what if he never tried?"

"Yes. This is true," Dennis said. "I will be glad to speak at the gathering of what I know."

Meeting with Dennis raised my spirits as it always does. His clarity in the face of personal obstacles is inspiring. Though we had only been together on two brief occasions, he felt more like a brother than a friend. I agreed to keep in touch over the month to let him know how every-

Gathering of the Healers

thing was progressing.

When I got back to the hotel I checked my e-mails and was amazed to find one from a guy named Alex Holden. He had been searching the Web and came across the Website for *Rasta Heart*, which had only been up for a few weeks. What was amazing was that he also lived in Blowing Rock, where we live. He wanted to meet Julia and I. When I e-mailed him back that I was in Jamaica he said that he was going to Negril in a few weeks and asked if he could bring me anything from home. I e-mailed back and said I would also be passing through Negril the week after him. I asked him to bring me another box of *Rasta Heart* books and leave them at The Rockhouse, the hotel where I would be staying. He e-mailed me back to say he too was staying at The Rockhouse and would leave the books there!

"You doan't 'ave to 'ave locks to be a Rasta—clean livin' an' a clean heart an' sharin' wit' your bredren an' sistren. You doan't really 'ave to 'ave de locks."
—Tasha

Chapter 3
January 4, 2002

Local Healers

The next day I headed along the coast road back to Port Antonio. Though I was feeling fairly certain ("fairly certain" as opposed to "certain") about this new direction, I wanted to reflect on it some more and discuss it with Scram. I love the three hour drive from Kingston to Port Antonio—nothing but beaches, ocean, hills, small towns and villages and very little traffic.

When I was about half way there near Hector's River, I passed a small shop where a few men, two with dreads, were chatting at the counter. The Rasta behind the counter looked up and our eye's met. He flashed me a big smile and I smiled back. Given my speed, it lasted no more than a second or two but I could sense the love and calm coming from him. I drove another few miles but I couldn't get his smile out of my mind so finally I turned around and headed back.

Pulling in front of his shop, he looked as happy to see me come back as I was to see him. It was as if we had always known each other, two good friends reunited. Smiling broadly at each other, we introduced ourselves. Tasha, as he was known, looked to be in his mid-twenties—tall, thin, handsome with two-foot long dreads and a radiant aura. I greeted the other men at the counter and we all started to reason together, something that is so easy to do with perfect "strangers" (actually new friends)

Gathering of the Healers

in Jamaica. I gave them all copies of the book and told them what I was planning for the press conference.

"Well, now," said one of Tasha's customers. "Dat is a good idea but I doan't see 'ow dat is goin' to solve de economic problems 'ere. Dat is our biggest problem."

"I'm not saying that I can solve those problems," I said, "but it's reasonable to think that if greater love permeates the culture, the employers, out of kindness, may pay more. The rich homeowners may pay their gardener or cook more. The corporate executives may be willing to be more generous in their corporate giving and in their pay scales. If the exploitation was created because there wasn't enough love in the system than more love will correct it."

I noticed Tasha remained quiet, calmly smiling. He understood where I was coming from.

"But if you caynnah change de government," the customer said, unconvinced, "t'ings will not change. So I doan't see dat de love cayn come toget'er wit'out some support from de government."

"Well, that's not my job," I said. "I'm not one of the people that play in the financial or political world. My tribe is the storytellers, the ones that go out there and say, 'Look, let's get the love flowing better.' Other people in those areas will have to solve the economic and political problems as this love touches their hearts. I gave books to Prime Minister Patterson and some of his people and maybe if they will read them their hearts will change some and they will treat the people better."

"If you just preach love to de people," he continued loudly, "it won't work. If you cayn build a factory, cayn build a plant, to 'elp de little people, dat will make a difference. Babylon will not be fair wit' us."

"That's not my tribe," I replied. "If I had to go out and put a factory together I would fail. It would crush me. It's not what I was sent here to do. I'm a writer, a thinker, a storyteller. It's what I love."

"But de leaders, dey no wanna change anyt'ing," he continued unabated. "Dey want all de money an' power fe demselves."

"They are changing, too," I said. "If you were a senator in the U.S., or a business leader, or even the President, on September 11th at eight in the morning, you felt like you were the safest person in the world.

37

Gathering of the Healers

Two hours later you realized you were the most vulnerable. You were the target and always will be. This has changed them. At first they will retaliate. That is part of human nature. But eventually they will realize that retaliation will no longer work and the only way to get that bull's eye off their back, off the whole country's back, is to make friends with our enemies, with every country that hates us. And when they decide to do that, they will realize that to make friends with our enemies starts with sharing our wealth, not coming into places like Jamaica and exploiting people for 10 dollars a day like they do in the free trade zones in the Kingston wharfs."

This has started to happen, though it may be just another charade. In a UN International Conference on Financing for Development held in Monterrey, Mexico in March, 2001, the nations of the world launched a major initiative to supposedly combat poverty, with rich countries promising to try to double their aid and poor countries agreeing to do more with what they get. Leaders of poor countries from Tunisia to Venezuela and rich countries from France to the United States all agreed that terrorism will not be eliminated without a major push to help the world's poorest. However, in the early 1990s, when aid to developing countries represented .33% (less than 1%) of the GNP of the First World countries, The G8 countries pledged to double that to .7% within a decade. Instead, it has fallen to .22 %, a one-third reduction. The World Bank, IMF and the World Trade Organization has indicated as much. The September 21, 2002, edition of *USA Today* reported they "admitted that they are doing too little to help the world's poorest people."

"It's not about the American people exploiting the Jamaican people," I responded. "Or about the Israeli people hurting the Palestinian people or the English against the Irish. It's about the leaders everywhere leading their people astray, away from love. It's been that way throughout history and the leaders of the most powerful countries exploit the most, whether it's the Huns, Spanish, French, Dutch or English. The last super power befor the U.S. was the English and they sanctioned black slavery and colonized, for the benefit of a few powerful interests, a quarter of the known world. Now the U.S. is the super power and the greedy and misguided there are exploiting poor countries worldwide. But it is never

38

Gathering of the Healers

the average English or American citizen that benefits. They often don't even understand this dynamic. The people just follow. One day Israeli widows will hug Palestinian widows and weep together for what their leaders have led them into. Leaders everywhere lead their people into war and hate, usually because of the leaders greed and vanity.

Even Hitler's master propagandist Herman Goering, understood this when he said, 'Naturally the common people don't want war...but after all it is the leaders of a country who determine policy and it is always a simple matter to drag the people along...All you have to do is tell them they are being attacked and denounce the pacifists for lack of patriotism and exposing the country to danger. It works the same in every country.'

"But why you t'ink you as a white man from de states cayn come 'ere to our island and tell us to forgive? Dis is nah your country or your people," he responded.

"If you are trying to heal the planet with love," I said, "then I'm not a foreigner to you. I'm your tribal brother, your co-worker. I'm just on loan to Jamaica to do this just like Bob Marley was on loan to the world. Even though he was Jamaican, he had the assignment to bring his message everywhere he could. And what if I'm wrong and the individual acts of forgiveness do not heal the island? Are you going to call me in a year or two to tell me you're angry that you forgave people because most of the people here didn't join you? This is a no-lose proposition. If I'm right you win. If I'm wrong you win."

"But if we 'ad some of your money, it would make a big difference 'ere," he responded.

"I understand that and we definitely need to move to a more equitable system," I answered. "But I think we can only get to that with a change of heart, a change that puts people first and profits and possessions second. And that's what One Love does. But in many ways people in the States are not as happy as people here. The suicide rates for Americans is many times greater than for Jamaicans. And you live longer even though your health care is not near as good as ours. That's true for many of the poor Caribbean countries. That tells you a lot about whose enjoying their lives more. We've got all the things but things don't make you happy. Jamaica's got all the heart vibes and heart vibes *do* make you happy."

"An' de only reason you cayn see dat is dat you got de choice," he said.

"Well, actually I don't have the choice, " I said. "I'll always be here as a stranger, a visitor, enjoying your heart vibes."

"Of course, you cayn," Tasha interjected, "Just move here. Or if you cayn't do dat, just come an' 'ang out 'ere wit' us. Anywhere you go, mon, you will fit in. You got to come 'round here."

"Thanks for the invitation," I said. "I will."

"Yeah, mon," said Harold, a handsome man now living in England but building a large new house on the hill above Tasha. "You are always welcome at Tasha's. Tasha 'as a lot of love. Everybody love Tasha, especially de kids from de school dere dat come by de shop every day. Dis mon is a true Rastamon and it's not me I'm talkin' about. It's some-body else."

After an hour or so, I was ready to continue on to Port Antonio and settle in my hotel. I had really wanted to connect with Tasha but as hap-pens so much in Jamaica, the loudest voice tends to dominate. Knowing I would be driving back by soon, I said goodbye telling Tasha I would see him in a few days. I headed out knowing I had just made a new friend.

An hour down the road, I arrived at the Frenchman's Cove Resort, my home for the next week. It is an amazing place that can only be experi-enced, not adequately described. Frenchman's Cove consists of 45 acres of rolling landscape with huge tropical trees and plants everywhere. A small river runs through the grounds down to its own sheltered, white sandy beach. In addition to a small hotel, there is a collection of 17 unusual secluded stone villas scattered among the cliffs and on a park-like setting above the famous Frenchman's Cove Beach, where lunch is served daily. It is a magical place.

I settled in my villa which had a large deck overlooking the beach and river. Tropical shade trees hung over the deck. The villa consisted of a large living room, a smaller air-conditioned bedroom, bath and kitchen. It was a ten-minute drive from Port Antonio and Scram's and directly across the street from the San San Tropez, where I could always get a

Gathering of the Healers

good vegetarian pizza and hang out with friends.

Late in the afternoon, I walked up the hill to the Fern Hill Hotel for dinner in their restaurant overlooking the ocean. Ronald, our friend from previous trips, was now working there as the chef. It was good to link up with him again. I talked with him and the other staff about the press conference and asked everyone the same question I would ask many times in the coming weeks, "Who on this island do you feel are the *national* teachers of One Love? Who do you personally feel loved by?"

Over the weeks of my asking many people, from waiters to business people, from farmers to politicians, from taxi drivers to shop owners, the same names were commonly mentioned. These included many reggae artists (Morgan Heritage, Bushman, Luciano, Abijah, Tony Rebel, Marcia Griffiths, and Beres Hammond), two politicians (Tourist Minister Portia Simpson-Miller and UPP President Antonnette Haughton-Cárdenas), and two college professors (Rex Nettleford and Barry Chevannes). Many other names were mentioned on a local level but these were the names on a national level.

In addition to giving me the names of people they thought taught love in their society, almost everyone I spoke with greeted the idea with big smiles and enthusiasm. Most people encouraged me to pursue it, even those that weren't convinced it would make a difference. However, most felt that these healers asking Jamaicans to forgive and heal their personal relationships *could* make a big impact on the island. No one questioned my motives or my right to undertake the effort. I encountered little of the cynicism I expected.

The usual response I got was something like, "Yeah, mon. Dis is a good idea. De people will listen to dese 'ealers. Jamaica needs dis now. Maybe it is better dat a foreigner do dis becuz everyone 'ere is so divided." This response spoke volume as to the genuine loving hearts of the Jamaican people. It served as a daily source of inspiration, constantly reminding me how willing people were to be led into love.

Many times I presented the concept, it opened the door for a more extensive reasoning about the nature of forgiveness. The main objection was why should anyone forgive someone who had hurt them unless that person asked for forgiveness and made amends.

"Look, I didn't design this system. God did." I would often respond. "If you want to be truly happy, you have to forgive, whether the other person asks for your forgiviness and makes amends or not. It's that simple. It may not seem right or fair or just but you just can't be happy with a bitter heart. If you wait for the other person to ask for forgiveness, it may never happen. So you have to do it anyway. I'm just the messenger. If you have a problem with this basic design, you've got to talk to God about that."

As I was walking down down for dinner, I met Donald, a local man cutting shrubbery on the road and loading it into his truck to feed his 15 goats. He was a gentle, seemingly educated man, with a loving gleam in his eye.

"I never eat my goats," Donald said. "I am a vegetarian. I keep the goats for pets. I love them."

"I see so many goats and cows wandering freely in Jamaica. How do their owners find them?" I asked, hoping to clear up what had been a mystery for me.

"Technically, it is against the law to let your farm animals run free but everyone does it," Donald said. "It's much cheaper to let them roam than to buy feed. When you want to milk it or butcher it, you just go out looking for it and ask neighbors. Everyone kind of knows whose animals are whose. If you hit one with your car and kill it, it's yours. You can take it home and butcher it in exchange for whatever damage it did to your car. Sometimes you see the butchered carcass by the side of the road (I had seen several). Around Christmas, there are a lot of goats missing because curried goat is a big Christmas meal here," he said laughing.

I told him about what I was planning, wanting as much feedback as I could get.

"I like your idea. I think this island needs this now and people will listen," he said, enthusiastically. "If you could get Muta to jump into this One Love thing it could make a big difference. Don't evade this. The fact that Muta wasn't openly hostile to you is a good sign. Keep pushing on him. Sometimes he leads people into anger but he has a good

Gathering of the Healers

heart. If he would offer love it could make a big difference."

I spent the evening alone, wandering the property and reading. It was rainy and cool and I began to feel a little lonely and uncertain as to my ability to pull off this vision that I thought God had given me. I had the next six weeks alone in a series of hotel rooms (not my favorite places to hang out) and I had no idea how well my concept would be accepted. I was asking to join me, the press or the Jamaican people. After awhile I wandered inside to watch "The Color Purple" on my camcorder. (I had recorded various movies on blank tapes to watch during my travels.)

Watching "The Color Purple" was perfect for me. The movie's theme is about feeling good enough about yourself to stand up to people who abuse you and, after stopping the abuse, eventually forgiving them. Both of these themes were integrated into what I was doing. Watching the movie made me realize what a large effect one act of love and forgiveness can have on many people. I recommitted to my goal.

The next morning I headed to Reach Falls. I hadn't gotten a chance to give JAH Priest and Renny, two of the Rastas featured in *Rasta Heart*, their copies of the book the week before and seeing them and visiting Reach Falls was always refreshing. Plus I wanted to find out what they thought of the idea.

JAH Priest was at his stall a mile or two before you get to Reach Falls. JAH Priest is a seventy-something Rastaman with long white dreads and precepts (the Rasta word for an uncombed beard). He looks and feels a lot like an Indian sadhu or holy person. He is a craftsman, making wood carvings, and also teaches African drumming and dancing to the local youths. He often appears with them to perform at local hotels and dances like he is a teenager himself. He is very kind and very gentle and talks like a man who is well-educated and well-read.

He was glad to see me and said he heard I was in the area earlier. He had borrowed a copy of the book from JAH T, another Rasta in *Rasta Heart*, and had read most of it and liked it very much. I told him how

Gathering of the Healers

Julia and I had become vegetarians and had lost a lot of weight and we both felt a lot better.

"I am glad fe you," he said, sincerely. "I also made a change. I stopped smoking herb (ganja) six months ago." In Jamaica it is estimated that three-quarters of the population smokes ganja.

"You did?" I asked. "Why?"

"Well, I t'ink I reached a different level," JAH Priest replied. "I doan't want to be depending on not'ing apart from self. Not dat I would tell anybody not to smoke herb."

"But it's a tool and when you don't need the tool anymore you put it down," I said.

"You got de point," he said.

"How many years have you smoked ganja?" I asked.

"Fifty," he replied after some thought. "But I needed it then because it is so tough 'ere. I 'ave twelve children. An' when people come around, it makes us more respectful becuz I cayn offer a spliff to dem. It's mystical."

"What made you decide now was the time?" I asked.

"It's like in music," he explained, "you need the fundamentals at the start but you get to a point that you deviate and you go on your own now. You don't have to follow de fundamentals anymore."

"So now you're making your own music," I said.

"AHHHHH!" he replied, enthusiastically.

"What have you noticed since you stopped smoking?" I asked.

"Well, there's a lot. I have more functions for one t'ing. I feel my lungs better. I 'ave more speed. I used to 'ave a little pain walking an' dese t'ings are all gone, ya know. I have more flexibility," he says swaying his hands and body rhythmically.

"When you were smoking, how did it make you feel?" I asked.

"Well, you 'ave dis general 'igh, you know," he answered. "You feel real good but now I'm feeling better."

"What do you think this says about ganja?" I asked.

"Maybe it's the amount you use," JAH Priest answered. "Because I really was in it. I used to smoke everyt'ing—pipes, challis, spliffs."

"What would you tell a youth about ganja?" I asked.

Gathering of the Healers

"I doan't t'ink I would 'ave anyt'ing to say becuz ganja was good fe me in former days when we 'ad not'ing else to rely on to ease de pain and de frustration. It 'elps you to bring you to a point at lookin' wit'in yourself."

"So it's like all therapy. It's meant to end," I said.

"Yes. I t'ink dat's a good description," he replied. "And I'll never smoke again. It's like I and I am on a spiritual trek an' I reached a crossroads where I feel I in Iself is sufficient. I come to discover dat it's not working fe immortality."

("I and I" or "InI" is a term Rastas often use when referring to themselves or others and often replaces "me," "you," "we," "them," etc. It means the person as a human *plus* their Divine connection to God. It reminds them that we are all one and connected to Divinity. Often they may refer to themselves or others simply as "the I." Also they change many words to reflect greater spirituality. They change universe to "Iniverse," vital to "Ital," Ethiopia to "Ithiopia," creation to "Iration," ever to "Iver," eternity to "Iternity," etc. Also to keep the emphasis on life and not death, words like appreciate becomes "apprecilove," dedicate becomes "I-dicate." To add clarity, words like understand becomes "overstand" and oppression become "downpression.")

"Explain that thought that it's not working for immortality," I asked.

"In de Christian religion you were told dat you 'ad to do certain t'ings to reach God and escape hell but I come to find out dat we all are immortal and I come to know dat dey lie about my birth being my beginnin' an' my death being my end. It gives me a different going through, you know. Dat everyt'ing is dependent now on I of myself. I doan't want to depend on no mon, no womon, no herb, no alcohol, no not'ing. My high is myself, as a Christ. I'm my own Christ—wrapped up in my Christ."

"Was there any one event that made you decide to stop?"

"Well, you know it's funny 'ow I stopped. Marcia (Marcia Henry, a local artist featured in *Rasta Heart*) an' her 'usband, Phillip, were comin' from Ocho Rios one day an' I was in de back of de car tryin' to light a spliff. We drive maybe a mile wit' me tryin' to light a spliff an' I couldn't an' I just threw it out de window an' dere goes. I'm certain now

45

Gathering of the Healers

I will never backslide. Now every time I eat an Ital meal, it's like I smoked a spliff. It's miraculous."

I told him about the press conference and asked him what he thought.

"I t'ink dis is a good t'ing an' it may work but you know what I'm afraid of, if dat employer you ask to give two dollars instead of one an' he doesn't and you go back an' ask him if 'e loves 'is staff, what you t'ink 'e would answer?"

"Yes," I answered. "He would say he loves them."

"AHHH! No respect, mon. Lately, though, I been t'inking de word I use is not 'love' but 'respect.' I cayn't always say me love a person but I cayn respect dem. It different from when I look an' know what is goin' on in dat person. Den even if 'e 'urt me I cayn respect 'im becuz I know dere is no ot'er way. Let me give you a personal experience. De o'ter day when I went to my house, dere was a yout' dere, maybe 15 years old, tryin' to steal my t'ings. An' when I caught 'im 'e beg me not to tell 'is father. Most people couldn't love a mon fe dat. So I asked 'im, 'Why you come to my house an' take my t'ings?' An' 'e said dat 'e works fe 'is father but 'is father will not pay 'im not'ing. An' immediately, somet'ing else 'appen to me," he said, touching his heart gently with his fingertips. "Which is not love. I respect him."

"That's One Love," I said, "unconditional love. You love, or as you say 'respect,' him with no condition even though he tried to steal from you. I think we're just using different words for the same feeling."

"No, mon. Dey are different," he said. "A lot of people will love you but not respect you. Dey not see your position. Dey not see your need. To respect a person you 'ave to go into yourself an' ask 'What would I do if I was in dere place?' Dis is a new millennium, a new time, a new world, so we need new administrations."

"A world of greater respect," I said.

"AHHHHHHH!!" JAH Priest replied, smiling, his eyes twinkling. A chicken cackled in the background, a truck noisily sped by, beeping its horn in greetings. "Respect make you look away. Dat cause you not to bot'er. Most people are so poor 'ere but maybe dey got no education but dey got 'headucation.' What we need now is a good brainwashing and wash out de brain. When I was just comin' in Rasta an' de whole t'ing

46

Gathering of the Healers

and I 'ad to leave all my children, my house, when I come out on de street I said, 'Well, dere's no where I'll be able to get work' and at dat time I wasn't all dat poor. I was middle-class Jamaican. An' I throw down everyt'ing an' decide to become Rasta."

"What were you doing then?"

"Music. Same as usual an' I 'ad two barber salons goin' in Port Antonio. I 'ad de first all night place in Port Antonio, where I sell food. I wasn't doin' bad. It was just a job out dere but dat was leadin' me out of de life I need. So I 'ave to leave dat an' live my life de way I see it."

"What made you see that?" I asked. "Was it an event, someone you met, or just realizing your old life wasn't going to make you happy?"

"I was searchin' fe God," he said.

"And you weren't going to find Him in a barber shop," I interrupted and we both laughed. At this point his stall partner's 10 year-old son joined us and started feeding his two young puppies milk out of a coconut shell—a gentle touch to our reasoning.

"Fe as long as I remember," he continued, "I 'ad de fear of God in me. Dey tell you what will 'appen to you if you do dis an' dat. God will send you to hell, an' de devil will do dis an' dat. Well I didn't want to make no bad relationship wit' God so I tried to search in ev'ry way dat I would live to please God. I see dat de religions weren't helpin'. I even gone to some kinda of school in Kingston connected to de Jehovah's Witness fe five and a 'alf years before I was expelled fe being a difficult student. It couldn't satisfy me."

"What about Rasta appealed to you?"

"Fe one t'ing de Rastas were sayin' at dat time dey wouldn't die. I didn't understand it in dat way so I wanted to know. So I wanted to understand what dey were really sayin. I saw a Rastamon one day an' when I look at 'im, 'e was just in a swim trunk, not'ing else. But dere was such an' aura dere dat I say, 'Whatever it takes to be a Rastamon.' An' from dat day, I been checkin' out, checkin' out, checkin' out an' I find it to be more conducive to what I am t'inkin' wit'in myself. I just give my wife all de shops, de keys. She wasn't interested in dis. Funny enough now, she's starting to see what I am like. I try my best to keep my relationship wit' 'er."

Gathering of the Healers

"You didn't throw her out of you heart?" I asked, knowing the answer.

"No, mon. Dat not my way. De ot'er day I look around fe someone dat I hurt an' I doan't find nobody," he said and laughed. "Wherever I go an' live, dere's no one dat I cayn't learn from, no child, no big person, no one."

"And that to me is true Rasta," I said.

"You know what I 'ave come to see," JAH Priest continued, "is dat each of us is born *is* an' de only way we cayn truly be happy is to live dat *is*. Dere are certain people who come to teach like Bob Marley, John de Baptist, Jesus Christ. Dey come fe a purpose. So I find my purpose, to contribute to dis kind of knowledge of havin' people become Christ. An' a lot of people doan't like it when I say dat. But I say I doan't want to 'ave Christ in my heart. I want to *be* in de heart of Christ. I want to be *wrapped up* in Christ," he says, drawing his hands together to his chest and cuddling his shoulders, the puppies whimpering contently in the background.

"JAH Priest, it's been great being with you again," I said as I rose to leave and continue on to Reach Falls. "Let me ask you, what was your name before it was JAH Priest?"

"It was Ezekiel Oakley," he said smiling.

"How long have you been JAH Priest?" I asked.

"Maybe, 40 years."

I drove on to Reach Falls and Renny's craft stall, where he sold bamboo ashtrays, cups and water pipes. Renny, another Rasta in *Rasta Heart*, greeted me with his usual big smile. Though not the deep philosophical thinker like JAH Priest, Renny has a beautiful, gentle nature that is easy and comforting to be around. He always comes up with very wise sayings, like when he told me that after Emancipation, Babylon still kept everyone enslaved by "using dere brains instead of dere chains."

We started to talk about the World Trade Centers attack.

Gathering of the Healers

"All dese t'ings are prophesy, you know," he said. "When I was a little bwai, dis guy dat was a prophetman said dat de 'ighest buildin' in New York gwanna get licked two places. I heard dat all de time when I was a little boy. An' people hear dat but dey doan't put it in dere mind until dat day. Since I was a little yout' I nevah t'ink about it but when it hit now I remember. Dat 'ow it go, you know. Dat was about t'irty years ago, when dey were building dos buildings. Dis mon say dey were gwanna get licked, one buildin' an' den de next."

I later heard this same story from other people in the area.

We chatted awhile and then I headed down to the falls to cool off. I went for a long swim, incredibly invigorating as always. Reach Falls is truly a power spot.

Before heading back to Port Antonio to catch up with Scram, I figured I'd drive the short distance up to Tasha's shop and see if I could get him in a private reasoning. Tasha was very mellow, very loving and I wanted to hear more of what he had to say. As I parked in front, Tasha was just opening up and there was no one else around. I got some coconut milk and we walked across the street to a high bluff overlooking the sea and settled in.

"I was readin' your book last night," he said, "it is very comfortable read."

"Thanks, me bredren. Tell me a little something about yourself, Tasha," I said. "Are you from here? When did you get interested in Rastafari?"

"Yeah, mon. I'm from here. I started out in Rastafari at about nine."

"How old are you now?" I asked.

"Well, now I am 41," he replied. He looked like he was in his early-twenties.

"What happened at nine?" I asked.

"I knew a group of Rastas. Dey were farmers, elder dreads, so I knew dos Rastas since I was a little yout'. An' my mother died an' I grow up wit' dis lady dat was workin' at de farm where de Rasta guys worked an' dey guide me and stuff so dat's where I started. An' after awhile dere was rascal vibes, not Rasta vibes, so we leave an' I travel all over wit' dem. Dere was five of us and we travel wit' de Twelve Tribes of Israel.

Gathering of the Healers

But soon I quit an' be wit' de Nyabinghi because de Twelve Tribes eat all different kind of meat. Dey doan't specialize what dey eat. Dey eat anyt'ing as Rasta. I just couldn't keep up wit dat. Dere was fish cookin' 'ere, mutton cookin' dere, chicken over dere. An' dey drink alcohol. To dem it doesn't matter. An' I wanted a version dat would change de system so I become Nyabinghi where dey eat Ital, organic, no meat or pollution stuff. No fish, no shell food, not'ing wit' bones. I t'ink it a better livin', ya know. But de Rasta life of livin', most people, especially de yout's, will not do becuz dey want to eat everyt'ing. De last time I had fish, I got so very sick from de copper in de fish. Every joint was weak."

Though most Rastas follow their own divine guidance in adopting a Rasta way of life and belong to no group, there are several large "sects" on the island (Nyabinghi, Twelve Tribes, Bobo, Ethiopian Coptics, etc.), each with its own individual interpretation of the faith.

"Last week I met a man, a tourist, at my hotel," I said, "that ate an amberjack an' he got so sick they had to carry him into the hospital."

"Dat is what I ate, an amberjack. It took six months to get dat poison out and dat was de t'ird time I get poisoned. Mash me up. An' de fishermon dat sold me dat fish knew it was a sick fish becuz de fish didn't fight. Dere was no fight, no struggle. So dat show's dat de fish was sick when 'e caught 'im."

At this point a young Israeli tourist and his girlfriend stopped to ask directions to Port Antonio and ask for a recommendation for a hotel. I suggested the San San Tropez and invited them to join our reasoning. Declining, they continued on.

"So the Twelve Tribes and the Nyabinghis are pretty different?" I asked.

"At a Twelve Tribe gatherin,' you 'ave more Babylon. You would 'ave de police goin' right t'ru but at a Nyabinghi, we doan't 'ave no policeman, just drummin' an' singin' an' dancin'. As long as you 'ave Rasta congregation toget'er as one, you doan't need no police. You no provoke. De police drive by but dey doan't come in. But you doan't 'ave to 'ave locks to be a Rasta—clean livin' an' a clean heart an' sharin' wit' your bredren an' sistren. You doan't really 'ave to 'ave de locks."

"Is Rastafari getting to be like Christianity where each sect argues

Gathering of the Healers

about who's right?" I asked.

"Well, de Nyabinghi doan't say we are de best. We just read our Bible and give t'anks an' praise an' unity an' each one teach one dis love. An' everyone come toget'er an' read an' play our drums an' t'ings. In de Nyabinghi we doan't 'ave no time fe criticism, just love."

"Tasha, do you believe that Haile Selassie is the living God like some of the other Rastas do?" I asked. Haile Selassie I, who's title before his coronation was "Ras Tafari," is believed to be a messiah by some Rastas.

"Dat is what I was goin' to reason about wit' you. I truly believe wit'in Iself dat 'e was a great king rulin' Ithiopia (Ethiopia) fe many years but when I research it out an' look I know dat 'e is a true an' livin' creator an' I reason wit' a lot of bredren dat say Selassie is God but in my belief dere is some ot'er Irator (Creator) above Selassie I. Dat is de Almighty God. 'E is not a black mon or a white mon. He is de Almighty God an' 'is will fe me is to love everyone an' if you doan't 'ave dat love goin' t'ru you it's like you doan't 'ave not'ing at all."

"So to you, Haile Selassie not God incarnate any more than you or me?"

"Dat's right. Just a mon," Tasha replied.

"That's what I've concluded," I said, "but I think God sent Haile Selassie to give blacks, especially those in the West where they were taken as slaves, an image of a black messiah and that image was needed to begin Rastafari. Until then, tens of millions of displaced Africans did not have a figure of the divinity that was black like them. All other cultures had representation of God in *their* image. Jesus was probably black. The Bible says he had hair like a lamb and the bottom of his feet was like burnt bronze. But that was changed as it came through the white churches. I believe we all have a divine destiny like Haile Selassie but most people never claim theirs. To me, we are all expressions of the Divine on earth. Some, like Jesus, Buddha, Mohammed, and perhaps Selassie I, just remember this and live true to that reality. I don't believe there is only one true messiah or one true religion. We are all messiahs in embryo. My whole journey and these books are still about One Love. Whenever I leave that base it causes separation and arguing. Even

51

Gathering of the Healers

Selassie, who was Christian, said, 'No one should question the faith of others for no human being can judge the ways of God.' So a true Rastafarian would have to live by these words since they were spoken by their spiritual master."

At this point a group of school kids where gathering around Tasha's shop for after-school treats so we wandered back over. Until the school stopped off-campus lunches because their cafeteria was losing money, most of the students and their teachers would come to his place for lunch every day (he reluctantly cooked chicken even though he didn't eat it). Dressed in their school uniforms, they were laughing and playing. Obviously coming to Tasha's was one of the highlights of their day. We wandered over. It was a pleasure to watch Tasha interact with them like a kind older brother. You could tell it was one of the highlights of his day too.

After I left Tasha's, I headed toward Port Antonio. As I drove along the coast I passed a sign that read, "Ras Johnson's Ital Food." I had noticed it several times before and had often considered stopping but this time something said "Stop!" I pulled down the driveway and was pleasantly surprised. Set in an opening surrounded by a small beach in the front and the Christmas River wrapping around the back, was two well-built thatched-roof round buildings under some beautiful shade trees—very roots, very mellow. One building was a tee-shirt design studio and the other an open-air restaurant. Its large shutters were closed.

The place was empty except for Ras Johnson, who was raking leaves in front of the restaurant. Ras Johnson had two-foot long dreads and a black beard. One arm stopped just below the elbow. He handled the rake with the dexterity that showed his disability wasn't one. He was a well-built, vibrant looking man. A newer model Honda sat in the driveway. I got out of the car and he greeted me with a big smile which lit up his face.

"Ras Johnson, me brethren," I said, putting my right fist over my heart, "can I get some lunch?"

"Well, now, I'm really not open today," he said, smiling. "But if you

Gathering of the Healers

come back tomorrow, I can make you some Ital stew. If you just tell me what time you're coming, I'll meet you here."

He was humble but powerful—a nice combination. Usually I wouldn't make commitments like this, never knowing what the next day may bring but there was something about him and the setting that made me want to return. We agreed on eleven the next morning. Another man wandered over and introduced himself as AJ. He was an intense man, tall and clean-shaven with short hair and looked to be in his thirties. He would look away when I talked to him and then suddenly turn back to me and fix my gaze. He seemed both troubled and searching. However, the more he talked, the more I was impressed by his intellect and spiritual insights.

We chatted awhile longer and Ras Johnson showed me pictures of his wife and kids. He was married to a German woman and had two children in Germany and another child in Greece. They spent most of the year in Germany and the rest here in rural Jamaica. He showed me pictures of him in Finland where he plays in a reggae band and skis cross-country. By the time I left, I felt even stronger about my decision to return the next day. I gave them both a book and headed out to find Scram.

I found Scram at his shop and settled in there while he cooked us dinner. It's always amazing to watch Scram prepare food. To him it is a meditation and a gift. He loves to cook big meals for me. Since he was once the chef at Dragon Bay Resort they are delicious and beautifully presented with everything arranged on the plate just so. There is never a sense of rush around Scram (as there always is around me). He might take ten minutes to grate the coconut to make coconut oil; slowly grating it, soaking it in water and forcefully squeezing it between his powerful hands. Sitting in his makeshift kitchen, watching him cook over homemade charcoal in a stove made from an old tire rim supported by three pieces of old rebar, you couldn't feel more catered to if you were in a five-star restaurant watching a master chef.

Even when we went out for the day Scram would do our cooking. He would usually bring a small sack with a few yams, potatoes (which he called "Irishes") or breadfruit. If he didn't bring any he would buy some from a local. Then he would build a small fire while we talked with someone and roast our lunch—a picnic, roots style.

After dinner, Scram and I drove over to the Frenchman's Cove so we could reason awhile without interruption. We settled in on the deck and I told him of the idea of the "Gathering of the Healers." We discussed the highly volatile political issues involved. I wasn't sure we should keep pursuing Prime Minister Patterson and his rival Seaga.

"Dis political violence is recent. We want to bring t'ings back into dos days when two parties would be in one village an' not a person would get a scratch. If de people go back into dere real moral mind, dey will know how to act. We need dis love to motivate amongst us. Seaga and Patterson, dey are supposed to be toget'er hand-in-hand to show de people dis. Dey are ready fe dat."

"So you really believe Seaga and Patterson don't want all this fighting?" I asked.

"No. Dey doan't want all of dis. But right now it's 'ard fe dem to stop it. De people need to 'ave de love to stop it. People need to see de two men workin' toget'er. An' all across de wurld now, de big leaders like Bush and Blair, dey will one day want de violence to stop because it 'as 'urt dem, too."

"So you think we should try to get the politicians to come?" I asked.

"Yeah. Yeah, mon. We invite dem an' see if dey want to come."

"Next Saturday night is the Rebel Salute," I said. Every year, Tony Rebel, a well-known reggae artist, has a huge concert with all the best known Jamaican reggae artists. "Let's go there and see if we can link up with Tony and Luciano and ask them to join us. We can stop in Kingston on the way and see Muta and the people at the Marley Museum. A number of people have told me if we can get Muta to join us it could have a big impact because so many people listen to his weekly program."

"Yeah, mon," Scram said. "Muta's doin' a good job 'ere. We reason wit' dem. I believe de way you are doin' it is de right way. De people will 'ave a better vision to overstand all dese t'ings. Dey will join our cluster."

After awhile we started talking about the low wages and the extreme poverty in which most Jamaicans live. The minimum daily wage in

Gathering of the Healers

Jamaica is 360 Jamaican dollars (about US$10) and yet their cost of consumer goods, from gasoline to toilet paper to sugar, is the same as in America, often higher as most things must be imported. For instance, my cell service in the U.S. is a fraction of the twenty-five cents *per minute* I must pay for my cell calls in Jamaica. And if I call a cell on a different service than mine, I pay seventy-five cents! Given that few houses in the countryside of Jamaica have electric or phone lines, many people use cell and must pay these exorbitant rates.

The average Jamaican earns US $3260.00 a year, making it one of the poorest countries in the Western Hemisphere. In budget year 2000-01, 68.6% of every Jamaican tax dollar goes to paying off debt, much to the IMF and the World Bank. The next year (2002) was no better with the government getting deeper into debt by borrowing the equivalent of 40 per cent of the $210-billion public sector expenditure planned for the fiscal year, according to finance minister, Dr. Omar Davies. Basically, Jamaica had to borrow 40% of the money needed to run their country that year. Each year it gets poorer and real incomes have declined since 1980. In a one year period when I was traveling to the island, I watched the value of the Jamaican dollar go from 40 to 46 Jamaican dollars per one U.S. dollar. That means every Jamaican's savings and buying power lost 13 percent in one year. In 1993 the Jamaican dollar stood at around 20 U.S. dollars.

It is estimated that 50% live in poverty and many more marginally so. Approximately one-third of the population is unemployed (there are no unemployment benefits) and another third freelances in the "informal-sector" by higgling, hustling and operating the thousands of tiny shops. Since there are few cars, these shops are every half mile or so, providing the local neighbors with daily staples, cold drinks, rum, beer, ganja and cigarettes. Government help for the poor is almost non-existent.

Though there is some malnutrition, there is no starvation in Jamaica. The island is too fertile for that, with fresh organic coconuts, breadfruit, star fruit, plums, bananas and other delicacies dripping off the trees. This liberates the island from the dehumanizing effects of starvation seen in other poor countries. Many rural people that make up the majority of Jamaicans have small year-round subsistence gardens that produce yams, carrots, potatoes, squash, etc.

Since independence in 1962, there has been a significant growth in the middle-class. However, economic opportunities, especially for the vast rural poor, are almost non-existent, creating frustration and anger, especially in young adults. Many have migrated to Kingston in search of work only to find themselves worse off living in the vast slums of Trench Town, Back-A-Wall or Tivoli Gardens. If they can obtain a much-coveted visa, the often go to the U.S. or England, living in the large Jamaican communities there. It is estimated that over two million Jamaicans now live abroad, almost the same number that live on the island.

However, poverty needs to be looked at holistically. People *every-where* struggle to find meaning, love and happiness in their lives. Though it might be more obviously true in "poor" countries, it is also true in "rich" countries. As an American, I can testify to that. Enough money is only one element needed for a full and happy human life. We also need health, a feeling of connection to our families, neighbors and community, meaningful work, personal free time and enjoyable recreation opportunities. Also, we are learning more and more that a sense of connection to nature and the earth is essential. Spending most of our lives in man-made environments, no matter how opulent, will never offer us full "livity."

Living in *financial* poverty means you are missing one of the many needed elements. Many people are financially "rich" yet emotionally or spiritually poor and visa versa. In fact, finding the other needed elements is becoming more and more difficult for those of us living in an affluent, high-tech world. Or as Mother Theresa said after a trip to the United States, "Loneliness is the most terrible poverty."

"De people in de country, dey go in de jungle," Scram said, "an' dey plant up dere little stuff an' dey come into Port Antonio an' sell it. Dat is what dey do fe dere whole lifetime. An' even den dey cayn not pay fe dere children's school uniform and maybe dere children cayn't go to school. All dey want from de government is a good road an' some water in de pipe an' de government doan't even give dem dat. So we 'ave to get dis love to de leaders so dey will treat de small people right."

Gathering of the Healers

Scram and I talked until late in the night. Around midnight we watched some of "Malcolm X," another video I had brought. I especially wanted to show it to Scram but when I went to the video store to rent it two days before I was to leave so I could copy it, it was checked out. Disappointed, I headed home and turned on the TV. As I ran the channels, there it was just starting on HBO.

It was a great movie to watch with Scram. It follows Malcolm X's life from criminal to anti-white Black Muslim to peacemaker and an apostle of racial harmony. It is about a black man who, understandably, felt great bitterness towards whites until he later, after a spiritual transformation, understood the behavior that he hated was common among *all* races of people and *toward* all races of people. This was the message Malcolm X brought forward until his death.

"And the healing of the nation is not just a Jamaican thing. It's a world thing because the entire world is in turmoil today."
—**Denroy Morgan,** founder of the reggae group Morgan Heritage

Chapter 4
January 5, 2002

Denroy Morgan

The next morning I drove to Ras Johnson's arriving around eleven to find he had opened the shutters of his restaurant and was busily cutting vegetables for the stew. He was holding the knife in his armpit and deftly holding the vegetables with his one hand. I found it endearing that he had trusted me to return. The restaurant was spotlessly clean and very comfortable with a bar on one side and breathtaking views of the ocean and the river. AJ was at the bar and I joined him there.

"When did you start to lock-up and grow your dreads?" I asked Ras Johnson.

"Ever since I was a yout' me love de Rasta," he said. "Me love ta hear dem talk, yaunderstandme. It is an inborn concept. Not somet'ing like you turn or join like you join a church. Somet'ing what's inside. Ya 'ave ta be what you are. Always I knew dis was my path. It's a life. Ya get de fullness. But in my yout' you see one Rasta today and maybe it would be anot'er month before you see anot'er Rasta. Dey's around but dey back in de hills."

"So they weren't down here by the waterfront much?" I asked.

"No. Becuz in dos times," Ras Johnson continued, "if you were a

Gathering of the Healers

Rasta you get a lot of fight, you know. Police stick Rasta in de car and carry dem to de station fe no reason. Rastamon always love peace. Rasta love ta plant, love nature. But dere are still a lot of Rastamon up in de hills. But now you may look around an' see a lot of men dat look like Rastamon but dey nah Rasta. De are de wolves, de dreads. An' if dey do somet'ing bad dey just cut dere hair and hide. I and I know it's what's in the inside. Anot'er mon may look like I but 'e doesn't live de covenant. When you put on de faith an' you see de light, it's continually. Ya nah turn back. Rasta is just Rasta. All I look fe is inside. I just look wit'in. All de fullness is in 'ere," he said putting his hand over his heart.

"And you knew that since you were a kid?" I asked.

"Yes," he said, "but it was always a problem wit' me parents. When you grow up wit' parents, you 'ave to do like what dey do. My 'air was always a problem wit' dem. Even my grandfather. But I love dem. Dey 'ave good hearts. Ya parents grow you but as soon as you know yourself an' know dat, yes, I will lead myself. An' when you start to put on dese dreads you lose all friends, all family. Ev'ryone turn against you. It still go on but now it becomes a little lighter becuz now dey are seein' dis One Love dat 'as been Rasta from de beginnin'. It 'as been preached to de people, teached to de people. Now dey are seein' de light of dis One Love."

In my many talks with older Rastas I heard similar stories of persecution by the Jamaican authorities and discrimination by the general population. Rastas are highly visible on the island. There are an estimated 100,000+ dreads but how many of these are true Rastas no one knows. Almost every Jamaican knows of many people within their family or community who started growing locks, smoking ganja and abandoning their desire for material success and then left the fold forever. It was, and is, a common scenario and one that is not embraced by most Jamaicans and almost no government officials. And what is even more alarming to many, Rastas numbers are growing.

Though this persecution has abated since the 1970s when then-Prime Minister Michael Manley officially ordered the Jamaican police, army and court system to treat Rastas with the same respect as all Jamaicans, it still persists to some degree today. In the early years of the Rastafarian

Gathering of the Healers

faith, from the 1930s to the 1970s especially, it took great commitment to wear dreadlocks and keep your covenant with the Almighty—a commitment not unlike that of the early Christians.

In the past, Rastas were stopped at roadblocks and the police would force them to cut off each other's dreads, often using only a broken bottle. You couldn't take a plane off the island with dreads or get a job. Since they often look almost ferocious with their huge dreads (until you see their smiles or feel their vibes), people convinced their children Rastas were "black-heart" and to run away if they saw them. Police arrested them, often even killed them, and asked questions later. Yet they held to their covenant, refusing to trim their hair and adopt "Babylon's values."

Jamaica is very much a tribal culture and almost everyone in Jamaica now knows a "heartical" Rasta and because of this respect for them is established. To this day, the true Rastas walk the island teaching love and peace to all they encounter. Because of their total commitment to their way of life (much like the early Christians), they have the authority to call to us to teach love as they are doing. Or as Morgan Heritage sings, "Could you live through what the ancient Rastaman lived through? Would you hold on to your faith after what they've been through?"

"And when you say One Love, what do you mean?" I asked.

"We mean blessings from de heart," AJ answered. "Love is God. We mean one brother, one sister, one God, one blood."

"It doesn't matter the race or color," Ras Johnson said. "We are all JAH's creation. Ev'ryt'ing on de face of de earth is JAH's creation. But let me ask you, why do you t'ink so many people don't 'ave love in dem?"

"Well, I think that everyone was created in their Creator's image," I answered, pleased to be given the floor, something that rarely happens when talking spirituality with Rastas. "The Creator is Love, One Love, and we are created in His image so we are love but we have forgotten this because our fears and our attachments. So we are spiritual beings who believed ourselves to be separate from our Creator and everyone else. With this false belief in separation we create a physical body,

Gathering of the Healers

which is the symbol of separation and we incarnate on this planet with six billion other beings who also believe they're separate. Because of free will, all of us here are going through this detour into fear so we can learn this is *not* who we are. We are not separate but One. But all our lifetimes here are not even real. They're just illusions of separation, as Eastern religions teach. Most people are still sleepwalking. We are always One, always Love. We have never left our Creator. We just temporarily dreamed we did. It's a journey without distance. Love is the only thing that is real. Everything else is illusion. We're either extending love or asking for love. Every form of fear is an asking for love, no matter what form it takes. So to me the whole goal here is to remember that we—that everyone—is love and we do that by loving ourselves and others. Then we help to remember as well as helping everyone we meet. If we treat someone unlovingly or judgmentally we reinforce their false belief in separation and we reinforce our own. We extend the pain for both and keep each other asleep. That's why so many people don't remember this One Love. They're just the younger spirits who have little awareness of who they are or why they're here. We're all still learning and all at different stages of remembering, different grades in this one-planet schoolhouse. But none of us are bad or evil. We're just forgetful. I think we keep doing this lifetime after lifetime until we remember who we really as Jesus did. He's our older brother showing us the Way, the Truth. Eventually, we're all going Home because we never really left."

"Yes. We are 'ere to share love," Ras Johnson agreed. "We must seek fe love, seek fe peace."

"I believe the species can all wake up together," I continued. "And One Love, can reawaken in the hearts of humanity. And even though things look rather strange on earth now, if you look at it from a historical perspective, the universe is moving quickly toward greater love. Up until 250 years ago, almost every person born lived under the control and whim of a warlord or king. Now over half the world lives in democracies. Throughout history, slavery was an accepted, even legal, institution until the 1860s. Most of the people who lived on this island 160 years ago were slaves. Now it's unthinkable. Racial, religious and gen-

61

der tolerance is growing in many areas. So historically the arch of the universe is toward greater and greater levels of love. Babylon *is* getting weaker and weaker. And now after the World Trade Center fell, even the big guys will soon want the violence to stop. And when the big powers want it to stop, it will. The whole system is spring-loaded and ready to snap to correction because whether they know it or not, love is what everyone is seeking. They just mistakenly believe it's in money or power or accomplishing or belonging or pleasuring. So we may be at the point where the planet is ready to move into One Love."

I told them about my plans for the press conference and that I still had no idea how to meet the healers. AJ eyes brightened immediately.

"Ya know, my full name is AJ Brown," he said, enthusiastically. "Dennis Brown was my uncle and I've known Denroy Morgan since I was a kid. I cayn take you to meet 'im becuz 'e is a friend of mine, almost family becuz we share lands together in St. Thomas."

Dennis Brown, known as the "Crown Prince of Reggae," is a reggae singer who had died three years earlier. In Jamaica he had reached near legendary status. Denroy Morgan is the founder and head of Morgan Heritage, an internationally acclaimed reggae group.

"Really," I said, somewhat suspiciously. In Jamaica almost everyone is, or claims to be, a relative of someone famous. I didn't really want to pursue it any further because I was afraid I might be getting hustled.

"No, really, mon, I cayn tek you dere after you eat," he said, more emphatically, probably picking up on my suspiciousness. "Ya know, you are a real Rasta like Morgan Heritage. People ev'rywhere love, respect, an' cherish Denroy Morgan. De father, Denroy, 'e used to sing dese t'ings an' he doan't get not'ing becuz some necktie mon take all de money. But you do dese t'ings becuz you love. It's somet'ing inside of you. Ya just do it. But now 'is younger artists are doing better. Dey 'ave dere own company."

"Does he live near here?" I asked.

"Yeah, mon. 'E lives just down de road near Bath. He is building a studio near dere," he said. "Today is Tuesday an' 'e is dere today. I t'ink what you are doing' is very much important an' Jamaica needs dis now. I know dat JAH has sent you here ta do dis work. Last night seven of us sat in my friends shop an' read your book until eleven o'clock. An' de shop owner gave it to his daughter who teaches at Passley Gardens College fe 'er to read to 'er students. She said it is de best book on Jamaica ever."

It seemed like the statement someone might say to flatter but I sensed that he really meant it. I felt I was awaking some long suppressed sense of hope in him.

"OK. Let's go after lunch," I said, figuring I had nothing to lose and everything to gain.

Morgan Heritage, often referred to as the "Royal Family of Reggae," is made up of five of Denroy Morgan's 29 children: baritone singer/songwriter Roy ("Gramps" or "Grandpa"), soprano and key-boardist Una, who also serves as the group's executive manager and tenor Peter, Lukes and Mr. Mojo. Denroy, a leading reggae producer and internationally known for his 1981 hit, "I'll Do Anything For You," also performs with Morgan Heritage. Three other siblings have another recording group, LMS, named after Laza, Miriam and Shypoo, which has just released the album *Zion Gate* on the VP label.

"He kept us away from violence, kept us away from the streets," Gramps recently said. "He did a great job as our dad to keep our heads straight and let us know we can do this music thing."

Denroy also taught his huge brood to pray every morning and to keep "JAH in our midst" to serve as mediator and referee when family arguments inevitably happened.

They released their debut album, *Miracles*, in 1994 through MCA records, and then later released *Protect Us JAH* and *One Calling* through VP/71. "The record company (MCA) was trying to sell it the way they wanted to," Gramps said recently. "They didn't want us to be different...We didn't have much to say."

In 1993, Denroy returned to Jamaica to rest and stayed at the Bath Fountain Hotel in St. Thomas Parish. "During my stay at Bath Fountain," he said, "I was given the inspiration to write 12 songs in the space of two weeks. The lyrics came to me early in the morning and they represent my life. My livity with my family is based on spirituality; therefore, there's spirituality within the songs."

In 1995, the entire family moved back to Jamaica, their father's homeland where he was raised in the countryside, all agreeing that they needed to return to their roots and the grounding of their musical inspiration.

"It's brought us closer to the roots of the music, to the depth of the music...You feel the reggae vibe here on the island," Peter said in an interview. "Reggae is the heartbeat of these people; it comes from their pulse."

Forming their own production companies, HMG and 71 Records, with Denroy as executive producer, the group released *Morgan Heritage: Friends & Family, Vol. 1* and then the breakthrough roots-reggae hit came in 1999 with the single and album *Don't Haffi Dread*, which, much to the anger of some Rastas, was a call to spiritual unity and reminded the world that, "you don't haffi dread to be Rasta. Dis is nah a dreadlock thing. It's a Divine conception from the heart."

They have recently released their newest and best album, *More Teachings,* referring to the teachings of Emperor Haile Selassie I. " 'JAH Seed' is a testament of how God has been in our lives," Denroy said in a 2001 interview about the songs on *More Teachings.* " 'Always On My Mind' is a love song. 'Helping Hand' shows us how to help our brothers and sisters in need and 'Meskal Square' is a history that unveils the finding, in Ethiopia, of the true cross that Jesus was crucified on."

"We are keeping roots music alive," Peter told the *North Coast Journal* in 2001, "and at the same time bringing across a humanitarian message of love and peace for all people no matter what color or creed. We have enough people today doing music talking about sex and jewelry or whatever. Reggae talks about social issues, spiritual into the world...It's about helping to find a solution to bring forth change."

Their music has won virtually every music award named for the reggae genre, including: the International Reggae Awards for Reggae Album of the Year, Tamika Awards; the Nelson Mandela Award for Most Conscious Lyrics, Reggae Album of the Year, Reggae Soca

Gathering of the Healers

Awards for Reggae Group of the Year and Most Cultural Artist of the Year.

In 1995 and 1996, Denroy Morgan and Morgan Heritage was invited to perform in West Africa, an experience that further blessed their lives. Denroy reflected, "We have been to Africa. Africa is the foundation roots for the Black man. It's a family oriented life-style and I see where the family structure is being broken down in Africa. They have seen what I am trying to do in the West with my family and if the motherland's family structure is being destroyed then they know how much of a struggle I have been through to maintain my children, to become a successful family, and to have seen my children become adults where now my grandchildren are being raised in the same home where I'm still raising children. It's just phenomenal. It's such a great blessing from the Almighty!"

Says Una, "The advantage is that is everything stays within the family business—management, the writing, production. Even if there's a disagreement, we're right there with each other. We believe that the Creator has blessed us with this mission of music, and we believe our message is universal because everyone understands and feels love in one form or another."

Their songs offer a humanitarian, deeply spiritual, and positive message of peace, consciousness and love with a strong, almost tribal, thread of African and Jamaican vibrations. Their music is much more than their creative expression and livelihood. It is even more than a calling. To Morgan Heritage, dynamic and powerful on stage and off, their music is a fulfillment of a prophecy. As a recent article stated, "Morgan Heritage is surely roots reggae's strongest link to the past and brightest beacon for the future."

After saying goodbye to Ras Johnson, AJ and I headed out. We drove about a half-hour into the hills above Bath until we came to a large compound high on a hill with a sculpted concrete entrance gate that read, "Heritage Estates: Welcome Jah's Children." There were several Rases sitting near the gate that knew AJ and they talked in Patois for a few

Gathering of the Healers

minutes.

"Denroy doesn't live 'ere yet," AJ said to me. "Dey are still building dis place but we can go over to 'is 'ouse in Morant Bay. It is only about a half-hour from 'ere."

"Are you sure you know how to get there?" I asked.

"Yeah, mon," AJ said. "It is not far and I know where it is. I've been dere many times. I know dis man since I was a little pickney."

We drove another 45 minutes along the coast highway toward Kingston until we came to the outskirts of Morant Bay, where AJ told me to turn left into a subdivision area. The subdivision was set back from the ocean, a flat piece of land, sparsely treed with several mid-sized homes scattered around. We drove a half-mile or so in and AJ told me to pull into the drive of an attractive one-story stucco home, part of a two house compound with a large bay in the back yard.

"Dis is Denroy's 'ome," AJ said. "Ya cayn pull in dat driveway."

We got out of the car and walked up to the locked iron gate that led to a small inner courtyard, a common fixture in most middle and upper-class homes everywhere in Jamaica. Though violent crimes are rare toward strangers in Jamaica, theft is an issue in most areas. AJ yelled something in Patois through the gate and soon a very attractive young Jamaican woman appeared. She looked to be in her early twenties, tall and erect, proud and gentle. She and AJ talked in Patois and then she looked at me for the first time. Her eyes had such a kind, almost celestial quality, that I was instantly taken aback.

"I'm Taliba. Denroy is my father but he's not home right now," she said in perfect English. Her voice was as gentle and soothing as her eyes. "I don't know when he'll be home."

I began to tell her why we had come and just then another young man in his twenties appeared from the house and joined us at the gate. He introduced himself as Taliba's brother, Shypoo. He was thin, almost petite, with dreadlocks and a beard. Like his sister there was almost an angelic quality about him that radiated love and kindness. I continued my story, feeling like I could spend all day in the presence of these two. While Shypoo went back in the house, I gave Taliba a copy of my book to give to her father. Shypoo soon returned with a CD in his hand.

Gathering of the Healers

"This is a copy of our new CD, *More Teachings*," he said. "I want you to have it. I was at the Bob Marley Museum yesterday and I saw three copies of your book there and I was looking at it and liking it. I think my dad will like what you are doing. Here's his phone number."

Neither Shypoo nor his sister seemed to have Jamaican accents. I later learned that all 29 Morgan children had been raised between Brooklyn, New York and Springfield, Massachusetts, having moved there from Jamaica in 1965. Ranging in age from 40 to 6, and including 55 grandchildren to date, Denroy's offspring already includes two nurses, a teacher, flight attendant, accountant, record producer, two social workers and a business consultant. Being raised by Denroy, a 30-year veteran and one of the foundation builders of reggae who helped spread the music around the world, their home was infused with this musical vibe.

"This family thrives on God...My father keeps God at the center of his life," Una Morgan, the group's lead female singer, said of her upbringing in a recent interview. "He has vision and is divinely blessed...When we were at home, it was a Rastafarian culture. Going, outside, it was a different story."

Disappointed that I had missed Denroy, but elated that I had made a solid connection for a follow-up, AJ and I headed toward my car. As we were about to get in, a large, shiny new pickup pulled up, a rather incongruous sight in this part of the island where most vehicles are small Japanese cars or vans.

"Oh, there's my dad now," Taliba said.

I approached the pickup but because of the tinted windows I couldn't make out who was inside. No one opened the doors for a minute and I began feeling a little awkward, like a kid waiting for the school bus doors to open. I knew the people in the pickup were sizing me up and probably wondering what I was doing in the drive and what I wanted from them. Just then, the doors opened on both sides and two children crawled out of the seat behind the driver.

Denroy was driving and he looked at me from behind dark sunglasses. Denroy looks to be in his mid-forties (though he is actually in his late-fifties), a tall solidly built man with jet-black two-foot long, rope-

Gathering of the Healers

like dreads and a full beard with hanging precepts that accent a round expressive face. He cut the engine and stepped out of the truck almost reluctantly and looked me over. He nodded to AJ but I couldn't tell if it was from recognition or politeness. I had a sense he was thinking, *I guess there's no way I can get on with my busy day without talking to this guy. I just hope he makes it short.*

His personal power was obvious, almost overwhelming. He moved with the grace and confidence of a man accustomed to being in charge and respected yet with the aloofness of a man who had learned to protect himself and his loved ones from takers and betrayers. From behind his dark sunglasses, I couldn't really get a sense him and it threw me off a little.

"Mr. Morgan, I'm Robert Roskind and if you'll give me a few minutes of your time, you won't regret it," I said, extending my hand to him, which he took in a firm grasp while still keeping a physical and emotional distance.

I explained to him my family's brief history in Jamaica and the concept for the "Gathering of the Healers" press conference. He stood still looking at me from behind his sunglasses, seemingly expressionless and unmoved

"So that's what I want to do," I said in closing, "and I want to invite you to be one of the healers and join us. Almost everyone I ask names you and Morgan Heritage as one of the teachers of love on the island and many commented that you are one of the few examples of upful family life. I think that you're being there would be very beneficial, especially in encouraging families to stay together."

"JAH RASTAFARI! All praise Emperor Haile Selassie I, King of Kings, Lion of Judah, Holy of Holies. In the beginning as it is in the end!" Denroy said in a loud commanding voice. He reminded me of Dr. Martin Luther King, Jr. at his best. "This is a vision that we share but before I say that I will join you in this, there are a few more things that I must know. I know that this blessing is not just for us to enjoy but it's for us to take seriously. We have to live this life and to fulfill the prophecy. So we live life so that man will see it and glorify the Father in Zion. I know that it is a ministry. Even as a Rastaman, it is more urgent for us to make this livity to go out to the public. We want the world to know that the Rastaman in this time comes with the redeeming power of Jesus Christ and the resurrecting power of Jesus Christ. Not the crucifixion power but the resurrecting power. Because we are the dry bones in the valley. We are the ones who the Almighty has put his fingers into. We are the ones who the Lion of Judah loosed the Seven Seals and set free with serenity, prophecy and priesthood, judge and governorship. All of this comes down to true faith which we are trying to live by and it must fulfill in a ceremonial purity. Whether in our sermon, whether it is in our home or it's in the field, it must be pure to the Almighty Creator! Now I must ask you do you believe that God can be flesh?"

"Yes. I do," I said. He still had his sunglasses on, so I couldn't tell exactly what he was feeling. He asked me a few more questions before his final one.

"We believe that there's only one Creator. We believe that there is no language or culture where His voice is not heard and we believe that there's only One that was set to be crucified that His blood may be shed. We know He *has* returned in the personality of his Imperial Majesty Emperor, Haile Selassie I, the first King of Kings and Lord of Lords. Without doubt or apology, 72 nations bowed to him and acknowledged him as King of Kings! Revelation has showed us that Christ *would* return in his kingly character so we want to see the unification of all Rastaman. And that is who we are reaching out to and crying to right now! What are we crying for? For the unification of all Rastaman. We are from the Royal Black House of David without doubt or apology so we want to fulfill the prophecy. We want to see the restoration of the Solomonic Dynasty based upon the Davidic covenant. That's why I say that our livity has become a ministry because within it there is divinity to pass on through generation to generation. Now I must ask you, do you believe that His Majesty Haile Selassie I, Conquering Lion of the Tribe of Judah, King of Kings, Lord of Lords *is* the Divine Messenger of the Almighty?"

I hadn't expected this when I came but I had expected it once he started talking. He seemed determined, almost fierce. I felt a little on trial, like I was being tested and this was the only question that mattered.

Gathering of the Healers

"I feel that he was divine like you and I and everyone is divine," I said, knowing I could only answer him with the conclusion I had reached after over a year immersed in Rastafari. "I believe he had a divine mission, like all of us do, and that he successfully completed his, as many of us never do. I believe God sent him to catalyze Rastafari by giving black people a proud, noble kingly image. There were almost none of those before Selassie. However, I don't believe he was operating at the same level as Christ, who was showing us an example of how to live a purely loving life. Though I think Emperor Selassie was a deeply spiritual man committed to helping all humanity, I couldn't point to his life and tell my children that it represented the highest level a life can be lived. He had armies, palaces, wore a military uniform and was a secular leader. I *could* tell my children to live like Jesus. He owned nothing, had no temporal power and spent his life teaching love. But I do believe what I was taught when I was a kid in synagogue: that there will be a Messianic Era when every person will be their own messiah."

I paused to register the impact of my words. Denroy said nothing.

"And I would understand," I said breaking the pregnant pause, "if because of my not believing in the divinity of Haile Selassie you didn't want to join me."

A comfortable silence settled between us. It was his time to decide and we both knew it. He slowly took off his sunglasses and for the first time I looked in his eyes and I knew him and knew what his answer would be. As the eyes are always the windows to the soul, Denroy's soul was untainted and incorruptible, the soul of a man totally committed to live a pure life as close to God's will as possible. He looked at me searchingly as if an inner struggle was going on between the man who had been all too painfully disappointed before and the man who knew with every fiber of his being that love was the only answer, the only reality.

"Well, you're neither a liar nor a hypocrite and I like that. I will come to your press conference if I am on the island then," he said, a relaxation coming over his face, his decision made. "And if I'm not, someone from the family will. Give me a call in a few weeks."

He extended his hand to me. Looking me straight in the eye, he shook

Gathering of the Healers

my hand, lowered his sunglasses, and got back in the truck. I walked over to my car to get another copy of *Rasta Heart* and brought it over to him, handing it through his now opened window. Gail Moses (Sister Pat to the family), the youngest of his two wives, was in the car with him and had been listening to our reasoning. As they began to pull away, she looked me in the eye and said, "Your journey will be well paid for. You keep going."

I headed back to Port Antonio feeling elated. I dropped AJ in Port Antonio, thanked him and headed back to my hotel. With Denroy's commitment, I knew it would be much easier to get others to join us. Denroy was a very respected personality on the island both within the Rastafarian community and the population in general. His joining would open many doors for us. Back at Frenchman's Cove, I called Julia and shared the good news with her. That very morning I had no idea how to get this thing going and now, seven hours later, it was launched and through no real effort on my part. JAH had sent AJ to take me to Denroy.

After talking to Julia and Alicia, I went for a swim at the beach, ordered a pizza from the San San Tropez and relaxed watching the rest of "The Color Purple". Scram came over around ten o'clock.

"Do you still think I should invite Patterson and Seaga?" I asked Scram as we sat out on the deck overlooking the beach later that night. "I'm still a little torn as whether we should mix in the politicians, even just to come and listen. The political scene here is a mess and can get violent. I can see where the opposition party wouldn't want things getting better here before the next election comes up later this year. Someone might even take a shot at us to get us to stop. They're shooting people for a lot less in Kingston."

"Dis time dey not goin' to kill de messengers like dey did de first time. Send de book to Seaga like you did to Patterson and let dem read it," Scram said. "We will still invite dem. It is only dem dat cayn skip

Gathering of the Healers

over us an' den we will still mention dem in de book. Dey see dat dis t'ing, dis killin' on de island, reach to a point where dey demselves would want everyt'ing to change. Dese guys are ready fe some kind of a peace an' even if dey just read de book an' doan't come, it will change dere hearts. Dey will try to pick de wisdom out of it fe demselves. We are tellin' de truth to dem."

"So we should call their offices when we get to Kingston and try to meet with Seaga and Patterson on this trip?" I asked.

"Yeah, mon. Even de politicians in Port Antonio are reading de book now an' dey are gainin' de right knowledge. Invite all dem. Who doan't come, dey in de next book," he said laughing. "But dis is de last call becuz dis nuclear t'ing and dis pollution is rushin' us now. We just tryin' to get the heart of de people ready before someone just press dat button. Only love cayn stop it an' we are tryin' to push dis love in to de 'ead-quarters so dese wurld leaders can soften dere hearts. Even now de Indians and de Pakistanis are on de border an' everone is tryin' to cool dem down so dey doan't use dese nuclear weapons. So right now it is only de One Love dat cayn change de vibes." There had been a major flair up between these two nuclear powers earlier in the week and the whole world was on edge as they both threatened possible nuclear retaliation.

"So we are just prayin' to 'elp change de vibes so t'ings will go our way," he said laughing. "Becuz dis One Love is so high dey cayn't get over it an' it's so wide dey cayn't get around it and it's so low dey cayn't get under it. Dey gotta come t'ru de door, dis One Love door, you know," and we both broke up laughing.

"I'm not a person dat goin' on a journey an' when I cayn't find de 'ead of de journey, I'm ready to turn back. Me keep goin'. An' I t'ink dat people will read our book an' want to 'elp us make dese different t'ings 'appen, all des t'ings like in Moore Town. But if dey 'elp us yes or no, it's still goin' push though."

Long after midnight we turned in, Scram sleeping on the couch in the living room. The following day we planned to go to Kingston to try to meet with Antonnette Haughton, Muta and Barrington Laing, the manager of the Bob Marley Museum. After that we planned to head across

Gathering of the Healers

the island to the Rebel Salute, Tony Rebel's big yearly concert, where we hoped to meet him and Luciano. The day after the Salute, I planned to drive to Nine Mile, where Bob Marley was born and buried. On Ras Barrett's advice, I had called Bob's mother, Cedella Marley Booker or Mama B or Mother B, as she is called, at her home there. I briefly explained to her what I was planning and asked if I could come visit her. After some thought, she agreed. I made arrangements to drive to meet her in Nine Mile after the Rebel Salute.

"I am not a Rasta. I am a Christian but I think that your efforts are not just for Rastas but for everyone, no matter what their beliefs."
—**Barrington Laing,** manager, Bob Marley Museum, Kingston

Chapter 5
January 11, 2002

On The Road Again

"**D**id I tell you about going to visit a Native American tribe?" I asked Scram as we headed toward Kingston the next morning.

"No, I doan't remember you say anyt'ing about dat."

"There is a tribe of Native Americans called the Havasupai," I said. "They have lived for centuries on the floor of the Grand Canyon and were known for their peaceful ways. They never warred like many of the other tribes. They live near the Colorado River near three beautiful waterfalls that are their sacred sites. It is the most remote place in the States. Until recently you had to drive way out in the desert to the rim of the Canyon and then go down four hours by horseback to get there. But now you can go down by helicopter in five minutes," I said and we both laughed.

"Back in the seventies," I continued, "somehow they got turned on to Bob Marley and for the first time they got small portable tape players and everyone started listening to his music. They believe he is a prophet. I called the tribal office and the guy there said everyone still listens to him but some of the youths have started listening to other singers. Julia and I are going to go camp there this summer for a week and meet with

74

their elders. If we like what we hear, we'll do a book on them, too."

"Yeah. Dat nice, mon" Scram answered. "becuz dey must 'ave a lot to say."

"Bob always wanted to visit the tribe that cherished his message of One Love," I continued. "He died before he could go but in 1982, a year after his death, his mother, Mama B, went there. It was a big celebration for the tribe. They brought a piano in by helicopter and set it in front of one of their huge sacred waterfalls. Two thousand people gathered around the waterfalls—on the beach, on the canyon walls, at the top—and Mama B played his songs until late into the night."

"That was a very much powerful night. I would have liked to be a Havasupai Indian dat night," he said and burst out laughing.

We stopped at a small shop run by Scram's cousin who I had met the summer before. He was a young man with a great build and a winning smile. Aside from running his shop, six months a year he worked tenhour days in the sugar cane fields for $10US per day, barely enough to pay for food for his family. However, his poverty didn't seem to affect his livity.

"Scram, when you're not in your shop, what are you doing?" I asked, always curious about his everyday life.

"Well, now, when I am not in me shop," he said, "I might go up into de mountains to see a few people an' do a little work fe dem. Dey might want some little t'ing fe me to do, you know. I might go to Moore Town or Cornwall Barracks. Becuz I doan't like to stay in de town everyday. An' I might bring some food back to sell and to eat. And I go around to check up on how to get de little cabins built near Nanny Falls. I talk wit' de colonel, Colonel Sterling. An' on Nanny Day, in October, I built some thatched stalls for de celebration so dey could sell dere t'ings when de people come. An' we were goin' to build a bamboo blockade between de school and de shop so when people are in de shop for a drink, de kids doan't get to see dat drinking."

We arrived in Kingston at mid-morning and drove directly over to the UPP office. The UPP is a new political party founded by Antonnette

Gathering of the Healers

Haughton-Cárdenas, a well-known attorney and talk show host. Many people I had asked had named her as someone who taught love on the island. Her political offices were located in the central business district of New Kingston. It felt like you were in the middle of any American city, complete with a Burger King, a Wendy's and a Pizza Hut. We parked down the street and walked over to the UPP headquarters, a spacious suite of offices on the second floor of a modern office building one block off the main street.

Several staff people were busily at work at their desks in the large open front room—a typical campaign headquarters plastered with party slogans and campaign posters. We introduced ourselves to the receptionist and took a seat. As we waited I picked up one of their brochures and read it.

<u>THE UNITED PEOPLE'S PARTY DEDICATED TO TRANSFORMING OUR NATION</u>

The United People's Party (UPP) has been formed in direct response to a major crisis in the Jamaican nation. It is a crisis which has deep historical roots as well as alarming modern complexities. It speaks to the fact that the majority of Jamaicans, who are of African origin, have had a social and economic experience of exclusion, oppression and discrimination. It speaks to a social situation which, on the national level, has been one of exploitation, dispossession and learned self-hatred.

The United People's Party commits itself to a policy of re-education, re-socialization and opportunities to transform the future social experience of Jamaicans to one of self-respect, dignity and healthy self-love. We commit ourselves to recognizing the contribution of every ethnic group to development and the search for social justice.

We make a very special commitment to the nation, and to

76

Gathering of the Healers

God, to create opportunities for our young people, and to invest fully in their development and well-being. As one of Jamaica's founding fathers, National Hero Norman Washington Manley, said: 'I affirm of Jamaica that we are a great people. Out of the past of fire and suffering and neglect, the human spirit has survived—patient and strong, quick to anger, quick to forgive, lusty and vigorous, but with deep reserves of loyalty and love and a deep capacity for steadiness under stress and for joy in all the things that make life good and blessed.'

Our Mission is to work to transform the society by empowering and inspiring our people to unite and build our nation; by working to ensure a system of justice, peace, and prosperity for all Jamaicans; and by creating a modern administrative system that is efficient, honest and accountable.

It went on to list 25 priorities including such things as upholding human rights, improving the educational and health care system and making it accessible to everyone; lifting the self-esteem of young Jamaicans by teaching African, Indian and Chinese history as well as Caribbean and Diasporic history; encouraging organic self-sufficient agriculture; developing herbs and health food resources; protecting the rights of the workers; promoting tourism by rapidly seeking to develop eco-tourism, health tourism and cultural tourism, and developing policies to protect and sustain the natural environment and to educate the population as to the importance of protecting the natural environment. A conscious political party! These were our kind of people!

After a short wait, Grace Alexander, the party's public relations officer, came out and introduced herself and ushered us in a pleasant conference room. Grace is an attractive, vivacious Jamaican woman in her twenties—warm and intelligent. Soon we were joined by Horace Matthews, the UPP's general secretary. Horace, a former aeronautical engineer, is a tall, handsome Jamaican, with a salt-and-pepper beard and a noble bearing. He has the look of a college professor and, much to our surprise, 18-inch long braided dreads hanging down his back.

I later learned that Horace was also the co-founder, along with

Gathering of the Healers

Marcus Garvey, Jr., of the revived UNIA, the United Negro Improvement Association, founded by Marcus Garvey in the 1930s, which now has divisions island-wide. Horace is currently President of the St. Andrew's Division of that Association in Jamaica. He also sat on the board of several schools on the island and was the founder of a school in Vineyard Town (later renamed the St. Matthews Basic School in his honor).

He is concerned by the shame which many Jamaicans of African descent feel about their ancestry and has worked consistently to help foster cultural identity and pride in the Jamaican youth. A widower, he is the father of several children including a son studying architecture, another studying computer science and a daughter who had just graduated as a doctor from the University of the West Indies (UWI).

Grace and Horace were both excited to see us and their enthusiasm for our efforts was apparent. We talked for almost an hour, being joined by other available staff members coming and going. It was a pleasure, like an oasis in the desert, to be with other people who shared our vision that the world could be healed with love. They felt sure that Antonnette would want to join us and we made arrangements to meet her on our next swing through Kingston.

After our arranged meeting, we headed over to The Bob Marley Museum for our meeting with Barrington Laing. We parked in the enclosed lot and headed toward his office. As we walked in the front door, Julian and his brother Damian Marley were talking with some of the other Rastas. I waved hello to Julian but barely got a response.

Damian "Jr. Gong" Marley (after his father, "Tuff Gong") was born in 1978 to Bob and Jamaica's former 1977 Miss World, Cindy Breakspeare. Damian has his father's build and dreads and has inherited the good looks of both parents. He seemed to have a thoughtful and gentle, yet dynamic, nature. The youngest of Bob's children, he grew up in the musical atmosphere of his father's Hope Road home. At 13, he formed a band, the Shepherds, with the son of Cat Coore from Third World and soon started to play at such big-time events as Reggae Bash '92 and the Sunsplash '92 Bob Marley Tribute. He played the Sting show the same year, then in 1993 played at Sunsplash and toured with

Gathering of the Healers

the Shabba Ranks World Unity Tour.

Damian has also performed on the same bill with Julian. In 1996 they opened for Ziggy Marley and the Melody Makers, a tour which took them throughout the U.S., Central and South America. His debut album, *Mr. Marley*, one of the first projects undertaken by the Ghetto Youth International production label and recorded at the newly renovated Marley Music Studio at 56 Hope Road, was produced by his brother Stephen. Released in September 1996, it drew acclaim from both reggae and hip-hop fans.

Damian calls his new album *HALFWAY TREE* because, "my father is from the country and the ghetto and my mother is from uptown so I come like a half way tree, like a bridge because I can relate to both sides." The album was then nominated for, and subsequently won, a 2001 Grammy, up against albums by his brother Kymani, Luciano and Beres Hammond.

Scram and I headed upstairs to the Barrington's office where he greeted us warmly. Barrington is a tall barrel-chested man, friendly and kind. We all liked each other immediately and we told him about our plans.

"I told Julian what we were doing and he said he didn't want the politicians here," I said.

"Well, now, I like your idea," Barrington said. "I am not a Rasta. I am a Christian but I think that your efforts are not just for Rastas but for everyone, no matter what their beliefs. I would support your using the museum but I cannot go against the family. I think you better speak with Stephanie Marley. She is here several days a week. Call me in a few days and I will set up an appointment with her."

As we walked out of the house, we stopped to talk with Damian, who, like his brother Julian, seemed disinterested. Several other Rastas were hanging around listening to us. I waved to Julian to come over and join us but he just looked away.

"Damian," I said at one point, trying to overcome his skepticism "we are calling you out to help make your father's words a reality on this island. You've always known this One Love. I can see by your spirit that you've never hated anyone, never thrown anyone out of your heart no matter what they did. We're just asking people to step forward and claim their place like your father claimed his place and teach this One Love. It is your father's vision."

"I don't think that this will help the poverty here," Damian said. "This will not solve the exploitation that creates all this poverty."

"Ya are tired of de frustration of de poverty dat 'as come up into your eyes," Scram answered. "De poverty dat you complain about is true an' I like de way dat you observe it but it is just de love now dat cayn heal dis poverty. Becuz wit' dis love, de people dat pay dese wages will look into demselves an' see dat dese wages are nah right. Dey got to give more money. But first we gotta 'ave de love or we are puttin' de cart before de 'orse."

"Damian, just let me know through Barrington whether you want to join us," I said, "and I won't keep getting in your face."

"You're not getting in my face, mon. This is the kind of reasoning we like to have out here. I will think about what you said," Damian said.

We had wanted to try to get back over to reason with Muta at his bookstore but the traffic was too bad and we had to meet with Mike Henry at the Terra Nova Hotel so we decided to check-in at the hotel and try to catch Muta the next day at the Rebel Salute where he would be one of the emcees. We settled in our room and while Scram sat by the pool, I went for a swim, changed and then joined him. We lit up a couple of cigars I had brought and chatted while we waited for Mike. After a half hour, just as evening was falling, Mike joined us. We told him about the day and brought him up to date on our efforts.

Mike had been a Jamaican senator for 21 years and had recently challenged Edward Seaga for the leadership of the JLP (Jamaican Labor Party) party, the opposition party to the PNP (People's National Party). The PNP had been in power for 10 years with PJ Patterson as Prime Minister. Mike asked me to draft an invitation for Seaga similar to the one I sent Prime Minister Patterson, saying he would personally get it to him.

"You have known me only recently as a businessman," Mike said as we sat by the pool. "As a politician, I have tried to get Rastafarianism officially recognized as a religion in Parliament. I have talked to

Gathering of the Healers

Parliament that marijuana be made legal as a sacrament to Rastafarianism. All of that is in Parliament from me. Also I have published the book *Kebra Nagast*, which is the first ever modern English translation of the Ethiopian Bible. Based on the fact I was born in St. Catherine's and I visited Pinnacle (a large Rasta commune founded by Percival Howell in the late 1940s), I was around at the beginning of Rastafarianism. My position is clear based on the fact that I'm the only politician on the platform to begin and end with 'JAH Rastafari!' "

"So you have no problem being identified with all this?" I said.

"My position is that you let all ideas contend," he continued. "That to me is the strength of the developed societies. It is the weakness of the Jamaican structure that we do not let all ideas contend. In fact we almost shun ideas. I don't think that the Jamaican Labor Party would have a problem being identified with the gathering. And if it isn't identified at the leader level because of the certain things, my position is clear and irreversible. It's what I feel, I believe and what I will die with. I think that a party needs to be run by its conscience. And if anyone does not think that Jamaica needs love now then I'm not sure where they are."

"Tis true, mon," Scram agreed from the sidelines.

"Your problem, if it is a problem," Mike said, "is that you're not going to find everyone as liberal as I am. Our society is still steeped in colonialistic traditions and thinking. Some of the people will embrace you and yet distance themselves because of the criticism they think will flow. You must remember you're dealing with the most sensitive subject in the country which deals with the identity of the people. And the one thing Jamaicans are shying from is the identity of themselves."

"Explain that," I said.

"For may reasons we have not recognized the African structure of ourselves. We are therefore within the slave mentality of escaping rather than facing ourselves. That manifests itself in many ways. The Rastafarian religion has fought to find that identity by looking at their African roots, by going back to their roots and finding that within the structure of society. But the society itself is still steeped in colonial thought of the master against the slave."

The Rastafarianism I knew where things were all for the communal good rather than for the individual achievement. Contrast that with the slavery mentality where the house slave had a superior attitude to the field slave. In the Jamaican context, people still talk about 'we' and 'they' rather than 'us.' "

"Mike, let me ask you," I said, "where are Patterson and Seaga's hearts? Are they concerned with the welfare of their people?"

"Well, there is no doubt in the context of all I've said," he said, "both hearts are in the right place."

"Do you think Patterson and Seaga will attend?" I asked. "It seems straightforward enough—asking people to forgive and heal their country. Will the Rasta connection be a big problem?"

"That is what this society is afraid of," Mike said. "I have advocated all my life that Rastafarianism should be recognized as a religion. There is a whole body of thought from the Anglo-Saxonized, Roman-Catholicized body that are afraid and do not wish that. That's the area you are treading on, which the society has not come to terms with. Therefore you are generating a lot of reaction from the reactionaries. If indeed it appears that you are pushing this forward, you will have people that will object to it and be critical."

"I hope it doesn't appear I am pushing Rasta," I said. "What this is all about is One Love. That's why I am inviting anyone who is a teacher of love no matter what their religious beliefs."

"So you don't represent the Rastafarian aspect," Mike said. "You'll be in the middle. You must take that stand. But the fact that your book is called *Rasta Heart* is going to open up the critical aspect that you're promoting Rastafari. Maybe you should have a neutral moderator at the press conference."

"I've considered that," I answered. "The moderator sets the vibe and the tone and I don't know anyone that would set the vibe I envision that is not allied with any group. So at this point, I'm feeling my press conference is my press conference and I will take the lead."

"Well, now, if it is your press conference and not me as publisher doing it," Mike said, "you can do it any way you want. I'll do my own promotion because I'm here to sell books. You're here to spread One Love. Once you take the approach to heal our nation through love, then a lot of people will want to identify with that. Robert, there is nobody here that is not worried about the country now. The greatest problem that we face right now is crime and violence. If that is so, what can heal it? So there is no one in the country that doesn't want the nation to heal and be peaceful again. Bob Marley tried it. The churches continue to try it. Nobody has yet decided which is the best way to do it. The traditional churches will tell you it has to be through Jesus Christ. You are not taking any one position but including all. It is only through a moral awakening and a turning to God that you'll be able to do it. But you must communicate this to others. I'm still like Thomas."

"I was raised Jewish so I'm not sure I really understand your analogy," I said laughing.

"I'm Jewish, too," Mike replied. "My great, great-grandfather was the first Jewish Rabbi in Jamaica. My mother was a Jewess and it is only through the mother that one is Jewish. As you say, we are leaders of the world in One Love but we have not recognized it. You are trying to awaken that in your approach and you must understand that you have doubting Thomases, people in fixed positions, and you are going against tradition. And I think it is best to not let what you are doing get too diverse, get too caught up in the idiosyncrasies of everyone, because of what I think it could achieve."

Though Jamaica is a stable, even vibrant, parliamentary democracy, the political systems is riddled with corruption, greed, and, unfortunately, violence. Jamaicans call it "politricks" and travel writer Lynn Ferrin calls it "drop dead politics." Politics and guns are wedded together in Jamaica, especially in the ghettos of Kingston where entire sections are either the JLP or PNP territory. Just going into the territory of the opposing party can get a person killed.

2001 had been one of the most violent years in Jamaica's history. For over a year the murder rate had continued to climb until Jamaica had attained the ignoble honor of having more murders per capita than any country on the planet. While I was on the island in June, 2001, things

Gathering of the Healers

got so bad with escalating violence in the ghetto that the government had to bulldoze down hundreds of homes to create a buffer zone between PNP and JLP warring factions. (Most of Jamaica's violence is within local circles and seldom spills over into tourist areas. Violence towards tourists is extremely rare and tourists traveling on the island are quite safe. Violence toward young children is also very rare.)

Most of the violence was due to warring political camps and the active cocaine trade, two forces that are all too often mixed together. The two political parties fight hard and dirty to win the election. Many of the "dons," who are involved in both politics *and* narcotics trafficking, are able to deliver large blocks of votes in exchange for government contracts, jobs and housing. Their discipline is enforced by bullying and violence. In a country where jobs are hard to find and usually underpaid and where a quarter of the workforce is directly employed by the government, losing the election can mean losing the livelihoods of thousands of party workers. Graft, corruption, violence and cronyism is a way of life in Jamaican politics.

In August of 2002, the *Jamaica Observer* reported Jamaica's corruption score. "According to Transparency International's Corruption Perception Index (CPI) for 2002," the paper reported, "international and local business interests continue to view Jamaica as a country with mid-level corruption. The report, which highlights corrupt dealings between 'political elites' and their 'cronies' in the private sector worldwide, gave Jamaica a score of four on an index where 10 represents highly clean and 0 indicates highly corrupt.

This latest score, which inched forward from the 3.8 achieved last year, places the island at 45 among the 102 countries surveyed for this year's CPI. The United States, with its recent corporate scandals, scored 7.7."

After Mike left, Scram and I headed over to Caribe Theatre a few blocks from the hotel to see *Ali* with Will Smith. It was the first movie theatre Scram had been to since the 1970s when they closed the two theatres in Port Antonio. Like the Rastas, Ali had refused to play the government's game even at great personal cost. Ignoring the public outrage, he became a Muslim and changed his name from Cassius Clay (which

Gathering of the Healers

he referred to as his "slave name") to Mohammed Ali. He refused to fight in Vietnam by defying his draft call, for which he was instantly arrested and threatened with a long jail sentence (he was later exonerated when the U.S. Supreme Court agreed that he was a legitimate conscienscious objector).

Because of his opposition to the war, he was stripped of his heavyweight title. He was not allowed to fight for several years at the peak of his career. He lost everything—his title, his livelihood, his wife and his money—all for his beliefs. But still he did not budge and continued to speak out against a war that had "poor people killing poor people" and was supposedly being fought to "give South Vietnamese more freedom than the American black man has in his own country." It was a perfect movie to see with Scram.

After the movie, Scram and I stayed up talking in our hotel room about how our journey was going. We now had commitments from Denroy Morgan, Dennis Forsythe and most likely Antonnette Haughton. Using Bob's home still looked very iffy. The next two days were crucial as we hoped to meet with Tony Rebel, Luciano, Muta and Mama B. We had no idea what they would say.

"My intention is to contribute through our musical showcase, Rebel Salute, towards the promotion and the preservation of the healthier aspects of reggae music, as part of the mandate for nation building."
—**Tony Rebel**

Chapter 6
January 12, 2002

The Rebel Salute

T he next morning we headed out for the Rebel Salute, a four hour drive from Kingston to Fort Kaiser. Every year since 1994, Tony Rebel has hosted his "Rebel Salute," one of the many concerts on the island. It seems you cannot drive down a road anywhere without seeing colorful cardboard signs announcing the next major concert featuring local and internationally known artists and deejays. These concerts are Jamaica's main form of entertainment and since no part of the island is more than a few hours drive from anywhere else, the concerts are well attended.

However, the Rebel Salute is different from the many other all-night concerts that take place in Jamaica every year. It is also one of the largest, with the Rebel Salute in 2000 drawing over 30,000 people. Tony has designed the gathering to not only entertain with the island's best reggae artists but also to include a strong spiritual orientation and to further the Rastafari worldview. For many it is considered an annual spiritual Renaissance. The emphasis is on Rasta, roots music, His Majesty Haile Selassie I, vegetarian food (no meat is sold except fish), and being in a very good vibe.

There is a zero tolerance policy for both weapons and profanity and no alcoholic beverages are allowed to be sold. As Tony says, "Alcoholic

Gathering of the Healers

beverages impairs your ability to function at 100% and is responsible for a lot of the acts of violence and assault which occur at many stage shows." .

To quote the mission statement issued by Tony Rebel's Flame Productions which manages the event, the intention is "...to contribute through our musical showcase, Rebel Salute, towards the promotion and the preservation of the healthier aspects of reggae music, as part of the mandate for nation building."

In the past few years the concert has been held at Fort Kaiser in a very remote area on the South Coast near Lovers' Leap. It is several hours from all the populated areas but its remoteness allows the concert to continue until dawn without complaints from neighbors. Even with its remoteness, people come from all over the island, often driving on small back roads.

Scram and I arrived in the Fort Kaiser area around mid-day. We stopped for lunch at a beautiful thatched-roof restaurant, The Venus Sunset Lounge and Accommodations. It is set amid lawns overlooking the ocean. It was run by Clive, a very kind man who had been a businessman in Mandeville before returning to this area where he had been raised. He also rents out several modest, but clean, rooms for US$20 a night. A pool was being built next to the restaurant and a path led to a small beach below.

We ordered lunch and relaxed, chatting with Clive, telling him about our mission. Like so many other people we talked to, he liked the idea and thought we had a chance at making a difference. After an hour or so, we headed over to the concert area to see about linking up with Tony, Muta and Luciano. The concert was a short drive from Clive's and though it was early afternoon and the concert did not begin until eight that night, already the road leading to the stage area was packed with vendors.

Scram and I hung around the gate area looking for whoever was in charge. Finally we spotted the concert manager, a well-groomed businessman, obviously very busy. We told him we had come all the way from Port Antonio to invite Tony and Luciano to join our vision but he barely seemed to be listening. After our explanation, he said there was

Gathering of the Healers

nothing he could do to get us backstage. In fact, it was his job to protect the artists from people like us trying to get access to them. He suggested that we contact them at their offices in Kingston.

"Dat's OK," Scram said. "He is just doing 'is job but JAH sent us 'ere to do our job and to meet dem and we will. My spirit says just relax and wait."

"Well, as you know, my spirit always says hurry up and get it done," I replied, and we both laughed. "In this case, I think we better follow your spirit."

We decided to spend the rest of the day at Clive's. As we drove back, I stopped to ask directions from an elderly woman sitting on a bench. After she told me where to turn, I gave her a few dollars as she looked like she could use it. Her face lit up and she waved vigorously as we drove away.

"Ya know, anywhere you go and you 'ave done somet'ing to one person," Scram said as we drove away, "it cayn bring a great impact on your life journey, you know. Becuz sometimes you go to places an' see people dat is very, very much in need and what I notice, is dat every small item dat you give to a person, you cayn see it in de eyes of a person 'ow much dey give dere heart out in t'anks."

We arrived back at Clive's around mid-afternoon, showered outside under the hose and spent the afternoon lounging around his restaurant, me reading and talking with Clive and Scram sleeping in his chair. The vibes there were very restful, just what we needed. After dinner, we headed back to the concert. It was now shortly before dark and as we approached the concert, someone yelled out "Scramo!" It was an old friend of Scram's that now lived a few hundred yards from the concert and was renting parking spaces in his front yard. We parked the car, chatted with his friend, a very accomplished sculptor, and headed to the concert.

It was still an hour or so before the concert began and the crowd was very thin. We paid our entrance fee of 800 Jamaican dollars (about US$18) and headed in. The concert area was a large open field surrounded by a chain-link fence. The field was flat except in the back area where it gently sloped up a small hill. Higher hills were visible in the

Gathering of the Healers

distance. The office area was in the back, a low-slung, concrete block building with a large concrete veranda looking toward the stage. There were 20 or 30 policemen, in crisp starched uniforms, standing around the veranda chatting and laughing. To them it was a primo assignment. Everything looked rather low-tech, with a sort of roots feel to it, except the stage. It was 70 feet wide with a canopy, mammoth speakers and a giant picture of Haile Selassie I as the backdrop. Though roots, this was also big business involving big money. The only rather discordant note was a 30-foot high inflatable soft drink balloon off to one side of the stage. When the gates opened, there were only a handful of people milling around and I was beginning to think that the concert would be a bust with few people willing to make the three hour trip from Kingston, Mobay or Negril.

More vendors were set up inside around the periphery selling everything from Rasta flags, clothes and buttons, to Ital food, carvings and paintings. Almost every stall had a Rasta vibe, with many pictures of Bob Marley, Emperor Haile Selassie I, stars of David and Rasta green, red and yellow colors. Most vendors wore dreads and many were wearing long African robes and turbans.

We talked with some of the crew and Scram found someone he knew (as always) who said he thought he could get us to Tony later in the night. We wandered around chatting with the vendors and finally settled at a spot on the slope of the low hill where you could lay down but still had a great view of the stage over the heads of the crowd. We found two cardboard boxes and opened them up to lay on to keep clean. Behind us were several food stalls selling delicious Ital food, so it seemed the ideal spot to enjoy the show.

By eight o'clock, the official show time, there were only a few hundred people milling around to hear the opening act. I was convinced this concert was a bust. Though most of the top acts like Luciano, Sizzla, Capelton, Mikey General, Culture, Junior Reid, Marcia Griffiths, Mutabaruka and Tony were slated to appear in the early morning hours, the crowd still looked thin for the opening. Each singer or group was on stage for 30 to 45 minutes with the house band playing for all of them. As the concert continued, the crowd started to grow. Everyone gathered

89

Gathering of the Healers

as close to the stage as they could with only a handful of us sitting on the hill in the back with an open space between us and the rest of the crowd of 75 yards or so.

After the first group, Scram and I wandered over to the backstage area to see if we could find Tony and Luciano. The guards, two friendly female private security workers, said they couldn't let us backstage but Luciano wasn't there yet and Tony was outside the gate. They pointed to the area where they thought he would be. We wandered over and spotted Tony immediately outside the wire fence in a heated discussion with some people who wanted free entry. We wanted to go outside and talk to him but we were told if we went out we would have to pay the admission again. Scram, who had met Tony years before in Portland, called over to him through the fence and told him we would like to talk to him. He told us to try to catch him later, obviously preoccupied in the moment.

As I watched the interaction, I immediately liked him. Tony is a tall, muscular, handsome man, self-assured, with a kind but serious nature. He laughs easily but has a sense of guardedness about him probably developed from many years in the often highly unethical world of Jamaican music. He exudes power and confidence and when you hear him sing he reveals an idealistic and caring nature. His hits include such classics as, "Sweet Jamaica," "Fresh Vegetables," "Chatty-Chatty," and perhaps his best known album and song, "Jah Is Standing By My Side," released in 1997. His music is a strong combination of reggae and roots that blends singing and rapping with lyrics of wisdom and redemption, both personal and racial. His songs are infused with lyrical purity, race consciousness and emphasis on a healthy lifestyle. His *Realms of Rebel* album was a big hit in 2001 with "Just Friends," a song he recorded with Swade that hit the top 10 charts.

Tony performs worldwide often in front of over 80,000 fans. However, Tony Rebel is more than a singer and performer. He is a messenger for One Love. In addition to appearing as a singer, he is a motivational speaker and serves on several national committees, including one working on stemming AIDS in Jamaica. He is an untarnished Jamaican cultural ambassador for love and peace.

Gathering of the Healers

"Well, now," Scram said, "let's just enjoy the show and look for him later like he said."

"Sounds good to me," I replied. "I love this. This reminds me of the pop festivals I went to back in the sixties and seventies."

We went back to our spot and reclaimed our cardboard mattresses. After a few groups, I wandered over to the stalls and talked with Sister Faye, a Rastalady from Port Antonio I had tried to link up with in my earlier visits. We chatted awhile and then I wandered over to a few other stalls and talked with several Rasta vendors. They all liked the book and I quickly gave away the few extra copies I had brought.

When I returned to our camp spot around eleven I was amazed to see that the crowd had grown tremendously (it eventually reached 15,000). The space between us and the standing, packed crowd was now only about 20 yards. Many people were waving small red, green and yellow Rasta flags, swaying to the music as more and more artists appeared. Many blew whistles or held up lighters. Several people near the front had blow torches that they would ignite every few minutes throwing huge tongues of flames up in the air. Roving vendors were wandering around selling peanuts, bottled water, soft drinks, and cookies. Every now and then a vendor would come by selling hot nuts out of a rolling cart that made a loud shrill whistle from its oven that would almost drown out the music—the only discordant note of the night.

The crowd was very friendly. There were only a handful of white faces in the crowd but there were no weird vibes and people quickly returned my smile. The police stayed in the background, lounging around the office area prepared for any trouble (there was none) rather than attempting to patrol the area. The smell of ganja was everywhere. There were vendors walking around shouting, "Weed! High grade weed!" and carrying trays of large buds with more buds stuck in their hat bands.

For hours I just laid on my cardboard, often looking at the stars, listening to some of the best reggae music in the world. Reggae really is the heartbeat of Jamaica. It is the Motherland of this sound and many of the local groups sound like world-class performers. The sound system was crystal clear. There was little alcohol consumption nor it's accom-

Gathering of the Healers

panying obnoxious behavior. Though the scene was dynamic and charged with an almost palpable energy, it was at the same time, mellow—very, very mellow.

Every now and then I would sit up and look around just to watch the crowd. This was definitely a Rasta or Rasta-friendly group. It was for the most part young, black and male. Women made up maybe 20 percent of the crowd, reminding me of how problematic male-female relationships are in Jamaica. Concerts in the US are predominately couples. This crowd was a mixture: clean cut looking people, probably middle-class professionals from Kingston or Mobay, working class people enjoying a much-needed break, and full-dread Rastas looking like they had just walked out of the Bible, some complete with full dreads, precepts, flowing robes and staffs.

Everyone got along easily with a fluid crossover between groups, often around a shared chalis pipe. Many people were reasoning together in animated conversation punctuated by laughter and affectionate touching. I saw none of the sexual or drunken behavior I was use to at concerts in the States. What amazed me most was the sheer physical stamina of the crowd. The concert, which had started at eight in the evening, was over at almost nine the next morning. During these 13 hours most of the crowd was on their feet, as close as they could get to the stage, singing and dancing with each group. The livity of the crowd was phenomenal.

The more popular artists came on in the early morning hours, when the crowd excitement was at its peak. Most artists would start by shouting, "JAH!!!" and the crowd would respond with a loud "RASTA-FARI!!" Around five in the morning, Muta came on as the emcee and the crowd came even more alive. Dressed in a long flowing purple robe and black turban that flowed over his broad shoulders, he strutted across the stage in an animated fashion loudly reasoning with the crowd who responded enthusiastically, though not always in agreement, to his every comment or joke. He looked like a cosmic Othello, out of time, out of place, yet strangely perfect for this scene. He spoke in heavy Patois so I could catch little of what he said though I occasionally asked Scram to interpret. Though unintelligible to me, his words sounded fluid, poetic,

Gathering of the Healers

his delivery smooth and easy. At one time he started to get some cat-calls, obviously saying something that many in the crowd didn't agree with.

"What's he talking about?" I asked Scram, curious as to why the crowd's mood was changing.

"Muta is saying dat many of de ladies 'ere say dey are Rasta," Scram said, "but dat de way dey dress wit' de short skirts and de low shirts is not upful. A lot of de girls and dese guys doan't want ta hear dat. But I t'ink it is good fe Muta to tell dem to 'ave more respect fe demselves."

As I observed the concert, I was pleased to find myself in such a powerful yet peaceful experience. Though to most people in the crowd it was just another all-night reggae concert, one of many, to me it was indicative of how completely Rasta had captured the hearts and minds of the Jamaican people. Few of the people wore the outer markings of Rasta but people from all over Jamaica and from all socioeconomic backgrounds were there to enjoy the Rasta music, slogans, food and philosophy.

Perhaps what was most amazing to me was how effectively One Love had permeated this culture. Here were 15,000 people from the most impoverished country in the hemisphere, coming together peacefully and for the most part exhibiting "upful" behavior. There was no apparent racial prejudice toward me or the handful of other whites in the audience whom seemed as relaxed there as I was. If ever there was clear evidence of the healing effect of Rasta influence, it was the Rebel Salute.

This also confirmed what I already knew—that Jamaicans are a truly loving and forgiving people. Over the previous year, in five trips to the island, I had wandered, often alone, in the cities, villages and country-side of this 90-plus percent black country asking Jamaicans to join me, a white-middle class American, in my pursuit of One Love. Not everyone I encountered agreed. However, in all those encounters I never once was met with a bad vibe.

At one point late in the night, it seemed so overwhelming to me that I began to wonder whether I could really serve as a proper messenger for this powerful movement.

Gathering of the Healers

"You know, Scram," I said, leaning over to where he was laying next to me, "I'm not so sure I should even be doing all this. I mean it's one thing to go around the island reasoning with a few individual Rastas and being their messenger. But here I feel like I'm in over my head. I mean this is very powerful and everyone here fits in but me. I'm not sure I'm up to this task or even meant for it."

"No, mon. JAH has chosen you," he said, in his usual unflappable way. "Someone must come an' tell de wurld our story. Someone's got ta come in from de *outside* who is not a Bobo or a Coptic or a Nyabinghi and tell dis story. And you are a good storyteller who understands de truth when 'e hears it. Dat is why you are a good messenger for Rasta." With that, I rolled back on my cardboard felling more assured.

The positive vibes were not always consistent from the performers. Several of the singers drifted into angry, occasionally anti-US, anti-Babylon diatribes. Shortly before dawn a young reggae artist, Sizzla, popular both in Jamaica and internationally, took the stage. Along with his talent, he's known for his anti-white, anti-gay, anti-US rhetoric. At one point in his performance, he brought up some large plastic bags on stage filled with African ganja and started throwing large one-foot long buds into the cheering crowd. Jumping around in brilliant red pants, tunic and turban, he whipped the crowd into a state of excitement.

"What's he saying, Scram?" I asked, unable to make out his words.

" 'E's railing against Babylon," Scram replied. " 'E's getting every-one pretty stirred up. It is always easier to get people angry than have dem open dere 'earts to love. On dis island it is easy to get people angry. 'E's a yout' and 'e doesn't understand dis One Love business so good."

"Man, if this show ends on this note, everyone's going go out of here angry," I said. "They're going bum out everyone they meet today. These artists really need to guide everyone into a good place and not leave them with such anger. But then if I had been raised in the Kingston ghet-to, like most Jamaica's reggae stars were, I don't know what I'd be doing on stage. And his tribe is needed to call attention to the problems so we can recognize them and solve them. Getting angry at injustice is a great motivating force. Anger is part of our healing. Our tribe calls attention to the spiritual solution, reminding everyone that all the prob-

94

Gathering of the Healers

lems must be addressed with love or we'll just fight again. Most of us know the problems. We've been discussing them forever. We're asking people to bring forward solutions in whatever form they feel guided to do. And our message of love and forgiveness can anger people calling attention to the problem. But both tribes are needed."

"Yeah, mon. It is only dis One Love dat cayn solve all dese problems now," Scram agreed.

"It's almost like people have been trying to hack there way through the jungle of this human journey with a machete not knowing that right next to them is a wide, easy path called Love," I said. "And if they just step over on to that path their own personal journey becomes much easier. Everyone can step over to this path—no matter how much money you have or what your spiritual beliefs are. Rastas call the path "Rastafari." Christians call it "grace." Buddhists call it the "middle way." Native Americans call it the "beauty path." It's all the same. God made it available to everyone all the time. Many Rastas have shown that this joy and livity is not a function of financial status or even political oppression. It is something anyone can claim within themselves. And there will always be people painfully hacking there way through the jungle and there's nothing you can do about that but keep inviting them over to join you on the path. But you cannot make them come over. They must decide for themselves."

Just as the sun was lighting the eastern sky behind the stage, Muta came back on.

"Now, we have a different artist!" he yelled into the mike. "JAH'S MESSENJAH!!!-LUCIANO!!!"

To the wild cheers of the crowd, Luciano came on stage wearing his characteristic camouflage long-sleeved shirt and pants tucked into his combat boots—a soldier for JAH. His understated outfit seemed perfect to emphasize the message and not so much the messenger. For almost an hour, as the night slowly turned to day, Luciano mellowed the crowd and opened their hearts with one song after another singing about love and peace. His performance was commanding, sometimes soft and gentle, at times on his knees, other times dynamic and captivating as he repeatedly jumped two feet in the air doing full splits. His three female

Gathering of the Healers

backup singers, like Bob Marley's I-Threes back-up group, wore long, dignified African gowns and moved gently and rhythmically as they sang.

As soon as he finished, Scram and I headed towards the backstage area knowing it was now or never. Capelton, another well-known reggae artist, had taken the stage but for us the concert was over. As we approached the backstage area we were surprised to see the same female guards now letting everyone in freely. Capelton fans, mostly from the Bobo Rastafari sect, had pushed down the backstage fence. "Luciano and Tony Rebel are both back here now," one of the security guards said as we approached, pointing toward an area where fans had gathered around both of them.

"Thank you, my princess," Scram said, giving her a big hug. "Let's go talk to Tony first."

We joined the small crowd of grateful fans and waited our turn. As we waited I put a signed copy of my book in a beautiful royal blue velvet bag embroidered with the Lion of Judah and a Star of David. (Many Rastas believe they are Jews and members of the lost tribe of Israel, hence they often display the Star of David on their clothes, homes, shops and in their art. The Lion of Judah was a title for Emporer Haile Selassie I).

When it was our turn to talk to Tony, Scram addressed him. "Blessed, me brethren, Tony Rebel," Scram said respectfully, holding his fist over his heart and then tapping his knuckles with Tony's in the Rasta salutation. "My friend Robbie and I 'ave come from Port Antonio to invite you to join us in a vision we 'ave."

With this brief intro, Scram turned to me and I handed Tony the book. He looked at it with interest as he listened to our concept and invitation.

"We would like to come visit you in Kingston in a few days to tell you more," I finished, as a fresh group of fans were waiting to talk to him.

"Here's my phone number," he said. He seemed interested but unconvinced. "You come see me but I'm not so sure about this."

As we headed over to where Luciano was talking to his fans, I felt somewhat disappointed. We had been up all night and given Tony's rep-

Gathering of the Healers

utation for spreading One Love, I guess I was hoping for a more enthusiastic response. Luciano was sitting against the fence, signing autographs for 10 or so fans that were surrounding him on three sides. Again we waited our turn and after his introduction, Scram stepped back and I handed the book and bag to Luciano. I was excited to be so close to a man who's music had become the backdrop to our lives the last four months. Given the beauty and clarity of his musical message, Julia and I had been listening to him almost exclusively.

"Is this for me?" he said as I handed him the book and bag, obviously grateful for the gift. His humility was touching and unexpected. I told him of our plans and he looked me straight in the eye the entire time.

"I like this idea. Come see me when you are in Kingston," he said with a serious look on his face.

"Thanks," I said. "I thought you'd like it. We'll call you soon."

We looked around for Muta but he had gone. Feeling elated that we had gotten through to Luciano and Tony, we listened to Capelton for a few more minutes and then headed out.

"Dat went good," Scram said, as we headed toward the car. "Dos guys will join us. My spirit feels it."

"I think you're right about Luciano," I said, "but I'm not so sure about Tony. He looked luke warm at best."

"Dis is de first time 'e heard about it," Scram said reflectively. " 'E is a great teacher of love and once 'e hears more about what we are doin,' 'e will want to join us."

"I hope you're right," I said as we got into the car. "He has a very powerful voice here on the island. Let's stop by Clive's and shower and eat before we head to see Mama B's."

We drove back to Clive's. The usual 10-minute drive took almost an hour due to the bumper-to-bumper traffic. When we arrived it was almost 10 in the morning and Clive greeted us warmly. We told him about our meeting Tony and Luciano and ordered breakfast. As Scram napped in the open air restaurant, I took a much needed shower outside using his hose. After breakfast, we piled back in the car and headed to see Mama B in Nine Mile, a four hour drive north into the mountains.

"How he do things and prophesy things, he is not just by himself—he have Higher Powers, even from when he is a little boy. The way I felt, the kind of vibes I get when Bob comes around... It's too honorable."
—**Cedella Marley Booker,** Bob Marley's mother

Chapter 7
January 13, 2002

Mama B

We arrived in Nine Mile around two in the afternoon. The drive was beautiful, deep into the rugged interior hills of the island. The only populated area we drove through was the small city of May Pen, where I called Mrs. Booker to confirm our appointment. Nine Mile is totally out-of-the-way, nine miles east of the small hamlet of Alexandria. The roads leading to the area were some of the worst I'd seen but there was some road improvement going on, probably in preparation for the annual Bob Marley birthday concert held every year in early February near his birthplace.

As I rode through this remote and poor farming district I began to wonder how this place could have birthed such a consciousness as Marley's. But then as I sensed the peace of the area and saw the smiles of the locals, I thought, *Of course!*

Thousands of fans make this pilgrimage every year to his birthplace and final resting place. The site is run by the Bob Marley Foundation, which uses the proceeds to help the local community, the community where Mama B was born and raised and where Bob lived his early years.

The entire compound is surrounded by wire fences, a rather discordant but necessary note. There is a small hotel, the Wailer's Villa, across

Gathering of the Healers

the street from the home and a museum shop directly below his crypt. We were ushered into a small secured parking lot by a couple of smiling Rastas. The place looked empty with only a couple of other vehicles parked there. Mama B's home is private but for $10US you can tour Bob's birthplace and crypt. Explaining that we weren't the average tourists but had an appointment to meet with Mama B, our Rasta guides escorted us up the stairs to her home, a comfortable bungalow a little below her original small house, now called Zion, where Bob was born.

Knocking on her door, Mama B called for us to enter. Mama B was sewing in her living room, a cozy high-ceiling, medium-sized room, tastefully and comfortably decorated. Oprah Winfry was on the TV, which she turned off as we entered. Mama B, a proud, dignified woman who looks to be in her late fifties but is actually in her seventies, greeted us warmly. Her long, massive dreads were tucked under a colorful turban. She seemed both wise and child-like at the same time, still in some ways the simple country girl from rural Jamaica and yet at the same time sophisticated and worldly after the amazing life she has led. As we spoke, she seemed serious and thoughtful, as if struggling with a life that had dealt her both great joy and satisfaction as well as hardship and disappointment. I liked her immediately and felt at ease in her presence.

Born Cedella Malcolm in 1926 in Nine Mile, Mama B was the sixth of nine children of Alberta and Omeriah Malcolm. Both her father and uncle were accomplished musicians and by the age of 14 she was the star vocalist at the Shiloh Apostolic Church Choir. As a young teenager she had a relationship with Captain Norval Sinclair Marley, a 50-year old white overseer. They married in June 1944 when she became pregnant but he left for Kingston following the wedding and returned only twice while she was carrying their child. Bob was born on February 6, 1945 at two-thirty in the morning. Until he was six, Bob was raised in Nine Mile by Cedella and her father, Omeriah, with only occasional visits from Norval. Omeriah, a strong-willed, proud man, was a community leader and Bob soon fell under his tutelage and became his goat herder.

Gathering of the Healers

When Bob was six years old, Captain Marley convinced Cedella to let him take Bob to Kingston to live with his relatives so Bob could get a better education. Reluctantly she agreed. However, Norval actually farmed Bob out to take care of an elderly lady, Mrs. Grey. For over a year, Cedella had no idea where her son was and she was frantic. Finally, a neighbor saw Bob on a street in Kingston and told Cedella, who instantly returned to reclaim her child.

A few years later, Cedella moved with Bob to Trench Town in inner-city Kingston to join her boyfriend, Toddy Livingston, and Toddy's son, Bunny (who later became a Wailer). Captain Marley died of a heart attack several years later after having illegally married again thereby clouding his estate. Raising children in the crushing poverty of the Kingston ghettos and hoping to improve the family's life, Cedella moved to the U.S., hoping Bob would join her. Soon her daughter Pearl was born in Wilmington, Delaware, followed by sons Richard and Anthony, by her new husband, Eddy Booker.

Bob moved to Wilmington two years later and worked as a welder but not until he married Rita Anderson on the day before he left Jamaica. Bob stayed with Cedella for six months before a welding accident and the threat of being drafted and sent to Vietnam made him decide to return to Jamaica to pursue his musical career.

Throughout his tumultuous career, Bob maintained a close and loyal relationship with his mother, providing her family with a new home in Miami. In 1981 Mama B nursed Bob through the final stages of his bout with cancer. Mama B and Diane Jobson, Bob's lawyer, best friend and confidant, were with him as Bob made his transition. As Diane informed Mama B's Uncle Gibson that Bob had just passed on, Mama B saw a photo of Bob move slightly on the mantelpiece. Around the same time, back in Jamaica, Judy Mowat, one of the I Threes, Bob's backup singers, was sitting on the veranda of her home when a lightening bolt shot through her open window and struck a picture of Bob on the wall. Although Marley's death had not been announced, Judy knew that Bob was gone.

Her other sons, Richard and Anthony, formed the band Copasetic, who in 1988 released *Five And Dime*. In 1990, Mama B suffered anoth-

Gathering of the Healers

er tragedy when Anthony was shot dead in a Miami shopping mall. Cedella has since recorded a series of Rastafarian-influenced songs, including her album *My Altar* and has also organized and performed at a number of Bob Marley Festivals. She is an accomplished performer in her own right, singing in concerts internationally.

As Bob's mother she is greeted by loyal fans wherever she goes, almost like a superstar herself. Yet she remains humbled, perhaps even a little embarrassed, by the enthusiasm she engenders. She is quite aware of her son's impact and mission, telling an interviewer, "I'm hoping and praying that Reggae will reach many hearts because reggae music has changed so many people, the message that Bob has brought to the world." After all her personal heartaches, she remains strong and brave, saying recently in her book, *Bob Marley: An Intimate Portrait by His Mother*, "This is Jah's Plan. This may not be to my liking, but it cannot be otherwise."

Scram and I settled on opposing couches, with Scram next to Diane Jobson, who was also there. Diane, a light-skinned woman, looked to be in her fifties with long flowing dreads. She is intelligent and articulate and tends to dominate the conversation. She is aggressive and somewhat combative (she is after all a lawyer) but it seemed more due to past hurts than a mean-spirited nature. As Mama B says about Diane in her book, "...a truer, more loving heart than Diane's, Nesta (Bob) never knew while he walked this earth."

"Mrs. Booker, I'm Robert Roskind. This is Thomas Anderson, or Scram as everyone calls him. We've come to see you because as preposterous as this might sound, we believe we've been sent to help complete your son's work. It will take a while for me to explain but I think you'll find the time well spent."

"Go ahead. I'd like to hear this," she replied.

"I've just finished writing this book," I said handing her and Diane each a copy of *Rasta Heart*, as well as copies of my other books on unconditional love, *In the Spirit Of Business* and *In the Spirit of Marriage*. "A year ago, my family and I began a series of trips to find the true heart of Rasta, the heart that inspired your son. We met a lot of wolves, a lot of dreads and a few real Rastas. This book is about our

Gathering of the Healers

search, which includes a large section on your son. We had a vision to introduce the book during your son's birthday week and during the publicity campaign we will ask the Jamaican people to claim their position of teaching One Love to the planet by making Bob's words real. We plan to do this by asking them to do one simple thing: to forgive all their old hatreds as much as they can. We believe your son was sent here because Jamaica is the headquarters. This One Love vibration is emanating strongly from here."

"Why have you come to see me?" Mama B asked

"To tell you the truth, Mama B—can I call you Mama B?" I asked, as she nodded her consent. "As an outsider, I don't have a strong position to ask the Jamaican people to forgive and heal their relationships so we decided to go to people who did have that authority. So our concept is to have a press conference at Bob's home on Hope Road and have well-known Jamaican healers or elders, like yourself, to ask Jamaicans to claim their destiny and teach One Love. We're asking each person to begin to heal their relationships in their own lives. That's how One Love is taught. Denroy Morgan, Antonnette Haughton and Dennis Forsythe are joining us. We met earlier this morning with Luciano and Tony Rebel and they are considering. A few days ago we met with your grandsons Julian and Damian but they didn't seem too interested. We are asking PJ Patterson and Seaga to come, not to speak, but as chiefs to listen to their healers. We are hoping you will join us."

"What form would this take?" Mama B asked.

"It would not be a concert but a major press conference," I answered, looking over to Scram who was now fast asleep on the other couch. "And by the way, I met your brother at the museum and he said to tell you hello."

"Which brother was that?" Mama B asked.

"I'm not sure I remember his name," I answered. "He was a stocky guy with a big smile. When I asked if he wanted me to tell you hello, he said 'In any language.' "

"Oh, that's Brother John!" she said laughing.

"Well, now, this sounds very ambitious," Diane said, "and there's good heart behind it. But how effective is this going to be? Bob himself

102

Gathering of the Healers

had an original One Love Peace Concert where he held the two politicians' hands over his head and asked them to unite for peace. And many of these singers, like at the Rebel Salute last night, cry out for peace, cry out for justice and there still is no response. And these are heavy voices. Why do you feel that your press conference is going to have any greater impact than all of these other efforts?"

"That's a good question," I replied. "Probably the one that I ask myself the most. And I'm not sure how big our impact will be. The success is in attempting even if it isn't as successful as planned. So I don't know what the results will be but whatever they are, big or small, it will be a success. It will definitely be a success for each individual deciding to exercise more love and forgineress in their life."

"How is this different then from the annual prayer breakfasts where they all get together and pray to God?" Diane continued.

"When you only pray to God to heal the country," I said "you leave it all up to God without doing your part. We're telling Jamaican people to not only ask God for guidance *but* that each one of us, as His ambassadors on earth, must also do our part by forgiving our own personal animosities and bitterness. God loves us *through* each other. The prayer breakfasts, as well-intentioned as they are, may not be strongly emphasizing this human participation enough."

"The only power that we have is through JAH," Diane said. "Our power doesn't start with us. It only comes through us. So unless that divine inspiration is with it, your whole mission is doomed to fail. Bob's message must never be taken out of context in knowing that Bob was a Rastamon first and as a Rastamon his message was a message *from* the Father *through* him."

"I understand and I wish I could say that I remember that every minute of my day but I don't," I replied. "As much as I can, I try to live JAH's will but probably within about thirty minutes I will forget again and come from my ego or my fears. But I have God as my basis."

"We are all servants of good and we heed the instructions of JAH," Diane continued.

"And the tough part for me is trying to figure out just exactly what His instructions are for me," I replied. "I usually know by determining

Gathering of the Healers

where my passion is. Coming down here to put this thing together has become a passion for me. That's how I determine JAH's will for me. And many times, I wonder why I am driving around Jamaica trying to get people to join me in this. But every time my faith waivers, God reinforces it with a coincidence that helps me along the way. Like when I meet a guy at a small restaurant in Long Bay who knows Denroy Morgan and he takes me to meet him. Or when I find out my cousin Bobby is close friend's with Peter Shukkat, your family lawyer. Or when I was leaving the museum in Kingston and a nephew of Mama B's, who had heard me talking, comes over to my car as I'm about to drive out and gives me your number and tells me I should call you and here I am. So I just keep breathing into it and going to the next step."

"You are about enlightenment," Diane said, "a most powerful magnet, obviously this has to pass. To be totally enlightened, one has to reach Rastafari. I can see just from the various books you have written, going from your hippie stage and going from wherever it is, you are a person that is seeking Truth and the meaning of humanity. And as such your journey has to be true Rasta. We are the beginning and the end of the journey to enlightenment."

"And when you say 'we'?" I asked.

"I and I," she answered. "Noah got the message from JAH that He would destroy all of mankind because of their wickedness. But Noah still went out everyday and preached and warned people to stop their wicked ways and start praising JAH. He never lost faith that maybe mankind would heed his message but he also never stopped building the ark, knowing that there was an inevitable conclusion. This is where we are and we will continue to preach to everyone and tell them. But mankind has been so overtaken by these vast powers of wickedness and whatever, that you don't want to say they are beyond redemption, but there is an inevitable conclusion. There is going to be a second coming—this time with the fire. Looking and thinking of America, it is so engulfed in the evil, they are drowning."

"All expressions of Babylon in all countries create war and divisiveness," I replied. "It's the nature of Babylon and America just happens to be the strongest expression of this on the planet now, just as England was before us and the Dutch before them. Many leaders lead people astray and that includes our country and yours. Americans are being exploited and led astray just like Jamaicans."

"America is a war monger," Diane shot back.

"It happens in every country," I said. "Everyone on the planet, even the leaders, are in a personal struggle to free their minds from Babylon's inflence.

It's a planetary system of forgetfulness, of unconsciousness that has ruled this planet for a long time. But that may end soon because with weapons of mass destruction, over-population and pollution, this archaic, painful system in no longer sustainable. Wisdom is returning to the planet and Bob is a symbol of that return."

"It will be too little, too late," Diane replied.

"Well, in that case, I'll go down trying to change it anyway. Because if you start to hate Babylon, you become Babylon. Because Babylon is separation. It is anything that leads God's children away from Him, away from love. So if you hate, you are being led astray. You are weakened. You become what you meditate upon and if you hate, you become Babylon."

"But there needs to be separation of the wicked from the good," Diane continued.

"Well, I'll have to leave that to JAH because I never know what is in people's hearts," I replied.

"Yes. And by their fruits you will know them," Mama B added.

"But I hope you will not hold my being American against me," I said. "I know it seems strange that I would be the catalyst but if it was someone from within the Jamaican culture they would have a hard time pulling everyone together. If it was a Rasta, the Christians wouldn't come. If it was a Christian minister, the Rastas may not come. If it was a politician, nobody would come except people from that party."

"Can I say something now? Don't be offended," Diane said. "You are a white man and you represent the oppressor."

"I know," I said, "and all I can say is JAH sent white and the color of my skin won't matter to those who know One Love and are working to heal the planet. Bob was part black and part white and he went out and

105

encouraged people of all colors to love."

"Your mission is like trying to bring peace," Mama B said, for the first time joining the dialogue between me and Diane. Her voice was clear and certain.

"I don't know if you'll be in the country then," Diane quickly interrupted.

"I'm not sure about that," Mama B said.

"But this must not trivialize his message," Diane said.

"I don't think having the caliber of people at the conference with this invitation to forgive would trivialize his message at all," I replied. "I'm just saying let's call forth the healers of this island to heal it with One Love. Patterson and Seaga can't do it. They don't know this One Love. They're the administrators, the chiefs not the healers. And these healers, the elders, must teach people to exercise this One Love that your son spoke about. And to teach the people, we must tell them to forgive and heal their own relationships and we must do it in our relationships."

"People have to get to know that because they are hurting their own selves," Mama B said. "But like Bob sang from Haile Selassie's speech, 'Until the color of a man's skin is no more important than the color of his eyes, there is war.' "

"I think this is one of the greatest obstacles to people embracing One Love," I said. "They think exercising One Love means that you like a person or seek out their company or allow them to continue treating you abusively or unlovingly. It does *not* mean that you forego justice or reparations for past wrongs committed but only that you seek them without bitterness or a desire for revenge, only justice. One Love simply means that in your heart you try to remember that everyone you hold bitterly is also a child of God who may have temporarily forgotten who they are and gone astray. When my wife and I were working on *Rasta Heart*, we uncovered an ancient mystery that showed a true example of One Love. We began to feel there was some connection between the Maroon leader Nanny and the Rastas, even though there was a 200 year span between the two. Nanny led her people to physical freedom. The true Rasta leads people to emotional, spiritual and mental freedom. We asked many people, both Rastas and Maroons, if they knew of such a

Gathering of the Healers

connection. No one did until we asked Roy Scotte, a Maroon leader in Flagstaff. He told us that when Nanny made the 'Great Trek' where she marched with several hundred warriors from the Blue Mountains in Portland to Gun Hill in Flagstaff, it was not for the reason that the history books said.

The books said that Nanny marched for several months, avoiding capture, to tell her brother, Cudjoe, the leader of the Leeward Maroons, not to sign the peace treaty offered by the British. Mr. Scotte told us that this is not what he was told by the tribal elders. He said that his foreparents were told by their foreparents that the reason Nanny left her mountain hideaway and marched across the island, at the risk of being captured and killed, was to deliver one message to her tribal members in the West.

'Nanny came here,' he told us, 'to teach us One Love. She said that we must never hate the English or this hate would weaken our tribe. She told us we must love them even if we must fight them to keep our freedom. Nanny taught her people to love the slave master while still fighting them for their freedom."

"That is why there has been centuries of domination in Africa because of the love that was turned against them by the Europeans," Diane replied. "And that's why I say there is a lot of exploitation in the name of love. We don't come as lambs to the slaughter now. In this particular generation there are no lambs to the slaughter, brother. It don't work so. Not in *this* generation."

"But Bob also said that we could only win the revolution with Rasta, with One Love," I said. "If you win it in other way, like with guns, you're going to have to fight again. So to me, I think it's only One Love. I think that's why the Father sent us—to teach this One Love because it's who He is and who we are because we were made in His image. But that still means you can fight for your rights."

"But there are some who have ears and cannot hear and eyes that cannot see," Diane replied. "And JAH would say to separate yourself from them."

"But this message would be good for those that don't know," Mama B interjected thoughtfully. "This would be good for those that don't

107

Gathering of the Healers

have the knowledge of what Rastafari is. This gentleman has the ability to face it but you're going to have a hard time. There will be many obstacles. Bob couldn't do it. Bob had done his best to bring them together and still they are killing one another."

"But even if you knew the results would be what they've been," I said, "You still would have said, 'Bob, go out there and teach as much love as you can.' "

"But he had to because he was sent to do it," Mama B replied, her voice rising with power and clarity. "He had to. And with all the bruises, with all the beatings and with all he had gone through, he never stopped. When he stopped it was when he was ready to go."

At this point a young woman came in to tell us that she had lunch ready for us in the breakfast room. Leaving Scram fast asleep, the three of us went into the adjoining small dining room for a delicious Ital meal of vegetables, beans and rice.

"You see, what attracts you to Jamaica," Diane continued as we ate, "is that you can't travel to England and Europe as a stranger and get that welcoming spirit where people invite you to be part of their lives. You as an American probably have never been exposed to that degree of love that you've been exposed to coming to Jamaica."

"It's true," Mama B agreed.

"And that's what brings a lot of people back to Jamaica," Diane continued. "That spirit that you can actually live a social life, a human life, interactive with people. You don't get that in your country where you mostly relate with people on a business level but not with a sense of community. We still have unpolluted land, unpolluted water."

"That is why I love it here," I replied. "In our country people are becoming more and more isolated."

Over lunch, I told them about several more of the coincidences that had guided us on our journey.

"There have been so many of these JAHincidences that we feel this is under His guidance," I said, "but after hearing me what do you think?"

"Well, like I say, it is not everybody that has those kind of feelings, that kind of energy to go out there and say what you are saying and do

Gathering of the Healers

what you are doing here," Mama B said after a thoughtful pause. "If you really get that anointment to go out there and tell what you feel and what you think about bringing people together, you should do it. You should do it."

"And see where it goes?" I added.

"And see where it goes," Mama B replied, "because with faith you can move mountains. It's a wonderful feeling that you have there and I think it's a very good idea to think about bringing people together. The One Love that Bob has gone out there and preached so many times in his music, just talking to people and showing the people the right way in life and what is best for everyone because that was his mission. He has done a lot because he touched a lot of people—even you speaking here to me, he has touched you."

"Yes. I wouldn't be doing what I'm doing if it weren't for him," I said.

"And this is what makes me feel good because so many people all over the world, Bob has touched their hearts," Mama B continued, "and they come from faraway just to see where Bob's body lay. And I think that Bob has done so much for the world that it is up to them now to do their part, I would say. He has done his part. He can't do no more. And when man on earth has done their best, angels in heaven can't do no more. Bob has done his best and you have seen the results. The only thing I see the people lack is that togetherness. They're still not together and that is the only thing they need. But even when you see the people arguing with one another here in Jamaica, by the end of the day you see them sweet up again. Nobody holds anything against anyone."

"And Bob's message, which Jamaicans have been listening to for almost 30 years, is key for creating that," I interjected.

"Yes. They just love that and that's what's really keeping them, you know," Mama B continued. "They should appreciate all the good that Bob has done for them, how he opened up their mentality to the reality. And I think that if you can get people to just stop and think for a moment, then they would see and feel that greatness. But I guess everyone that is not even concerned does not see that. But those that are concerned are holding the fort. They're not going to let go."

Gathering of the Healers

"So in the end you just do what you can no matter what the results are," I said. "My family and Scram may be the only people at the press conference."

"But you could never say you didn't do your part," Mama B said. "And you are writing a second book, too?"

"Yes. This is book two," I answered. "That's why I'm recording this conversation. You'll be in it. Book two will chronicle our efforts to try to implement One Love at the level of society. The first book looked at exercising One Love in our personal relationships. Book two looks at it from a societal level. And sometimes I see clearly why JAH chose me, a white, middle-class American, to continue to bring this message forward. I understand the illusions that my culture is lost in and they may listen to me where they wouldn't listen to a black, dreadlocked Jamaican."

"Well, we are leaving the island Tuesday and I don't know if we will be back here on the day of your press conference," Mama B said.

"Well, what I'd like to do is let you think about what I've said for a few days and then I'll call you and see if your spirit is drawing you to join us at the press conference," I said. "If you can't come, you can send us a message to read out loud."

At this point Scram joined us, smiling, yawning and rubbing his eyes. "I'm glad you finally woke up," I said, "because I wanted Mama B to hear from you before we left. "

"Well, when I was sleepin' an' you people were havin' all de conversations," he said, "I was enjoying all dese suggestions while I was sleepin' becuz I was gettin' it like a food of wisdom. Dis One Love is dat Bob was talkin' 'bout, it is to a point dat people today are not living dis One Love de right an' proper way. Dat is why we 'ave so much killin' an' so much negative vibe around Jamaica. So Robert an' meself decided to probe dis One Love business to see if we could get de soft feelin's of love inside de people. So dat's why we try to pick up dis word dat Bob 'as said, One Love. And dat is why all dese people come to 'is concerts becuz Bob exercise dis love in dere presence while 'e was around. Dis One Love 'as a great virtue in it but people doan't cherish dis yet up to de right maximum way. So we are tryin' to put out de peti-

Gathering of the Healers

tion fe dis love."

"And we understand that this is what Jesus did and they nailed him to a cross," I said, laughing.

"But now dey won't nail us to de cross when we speak about love. It's not like de beginnin'. It's not like de first time. Now dey not goin' kill de messengers," Scram said and we all laughed.

As Scram ate his lunch and talked with Mama B and Diane, I wandered up the hill to Bob's crypt. I had hoped to go alone but that is not allowed so a Rasta guide accompanied me. Bob's body lies in a tiny chapel of traditional Ethiopian design. Next to the chapel is the tiny house where Bob was born—rebuilt and painted with Rasta green, yellow and red. Inside the house is a bed and graffiti and various items left by adoring fans. Behind the house is the "inspiration stone," on which Bob sat and learned to play the guitar. Nearby is another Rasta-colored rock, "pillow," on which he rested his head and slept, getting inspiration for some of his songs, including "Talking Blues. "Leaving my shoes outside, I reverently entered the chapel, asking the guide to wait outside.

Inside there is an 8-foot-tall oblong marble mausoleum. There is a beautiful Star of David-shaped window that is set so the rising sun casts its rays on his grave. At the base of his tomb is a large picture of His Majesty Haile Selassie I. Next to this is a smaller picture of Bob. A large bronze bust of Bob is against a wall, along with several of his instruments and a leather-bound book full of newspaper clippings reporting his funeral. A stained glass window of the Lion of Judah is set in another wall.

I had hoped to have some sort of profound experience at his grave, some major realization, or better yet maybe he would appear to me with further instructions. But between the constant chatter of the guide and being somewhat drained from the long drive and no sleep, I had none. However, as I sat putting on my shoes on the stoop of the chapel, I started to think about Mama B and what she had said and my spirits started to lift. She understood all too well how difficult it is to get people to express One Love in their lives and she realized how important it was to keep trying. This was her message, her gift, to me and it recharged

Gathering of the Healers

my spirits and re-energized my efforts.

I walked back down to the house feeling refreshed. Scram was finishing up his lunch, laughing and talking with Mama B and Diane. After getting directions from Mama B back to Port Antonio, we headed out, promising to call her in Miami in a few days.

"Mama B," I said, as she walked us out the door, "I cannot imagine what it must be like for you to sit in this house, on land where you were born and raised on, and reflect back on the amazing life you have led—a life I'm sure you could never have even dreamed possible as a young girl. JAH knew just what He was doing when He made you Bob Marley's mother. He knew that you could give your son something no one else could and whatever that was, it was good—very good. Bob could not have spread such a powerful message of One Love if you hadn't taught it to him as a child."

"When I was pregnant with Bob," she said, "I heard a voice that said to me. 'You are blessed.' "

"Much love and respect to the mother of such a one as Bob Marley," I closed, putting my right fist over my heart.

She smiled warmly and we nodded good-bye.

"If we can't imagine a new way of life or a way out of situations like war and crime, we can't resolve them."
—Luciano

Chapter 8
January 16, 2002

Luciano
"Jah's MessenJah"

Leaving Nine Mile in the late afternoon, we arrived back in Port Antonio after dark. I dropped Scram at his shop and checked in to the Fern Hill Club. Across the street from Frenchman's Cove on the hill above San San Tropez, the Fern Hill Club is a family-operated hotel that overlooks the Caribbean Sea. Individual villas and large rooms, most with dramatic mountain and sea views, are spread throughout the landscaped property. I was given a spacious room with a large deck overlooking the ocean. I ate dinner at the hotel's restaurant, with its open-air dining area looking over the sea and the distant mountains of Portland Parish.

During the next couple of days, I made phone calls trying to reach the other people we were inviting to join us. By Tuesday, I had appointments to meet with Luciano, Tony Rebel, and Stephanie Marley in Kingston.

Scram and I left early Wednesday morning. We stopped to reason with Tasha, always glad to hear of our adventures. An hour out of Kingston we stopped at the Morgan Heritage compound and talked with

Gathering of the Healers

Taliba and brought her up to date. We also met Taliba's sister, Tafire, equally as beautiful and serene and Denroy's oldest wife, Hyacinth, a loving and wise woman. Hyacinth said a wonderful prayer for us before we left. Both of these stops were like an oasis along the way where we would rest and get energized before undertaking our next challenge. We would also stop on the way back to let them know how things went—a kind of conscious debriefing.

After leaving the Morgan's, we called Luciano's office. He had not returned my call from the day before and I was getting concerned that he didn't want to meet with us but Scram said not to worry, which I did anyway. When Denica, his lady friend, got on the phone she said she had called my cell number several times and got no response but that Luciano could meet with us as soon as we got in town. She gave us instructions to the office and we told her we would be there in an hour or so. I was relieved and elated. I called the cell phone service and they said the person who sold me the phone had failed to activate the number in the main computer but they would do it immediately. No wonder none of my calls were getting returned!

We arrived about an hour later, shortly before lunch. Luciano's office was located above a small strip mall in New Kingston about a mile from the Terra Nova Hotel. We had to ring a bell to get someone to come down and unlock the iron gate and take us up. We were ushered into a small outer office directly across from a large open rehearsal room where four or five guys were hanging out. Denica, a beautiful, petite African-American with glowing eyes and a loving smile, dressed in a long African dress and matching turban, rose from behind the desk and greeted us. She had met Luciano while she was traveling with her own singing group, musically spreading her own message of One Love. You could sense her spiritual power and commitment. I felt right at home. She introduced us to Sonja, an attractive Jamaican woman with a warm smile and peaceful nature. Also, we met Moira Morgan, a white Englishwoman dressed in a white dress with her dreads in a white turban, who was there just to help for a few days while she was volunteering with some inner-city projects.

After a short wait, Luciano came out of his adjoining office to greet

114

Gathering of the Healers

us, giving us both an African-style greeting with a hand on our shoulders and nodding deeply over each shoulder. Luciano is a handsome, powerful-looking man in his late twenties, serious and intense but with a grace and a smile that reveals a kind and gentle soul. It is obvious that he is a man with a mission—a mission you can sense he is constantly planning and pondering. He was dressed in his usual army camouflage fatigues, clean and pressed. He has long rope-like dreads with a short black beard and mustache. What struck me most about him, something I had glimpsed when I met him at The Rebel Salute, was his humility and concern for you as a person. It's as if he's thinking, *I'm so glad and honored to be interacting with you and I hope that I can help you in some way.* In fact, he does describe himself as "a humble servant like anyone else who is willing to carry out the word." This man is a very clear light.

In his native Jamaica, Luciano is a superstar, filling concerts with enthusiastic fans wherever he appears. His fame is growing worldwide, especially in the U.S. and Europe. Since his remake of the McCartney-Stevie Wonder hit single "Ebony and Ivory" was released in 1991 and his *Where is the Life* debut album, considered by many to be one of the greatest reggae albums ever, his audience has grown every year. He writes most of his own songs, calling on an inner wellspring of joy, optimism, love of humanity and JAH. In 1994, his "Shake It Up Tonight" became his first UK reggae #1 single. He released another hit, "It's Me Again JAH" in 1995, a beautiful song of pain and piety coming straight from his heart and soul. Since then he has had a series of hit singles and over 15 albums, as well as appearing on songs with many other reggae and African artists. His biggest single, "Sweep Over My Soul," on the album of the same name, is a powerful, moving song—a celebration of hope, love and devotion.

He was born Jepther McCylmont in Davey Town, Jamaica, a small community in the country parish of Manchester, where he would sing while herding the family goats or picking breadfruits for his mother. A deeply religious youth raised in a household of musical parents, he sang in the local church choir. His father, a carpenter, built a guitar and taught him to play. He eventually moved to Kingston, where he worked as an

115

Gathering of the Healers

upholsterer while singing at sound-systems parties, mobile discos as they are called, in the evening. Soon he changed his name to Luciano because of his operatic-quality voice.

After a few years in Kingston with only limited success, he returned to Manchester to sell food in the market place. He returned a second time to Kingston, which he refers to as his "struggler's stage," to continue his musical career. Doing upholstery during the night and recording at the studio during the day, he released several albums that were critically acclaimed but went largely unnoticed by the public.

In the summer of 1993, tired from the stress of his budding career as a reggae star, he walked off the stage in the middle of his performance and headed for the Blue Mountains, as he had done in his youth when he needed to find refuge. After a few months of rest and meditation there, he returned a changed and reinvigorated man. He later explained his sabbatical by saying he needed to "take intervals off in order to cool out spiritually. You have to travel JAH road in order to carry JAH word."

Luciano sees himself as much more than an entertainer and a recording artist. Often reading to his audience from the Bible before performing, his main goal is to be a clear messenger for JAH. He refers to himself as "Jah's MessenJah." "The kingdom of God is within me," he said in a recent interview, "so true faith starts within me. I must have perseverance and strength. I ask God for that strength and will power, so God operates within me as inspiration and my willingness to comply."

Many others see him likewise noting that such a powerful message of love for all humanity has not been heard since Bob Marley. Like Marley, many fans have said that his music and philosophy have changed their lives. His music is positive, hopeful, conscious reggae, reflecting his spiritual, social and human concerns. Luciano's message is especially directed at the youths, ghetto youths in particular, to teach them about roots and culture and to lead them away from the messages of sex, drugs and guns that have led them astray.

His singles "Happy People" and "Road of Life" portray a future where people are motivated by One Love and are free of petty divisiveness. It was songs like these that made Julia and I know he was seeing the same potential future we were seeing. "Some of the songs like 'Happy People' are about people who live in their imagination," he said to an interviewer a few months before we met him. "If we can't imagine a new way of life or a way out of situations like war and crime, we can't resolve them."

In a 2001 interview with Sista Irie, a DJ on an Austin, Texas reggae show, he said, "Knowing how God intended this world to be and having that focus, I get energy just wanting to see the world becoming the way as God ordained it to be. This is one of many main sources of inspiration, to really use my talents that way, to bring forward that love...I really love it when I see people of all different races joining to the One that calls them...My greatest vision is to use my inspiration in a positive sense to encourage people to unite humanity and being about love and unity in the community."

It was his music and statements like this that made me know I had to invite him to join us. We followed him into his office—an attractive, well-lit room decorated with African art and comfortable chairs. Scram sat off to the side and I sat directly in front of Luciano in a huge over-stuffed chair.

"Luciano, you know how you sing, 'Father of Creation, come and heal this nation,' " I began. "Well, JAH has given us a plan that we think will help heal this nation and we want you to join us. And I want you to know that there is no one that I have been more excited about seeing than you because there is no one who I feel has been holding this vision more strongly than you. My family has listened to nothing but your music for three months."

"I like those thoughts, Brother Robbie. What is your plan?" Luciano said. I liked being called "Brother Robbie" by him.

I explained our concept in detail with Scram adding in his views. The sun was shining brightly through the window directly behind Luciano, obstructing my vision so I was unable to judge his reaction.

"Well, now, Brother Robbie," he started when I was finished, "I like your idea but what would this mean to efforts to get reparations for the years of slavery?"

"One Love doesn't mean that you wouldn't sue someone who had wronged you," I answered. "It only means you wouldn't sue them with hostility or bitterness. It's the difference between seeking justice as opposed to seeking revenge. Most people think if they exercise One Love and true forgiveness, it means they have to let people continue treating them badly or unfairly. Or they have to stop all efforts to right past wrongs, like seeking reparations. A lot of people won't forgive because they believe this. But One Love doesn't dictate any particular *form* of behavior. It only means that whatever you do, you do with love, even if you sue someone, divorce them, confront them, or decide never to see them again. Love dictates the *content* of the relationship not the form. The content is always love. The form can be anything—ex-mate, ex-boss, litigant in a lawsuit, whatever."

"Yeah, mon," Scram said. "It is nah what you do; it is what is in your 'eart."

"I do agree that we all need to forgive and Jamaicans are forgiving people," Luciano continued. "We need to forgive in order to have a free heart and to allow the power and flow of God's love to manifest in us. Love is a positive energy that can activate the hearts of all people. But this vision can only come about when there is justice because there can be no love without justice. And this justice must come from the heads of government straight to the little man."

"And I agree that people must confront these leaders and demand this justice but if they do that with love it will also transform the leaders' hearts and bring this justice about quicker," I said. "But you *can* have love without justice. You can have love without anything. But I agree you cannot have *peace* without justice because those being treated unjustly will never be at peace nor will the people oppressing them."

"This press conference that you want to do," Luciano continued, speaking slowly and thoughtfully, "it is a good thing and I think that it will make a difference. We need this kind of forum. I will come and be with you if I am not singing that night. And the first issue that I am going to raise that night is the matter of reparations. I feel strongly about seeking reparations and as long as this doesn't detract from that, I can support it."

"I don't think it will detract from it at all," I said. "Martin Luther

Gathering of the Healers

King, Mandela and Gandhi were all able to demand justice but they did so with love and understanding for the oppressor, knowing that the oppressors too were caught in this Babylon system, which traps everyone—oppressor and oppressed into a system of hatred. It is easier for the oppressor to right his wrongs when you demand it with love, not hostility."

"Yes. Dis is true," Scram said. "And dey must right dese wrongs so dat dey cayn cleanse dere souls."

"But we can't wait until they do the right thing to forgive them," I said. "That's the whole problem on the planet. It's like saying I'll forgive the white man for enslaving the blacks once they pay billions of dollars in reparations. Or I'll forgive the person who betrayed me if they beg for my forgiveness and admit they were wrong. The reason we are not seeing love and forgiveness more on the planet is people are refusing to forgive until the people they think hurt them does the right thing. And usually those kinds of people don't come forward and make amends. If they were that evolved they probably wouldn't have done much to need to make amends for. True forgiveness is activating One Love in your own heart. Forgiving is *unilateral* not bilateral. It's a one-sided decision. Jesus didn't say 'Love your enemy *after* they make amends.' He said to do good to those that hate us and pray for those who mistreat us, whether they asked us for forgiveness or not. Forgiving is something you do to free yourself and hopefully the other person from the bondage of judgment and bitterness. And this gift of love awaits the other person, whether they are ready to receive it yet or not. This healed relationship still awaits them."

"Yes. That is true, my brother," he responded thoughtfully. "I am an ambassador for love *and* for justice too. So if I can be there, I will come."

"And I would be willing to try to adjust the date of the conference to be sure you can be there," I said. "That's how strongly I feel about your participation. I don't think there's a clearer musical voice for One Love in the world than yours. For as long as you can remember, from when you were a young child, you have known this One Love. It comes naturally to you, effortlessly."

119

Gathering of the Healers

We reasoned awhile longer and agreed to stay in touch. Luciano's openness and instant agreement to join us was refreshing. It was clear that he, like us, had been holding a vision of healing the planet with One Love and was eager to join with ours in this effort. I liked this man immensely and knew I had met a tribal member, a mighty co-worker.

After leaving Luciano's office, we drove the short distance to the Marley Museum and informed the office that we were there to meet with Stephanie. The receptionist informed us that Stephanie was busy but she would let her know we were there. We told her we would wait in the Queen of Sheba restaurant, the Ital restaurant in the front courtyard of the museum. Scram and I settled back, ordered some vegetable plates and chatted while we waited.

In a few minutes, we saw Damian Marley (Junior Gong) walking across the front courtyard. We told him we had just met with Luciano, who had agreed to join us, as had Denroy Morgan and, hopefully, Tony Rebel. Once again we asked if he would like to join us. He looked at us quizzically and said he would come talk with us soon as we ate. We waited for almost an hour before someone from Stephanie's office came to get us. Damian sat with some of the local Rases in the courtyard but never came over or looked our way.

We walked into Stephanie's office, a small room in the exhibit building in the back courtyard. Stephanie is Bob and Rita's daughter, born in 1974, seven years before Bob's death. She is an attractive, serious young woman who seems to have grown fully into the position that her father's fame has placed her. She handles herself with a sense of efficiency, integrity and caring—a rare combination in the business world. She is involved in many parts of the ever-growing Marley empire. Along with her mother, Rita, her grandmother, Mama B, and David Marley, she manages the Robert Marley Foundation, a non-profit, charitable organization created in 1991. She also works with the Marley Group of companies comprising Music Manufacturers Ltd., Rita Marley Music, Inc., Ghetto Youths United, Tuff Gong International

Gathering of the Healers

(Miami), Tuff Gong International (New York), and The Bob Marley Museum.

Stephanie gave us a cordial greeting and invited us to sit but reminded us that she was busy and could only give us a few minutes. She said she had seen copies of my book with Damian and Julian and would very much like a copy. I handed her the signed copy I had brought for her. I explained to her our vision and that her father's home seemed the appropriate place to launch such a venture. She listened intently and I could tell she liked our concept.

"I t'ink she overstands," Scram said, interrupting my long-winded soliloquy.

"I think your father would be smiling on this effort, probably laughing," I ended.

"In the past, we almost never have allowed a third party to use the home," she began, reflectively. "However, I like what you are attempting to do and I think my father would have liked it too. It's fine with me for you to use the museum but first I need to run this by my mother, Rita, to be sure she agrees. Call me next week after I talk with her."

"Also, we would love it if you would be one of the speakers." I could tell this woman was a teacher of love.

"I don't think I want to do that," she said, smiling. "I'm the only Marley that doesn't like the mike."

We headed over to Tony Rebel's feeling even more elated. Having the conference at Bob Marley's home just seemed so right. It was hard to imagine having it anywhere else. We could only hope Rita would agree but knowing that Stephanie would represent the concept in a positive light made us feel fairly certain that we would be allowed to use the museum.

Tony's office was a mile or two past Luciano's in a residential area where he had converted an attractive one-story home into an office. When we arrived, several women were cleaning up a meal that had been set up on the porch. Several Rastas were sitting around the porch and one went inside to get Tony. Tony came out, greeted Scram and I and joined us sitting on the low porch wall.

Tony was born Patrick Barrett in Manchester, Jamaica. Changing his name to Tony Rebel was appropriate as he has been a rebel in the Jamaican music scene, rallying against the emphasis on guns, drugs, violence and sex that has emerged. In a 1998 interview he stated, "There are a whole lot of my colleagues who have turned their musical vibe to a more positive vibe. And I am happy for that. There is also a lot of people who are still doing the slack music and gun lyrics. They are doing it more subtle this time, and it is very ambiguous and it is also getting a lot of prominence. And I think it is time now that they know they stop, because it is contributing to the deterioration of our music."

Before his 1988 debut with a tune called "Casino" for the MGM label, he spent 14 years on the local dancehall circuit, winning contests under the name of Papa Tony or Tony Ranking. His career took off in 1989 when he started working with veteran Jamaican producer, Donovan Germain. With Germain, he released the worldwide smash hit "Fresh Vegetable." In 1991 he was selected as the Best New Artist at Jamaica's Grammy's. He quickly followed with hit singles such as "Mandela Story," "The Armour" and "Instant Death." In 1993, Tony Rebel's popularity led to a contract with Columbia. His biggest hit is "Jah By My Side," chosen as the "Best Song Of The Year" in New York and Jamaica, is a compelling song acclaiming his faith that with JAH there is no reason to fear anything. He is also a gifted producer and now runs his own production company, Flames Production, which recently released his album, *Realms of Rebel*.

It was now late afternoon and with his workday over, Tony relaxed with us into a one-hour reasoning.

"I'm not so sure that this One Love thing will work," he said at one point. "A press conference is nice but how are you going to sustain it."

"We're not. *You* are," I said and we all laughed. "No. I mean that. Our vision is to just be the catalysts. Guys like you and Luciano and Antonnette and Denroy are out there everyday talking with thousands of people at your concerts and rallies. You're going to sustain it just as you've been doing by singing about this One Love. And we have other things planned after this press conference."

"I'm still not convinced you can get anything to work here because of these politicians," he continued. "These are the guys that are screwing everything up. They are the ones that are causing a lot of the killing."

"But dis love," Scram interjected, "dat you are singin' 'bout and dat we are talkin' 'bout, dere is not'ing stronger dan dis love. It cayn even change de hearts of de leaders."

"I smell a revolution," Tony said, and we all laughed. "I am still unconvinced but I will come."

It was now almost dark so we thanked him and headed back to the Jamaica Pegasus Hotel. The Pegasus is a tall Hyatt-like hotel and is not my first choice. When I'm in Kingston I always like staying at the Terra Nova, a three-story complex set in an attractive garden-like setting, a peaceful oasis in busy downtown Kingston. The Terra Nova was full that day but I kept calling hoping there would be a cancellation. After dinner, I made one last phone call and finally gave up.

"JAH wants us ta stay at de Pegasus," Scram said in his usual inscrutable way, "or we would 'ave gotten a room at de o'ter 'otel."

We checked in the Pegasus and sat on our balcony overlooking the city. We reflected on what an incredible day it had been. We now had firm commitments from Denroy, Luciano, Tony, Dennis Forsythe and perhaps Mama B, and hopefully permission to use Bob Marley's home. We were to meet with Antonnette Haughton before leaving Kingston the next day and we were fairly certain she would join us. A high profile press conference was now assured.

"It would be great if we could meet with Patterson and Seaga before we leave town tomorrow," I said, as we looked out over the city. "Meeting them in person would really make a difference. I'll call their offices in the morning but I doubt we can get an appointment."

"Well now, if JAH wants us to meet dem now, dey will 'ave to see us," Scram said and burst into a big belly laugh.

Gathering of the Healers

Me and Alicia at the Fern Hill restaurant.

Alicia with Scram, her Rasta grandfather.

Gathering of the Healers

Jah Priest near his stall at Reach Falls.

I

Tasha, a true Rastaman.

II

Gathering of the Healers

Tafire Morgan, Denroy's daughter with his grandchildren.

Ras Johnson's Ital
Restaurant near
Long Bay.

The view from my cottage at
Frenchman's Cove.

Gathering of the Healers

Scram reasoning with Damian Marley (Jr. Gong) in front of the Bob Marley Museum in Kingston. Julian Marley is in foreground.

Fern Hill overlooking the Caribbean Sea.

Scram relaxes at the Venus Sunset Lounge before we head to the Rebel Salute.

Gathering of the Healers

Scram talking with vendors at the Rebel Salute.

Tony Rebel (center, white shirt and turban) talking with fans after the show.

Gathering of the Healers

Luciano signing autographs after the Rebel Salute.

Jah Priest at his stall near Reach Falls.

Gathering of the Healers

Scram, Antonnette Haughton and author at the Pegasus Hotel.

The Rockhouse in Negril, my retreat.

Gathering of the Healers

Red (Maurice Lynch), the elder Rasta in Negril.

Red with Errol Chambers at Errol's restaurant, The Royal Kitchen.

Gathering of the Healers

Alicia with two of her "Rasta Grandfathers": Bongo Roach (above) and Red (below).

Gathering of the Healers

Bongo Roach (Joseph Roach), Sarah and Ras Thomas at the Original Mayfield Falls.

Bongo Roach reading my speech at The Royal Kitchen.

Gathering of the Healers

Scram, Bell, Julia and Alicia at the Terra Nova the day of the conference.

Alec, Red and Alicia.

Gathering of the Healers

Luciano rehearsing his song in front of Bob's statue.

Bongo Roach, Red and author reasoning before the conference.

Gathering of the Healers

The Gathering of The Healers Press Conference at Bob Marley's home in Kingston, Jamaica.

Luiciano setting the vibe for the conference.

Gathering of the Healers

Author explaining the vision.

Scram (Thomas Anderson), featured in *Rasta Heart*.

Gathering of the Healers

Luciano, the Ambassador of Love.

Dr. Dennis Forsythe, author of *Rastafari: For the Healing of the Nations,* left, and author.

Gathering of the Healers

Antonnette Haughton, founder of the United People's Party (UPP), Jamaica's third political party.

Reggae star Abijah, our youngest healer.

Gathering of the Healers

Denroy Morgan, Rasta elder and founder of Morgan Heritage.

Red entertains everyone with his closing song.

Gathering of the Healers

Sonya and Denica, friends of Luciano, join Red in singing.

Antonnette
and Red
after the
conference.

Gathering of the Healers

Mutabaruka and Denroy Morgan reason afterwards.

Luciano pays his respect to the elders.

Gathering of the Healers

Abijah, author, Red, Denroy Morgan and Luciano.

Sitting Denroy Morgan, Mortimo Planno, Luciano, unknown, standing: Red, Panner.

Gathering of the Healers

Standing (l to r): Antonnette Haughton, author, Abijah, Alicia Roskind, Julia Roskind, Red, Panner, Errol Chambers, Bell, Scram. Sitting (l to r): Hyacinth Morgan, Denroy Morgan, Mortimo Planno, Luciano, unknown.

Dropping Alicia, Bell & Scram off to catch the bus for Port Antonio.

Gathering of the Healers

Reporter Ras Bas (Basil Walters), author and Julia reason by the pool the day after the conference.

Rita Marley and I appearing on a panel for the Jamaican Cultural Development Council (JCDC).

Gathering of the Healers

Author speaking to Kingston high school students.

Reasoning with Abijah at the Terra Nova.

Gathering of the Healers

Julia Scram and I doing a radio interview on ROOTZFM, the inner-city Kingston station from the Bob Marley Experience.

Saying goodbye to Scram at the Mobay bus station.

Gathering of the Healers

Scram and I doing a radio interview with ROOTZFM, the inner-city Kingston station.

"Forgive your enemies. Do good to those that hate you and despiteful-ly use you and abuse you. Pray for them. Your prayer, honestly given from your heart, asking to heal them, is the most powerful weapon in this war against principalities, power and the rulers of darkness."
—**Antonnette Haughton-Cárdenas**

Chapter 9
January 17, 2002

Antonnette Haughton-Cárdenas

The next morning Scram and I left the room a little before seven to get some breakfast in the hotel restaurant. As we stepped out of the elevator in the lobby we saw Horace Matthews from the UPP walking across the lobby directly in front of us. He gave us a warm, enthusiastic hello and we fell in step with him, chatting as we walked down a side corridor where he turned right into a large ballroom. Scram and I barely noticed as he handed someone at the door a piece of paper and the three of us continued into the room. It was only then that I became aware of where we were. The room was set for breakfast for hundreds of people and above the stage up front hung a huge banner reading, "National Leadership Prayer Breakfast: Progress Through Prayer."

The National Leadership Prayer Breakfast (NLPB) was started in 1981, a year after the bloodiest election in Jamaica's history in which more than 800 people were killed. Every year approximately 400 leaders in government, business, church and civic organizations gather for the annual event, sponsored by the Victoria Mutual Building Society.

Gathering of the Healers

It's stated goal is to affirm and give spiritual support to the nation's leaders and to foster greater unity in the country. Money raised this year at the breakfast would go to flood victims near Port Antonio.

Reverend Raymond Cooke, the chairman, had called on church leaders to organize gatherings in communities and use live broadcasts so the entire nation can be at prayer during the breakfast. He also appealed to school principals and employers to do likewise. This year's event had already become somewhat controversial when the NLPB turned down a suggestion to have the annual breakfast meeting in a volatile inner-city community like 100 Lane (a place known for its gun violence), saying that safety was a major concern.

We settled in at our table and observed the crowd. Everyone was dressed in the usual business suits and ties. It was predominantly black and male with a minority of whites and women. Since this was a gathering of the leaders of the society, everyone knew each other and the crowd was animated and friendly, as you would expect at a gathering like this.

As Scram, Horace and I sat at one of the open tables, I noticed that many people were watching us, which was understandable since we didn't fit and were totally unknown to this invitation-only crowd. Horace, with his long braided dreads, was a little out of step but he was well-known. Scram had his dreads in a clean black turban. He was dressed in black pin-stripped dress pants and matching vest covering a white dress shirt with a black scarf with red, yellow and green Rasta accents over his shoulder. I was wearing beige long bush pants and a colorful Hawaiian shirt.

Behind us a radio station had set up for a live feed. The commentator left his station to come over to see Scram, who he greeted with a big hug.

"Who was that?" I asked, after they had chatted awhile.

"Dat was Ronnie Thwaites," Scram said. "E is a Jamaican senator and 'e 'as a talk show on de radio. We were friends when I worked at Dragon Bay an' was working on de movie *Club Paradise*." I was constantly amazed at the scope and breath of Scram's friends.

The ceremony began with a talk by Rev. Christopher Mason from the

Gathering of the Healers

United Church of Jamaica and the Cayman Islands, followed by the arrival of the Governor General, Sir Howard Cooke, and then by the singing of the national anthem. (Although Jamaica is independent, its titular head of state is Queen Elizabeth II. The Governor General, the GG, represents the Queen. Appointed on the advice of the Prime Minister of Jamaica, his duties are largely ceremonial.) Then there was a break in the speakers while breakfast was served. After breakfast, Horace left the table and returned a few minutes later saying that Antonnette was across the room and she wanted to say hello. We wandered over, again noticing that many people were following our movements, including Prime Minister Patterson and Opposition Leader Seaga who were seated at the head table with their wives. We chatted with Antonnette for a few minutes and all agreed to meet in the hotel restaurant later that afternoon for lunch.

As we headed back across the room toward our table, I instantly decided to walk by the head table. I could see that Patterson and Seaga were still watching us probably wondering, *Who are these two, how did they get in this breakfast and why are they talking to my political rival?* Our route took us along the aisle directly behind their chairs. As I got abreast with the Prime Minister I put my hand on his shoulder. He turned his head and looked me directly in the eye.

"Mr. Prime Minister, do you know who I am?" I asked, squatting down so we would be at the same eye level. The Prime Minister is a tall handsome man, balding with gray hair and warm eyes. He seemed to be a kind and caring soul.

"No. I don't," he said quizzically like it should be followed with, "And just who the hell are you?"

"I'm the man that met with Colonel Lindo and sent you the Rasta book," I continued, "and the invitation to our press conference."

"Yes. I got that book and invitation," he said, relaxing somewhat. He seemed pleased to meet me.

"Since I sent you the invitation," I said, "Luciano, Tony Rebel, Denroy Morgan, Dennis Forsythe, and Antonnette Haughton have all agreed to speak and we hope you will come to listen to these healers and also speak as the chief."

126

Gathering of the Healers

"We are considering your invitation," he said. "You should follow up by calling my advisor, Delano Franklin, in a week or two."

"Great," I said, "I'll do that. I hope you can attend."

As I got up to leave, I saw that Scram was also squatting a few chairs away talking to Seaga. I joined them and told Seaga the same thing I had told his political opponent.

Seaga gave us the phone numbers of several of his assistants and asked that we follow up with them. As I stood to go, I noticed that Scram was now one knee talking with the Prime Minister.

These two men, Patterson and Seaga, both probably in their last political campaign, had run the country for the last two decades. The 67-year old Prime Minister, or PJ as he is called, was Jamaica's first black Prime Minister. Due to his non-violent rise to power, he is sometimes referred to as the "Fresh Prince." A lawyer, he has been an active member of the People's National Party (PNP) since the 1950s. From 1972 to 1980 Patterson held various ministerial posts, including minister of finance. In 1989 he became deputy prime minister under Michael Manley and when Manley resigned in 1992 Patterson was appointed party leader and Prime Minister. He won the election the following year.

In a time of economic difficulties for Jamaica, Patterson has pursued privatization and other left-leaning free-market reforms. His first five years were marked by a dramatic economic turnaround through economic liberalization and tight macroeconomic policies. However, by 1997 the island was in financial crisis with crippling interest rates. That year, PJ was re-elected but many political observer remarked that his PNP party did not *win* that election but the disorganized and fractured JLP *lost* it. In 1998, with political tension rising and the country in recession with interest rates above 40%, the IMF issued a rebuke, warning that the government's policies were badly misguided. Two years later, PJ presided over a 30% increase in the gasoline tax and was forced to rescind it after riots, looting and arson broke out on the island leaving nine dead and airlines and cruise ships halting service.

The last several years under his administration have not gone much better. Key industries such as bananas, bauxite and agriculture are off. With election to be held by the end of 2002, tourism, the flagship of the

Gathering of the Healers

economy which accounts for a quarter of all jobs and 45% of Jamaica's foreign income, was off almost 30% due to the worldwide decline after 9/11 and the riots in Kingston the previous summer. Crime was at an almost all time high and Jamaica had acquired the ignoble title of "the murder capital of the world," having more murders per capita than any other country.

However, many of Jamaica's problms are beyond the control of their local and national leaders. Pressures, usually from greedy interests, affect the country constantly and strongly. Who knows what could be accomplished if the country was not influenced heavily by the U.S., the U.K., the World Bank, the IMF, and the local dons.

Opposition leader Seaga, 70, was Prime Minister of Jamaica from 1980 to 1989. Harvard-educated and born in Boston, Mass., to Jamaican parents of Lebanese descent, he was minister of welfare and development (1962–67) and finance minister (1967–72). In 1980, his conservative Jamaican Labor party (JLP) won the elections and he became Prime Minister, reversing most of Michael Manley's socialist policies and severing relations with nearby Cuba while promoting close ties with the United States.

In 1983 he called for "snap elections" while Manley was off the island and unable to respond. Outraged by the maneuver, the PNP boycotted the elections and the JLP won unopposed. However, by 1988 the JLP was losing popularity as the IMF forced strong austerity measures on the JLP administration that adversely affected the country's poor (by some estimates 80% of its 2.4 million). In 1989, the charismatic Manley won the election, defeating Seaga. Due to his failing health, Manley turned the reins over to Patterson in 1992.

We joined Horace back at our table only to notice Mike Henry was seated at an adjoining table. We went over and chatted with him. Needless to say he was surprised to see us there.

"Robert, you know a few minutes ago," Mike said, "I was telling the head of a local bank about the gathering and he wanted to know if he could be invited, too."

"Does he want to come as a speaker or to listen?" I asked.

"I think he wants to come to speak," Mike said.

"Well, I couldn't do that," I said, "because no one has named him as an healer. But give me his contact info and I'll call him to see if there is another way for him to participate."

By then the speakers were about to begin again so we took our seats. The Prime Minister read a short passage from the Bible regarding being our brothers' keepers. Then Seaga read a passage. Both seemed to just be going through the motions, very uninspired. At the end, everyone rose for the national pledge which ended in, "I promise to stand up for Justice, Brotherhood and Peace, to work diligently and creatively, to think generously and honestly, so that Jamaica may under God, increase in beauty, fellowship and prosperity, and play her part in advancing the welfare of the whole human race."

In all, 10 people spoke—all members of the clergy except for the two politicians and a high school girl. It was clear that everyone loved their country and was deeply troubled by its present state—politically, economically and socially. Their overriding fear was of the escalation of violence and crime that threatened to grow even more with the upcoming elections. In addition, every year the U.S. repatriates to the island over a 1,000 Jamaicans convicted of violent crimes. Since these felons have not committed a crime in Jamaica, they are set loose on the streets where they usually join local gangs. Crime is exacerbated by the fact that many Jamaicans have little or no respect for the police. Unfortunately, the fault often lies with the police force, which even the government has acknowledged is woefully corrupt. Many police are guilty of payoffs, summary justice and violent excesses.

In an interview in the August 15, 2002 *Jamaica Observer*, Jamaican Police Commissioner Francis Forbes vented his frustration at not being able to dismiss corrupt and drug-dealing cops unless he has a watertight case. "There is an inherent difficulty in dismissing people like those," Forbes told reporters. "'My hands are tied when it comes to dismissing them for corruption."

Many Jamaicans have become so frustrated with the police's inabili-

Gathering of the Healers

ty to stop escalating crime in their communities, that they have begun to take the law in their own hands. Calling it "jungle justice," citizens often become arresting officers, judge, jury and executioners—unfortunately only to often find out later that the victims were innocent. The article below from the *Jamaica Gleaner*, describes an example of this. This example is rather extreme but not that rare.

TWENTY-FIVE PERSONS were detained yesterday in Spaldings, Clarendon, as residents and the police remain at loggerheads, following Saturday's disturbance.

Residents, from as early as 7 a.m., took to the streets to protest against the detention of a taxi operator, Mark Robinson, one of three men injured when an angry mob converged on the police station on Saturday.

The community had erupted in violence after residents trapped three men in a roadblock in the Nine Mile area of Alston on Saturday. They accused the men of being gunmen responsible for the recent shooting death of 40-year-old Jean Donville from Alston, as well as several other robberies in the district.

One of the men, a licensed firearm holder, had to fire several shots in a bid to elude the angry mob. They drove towards the Spaldings Police Station and were later intercepted by a police unit, which escorted them inside the station.

The mob then swooped down on the station demanding that the men be handed over to them. During the confrontation, 16-year-old John Farquharson of Sunberry district was shot and killed. Several policemen were also injured.

According to a sub-officer at the Spaldings Police Station, at one stage, he and six policemen were at the station when the over 4,000 protesters attacked the station.

"People were using machetes to chop their way in, others were throwing bottles and stones. It reached a stage where they began to threaten to kill us, just to get the men. It was really frightening," the sub-officer said.

But, while the police maintain that the men were innocent people caught up in the roadblock on Saturday, residents are saying otherwise.

Gathering of the Healers

> According to residents, they are at times forced to take mat-
> ters into their own hands, because of the infrequent police
> patrols in the area.

Other problems besides crime were escalating in Jamaica. The economy was in a nose dive and socially AIDS was reaching near epidemic
proportions and most children were born with no father even listed on
the birth certificate. Eighty-five percent of children are born out of wed-
lock and few have the much-needed influence of a father as they grow.
In fact you often hear a woman referred to as someone's "baby mother,"
a common Jamaican term for a woman who has a man's baby but is not
married to or living with him.

Also, the young adults were in trouble with few job opportunities and
a 60% high school dropout rate. Of those that finish high school, more
than half are functionally illiterate as are most adults. (Officially the
adult literacy rate is 85% but this includes a large percentage who can
do little more than sign their name.)

No one at the NLPB had any set answers except to pray more, turn
back to God and treat each other better—good advice no matter what
the situation. However, you couldn't help but detect a certain sense of
hopelessness. The prayer breakfast had occurred for over 20 years and
things had not been getting better.

Another aspect of the prayer breakfast troubled me. It seemed to a
great degree cut off from the reality of most Jamaicans. Four hundred
leaders in business suits enjoying breakfast at the plush Pegasus Hotel
is something few Jamaicans can relate to. In many ways, it just made the
gulf between the leaders and the people, the "haves" and the "have-
nots," seem greater. Also there was not one Rasta in the group. The
prayer breakfast was for the spiritual leaders of the country but in reality it was for traditional leaders only. Yet when I asked many everyday
Jamaicans who are the real teachers of One Love in their country, mostly Rasta names had come up (Luciano, Morgan Heritage, Tony Rebel,
Mortimo Planno, Bob Marley, Dennis Brown, Bushman, etc.) and a few
Christian names (Antonnette Haughton, Abijah and Portia Simpson) but
not one church leader was named.

For seven decades the Christian community has ignored or fought

Gathering of the Healers

against the influence of Rastafari in their society for many reasons. Though many Rastas are devout Christians, others believe Haile Selassie to be the returning Christ. Their dreadlocks, ganja use, and anti-Establishment viewpoint are also problematic for many Christians. However, what I believe was unknown to this gathering is that the Rasta vibration now resounds across the island. In many ways it has captured the hearts and minds of the everyday Jamaican, a fact that is missed by the leaders. One Love was on the lips of many people I met with during my trips to the island. Many made a point of telling me that they had a "Rasta heart" if not the dreads and lifestyle. The Rebel Salute is testimony to the degree Rasta has permeated the country's thinking. To many, Rastas have become the spiritual leaders and moral compass. And yet not one Rasta had been invited to the prayer breakfast.

Also, many elder Rastas, true "heartical" Rastas, have paid their dues through decades of persecution and oppression as well as being ostracized from their families and communities. Still they walk proudly, shunning the materialistic world and teaching love to those with which they interact. Many are leading almost Christ-like lives and teaching and leading by example rather than by official status.

Nonetheless, I couldn't help remembering that many Rastas were also caught in the "we're right/you're wrong" game of spiritual separation. I reflected back on conversations I had with many dreads who railed against the church establishment and insisted that Rastafari was the only true way or that Haile Selassie was the only true God. More and more, I understood it was only One Love that could bring us all together, no matter what our individual spiritual paths may be.

After the breakfast, Scram and I hung around the hotel until our lunch with Antonnette. I called the Jamaican Council of Churches and left a voice mail for Rev. Howard Gregory, the Council's president, asking him to join us as a speaker on behalf of the Jamaican Christian community. I felt it was important to reach out to this segment of the population, especially since Jesus' message of love was the same as our own.

132

Gathering of the Healers

I decided to try Barry Chevannes also from UWI as a good representative from the Jamaican academic community. His name and Rex Nettleford's had been mentioned several times as UWI professors who were healers. Barry, Dean of the Department of Anthropology, had written *Rastafari: Roots and Ideology*, as well as other papers on Rastafari. I reached him after the breakfast and he immediately agreed to join us. I told him I would come by to meet him in person before the press conference so we could get to know each other.

Around noon, Antonnette joined us in the hotel dining room for lunch. Antonnette is an attractive, vivacious Jamaican woman, enthusiastic and animated. In her late forties, she has the energy, looks and optimism of someone in their twenties. She is electric to be around, a fascinating blend of a wise woman with a take-charge attitude and little-girl enthusiasm. She has a tremendous sense of empathy, an ability to feel other people's pain. She seems ready to mother the world and there are too many people who will take her up on it.

Antonnette is considered a champion of the disenfranchised and has made a personal crusade of public education on matters of human rights as well as providing practical assistance, on a personal level, to a number of her fellow Jamaicans facing serious challenges. Most notably, she is known for her love of children, and has cared for a number of youngsters, officially and unofficially, in addition to her own son.

Born in 1954 in the rural town of Islington, St. Mary, she attended the University of the West Indies where she gained a B.Sc. Honors in Government and was awarded two post-graduate scholarships. She took the one from the Jamaican Government to study law. She gained her LL.B., with honors from The University of the West Indies in 1977, qualified to practice law and was called to the Bar in 1979. It was during her legal studies in Barbados that she first met her husband, Cuban professor and businessman Osvaldo Cárdenas, who was then a diplomat. They met again many years later and married in 1994.

In 1980 Antonnette returned home to Jamaica to work first as a legal officer with the Ministry of Social Security and then, from 1980 to 1991, operated a private law practice that took her all over her home parish of St. Mary. She then returned to Kingston to join well-known

Gathering of the Healers

human rights activist, Lord Anthony Gifford, as a partner in the firm of Gifford, Haughton & Thompson. She established Haughton & Associates in 1998.

Antonnette's passion for social justice and her choice of law as a career was almost inevitable, given the very strong influences of her childhood. Her father is Kenneth R.A. Haughton, retired farmer, former chairman of both the Cocoa Industry Board and the All Island Cane Farmers Association and a well-known activist during Jamaica's struggle for independence from British rule. Her mother is Mistellie Scott-Haughton, retired school principal and dramatist. She still is an outstanding and dedicated teacher who runs the home school at the Haughton-Cárdenas home.

The second child and only daughter of four children, Antonnette remembers receiving powerful messages during her youth. "As a child," she says, "I saw that people were too poor to get heard and I had a sense that you could be part of what gave them a voice. I grew up in the St. Mary of the plantations, people working on the estates. But I was from a background of independent peasantry on both my parents' side—people who didn't sell their labor to the estate, who believed in owning their own land, taking responsibility for their own lives and educating their own children. My mother was the principal of the primary school I attended."

She was also inspired during her childhood by the late Prime Minister Norman Washington Manley, who gave children of the poor the first real opportunity for first-class education. However, this goal has never been reached. Public education is getting worse in Jamaica, where the government budget for education has shrunk from 18% in 1980 to 11% in 1999. Teachers are paid abysmally low salaries and causing many of the best teachers to seek employment abroad. (I talked to a couple, both high school teachers, who between them could not afford the cheapest used car). Many schools lack computers and some rural schools lack even basic sanitation facilities. The student-teacher ratio is very high and with no public school buses, parents are responsible to get their kids to school and buy the mandatory school uniforms and books, which many parents are unable to do. With all these problems, Jamaican

134

schoolchildren perform at very low levels in the Caribbean Examinations in math and English.

When Antonnette was a university student, Michael Manley was another powerful influence. "I supported Michael Manley as a young person," she says. "I came of age and supported his vision of Jamaica. Sometimes a man has a vision and can carry it only to a certain space. That doesn't mean it's not a good vision. Michael Manley came to power in the Cold War years and Jamaica became the center of the Cold War. The world has become less ideologically driven but the concerns are still the same today—poverty, dispossession and lack of opportunity and you need to bring marginalized people to the center."

In 1992, Antonnette was given the opportunity to serve a much wider audience when Radio Jamaica invited her to be a host on the popular talk show "Hotline" and on Jamaican television's discussion program, "Man and Woman Story." Here her public outreach developed into one specifically dedicated to the relationship between the sexes.

"This type of program offered a tremendous opportunity to speak to a lot of people," she notes. "I believe in public education. I believe in letting people know. People come to you for help and education from everywhere, and it gives you the capacity to help and empower them. The calls that come in give you an opportunity to explain things—legal matters, human rights concerns, self-esteem issues, etc.—not just to the person calling but to the whole nation. This allows you to provide a human service to help people in practical ways."

She used these public forums as an opportunity to focus specifically on one of her most urgent concerns—the lives, opportunities and status of women in her society as well as the relationships within families. Even with her busy schedule, Antonnette puts her family first, deriving much of her strength from her home life and strong family ties. Both of her parents live with her, her husband, their ten-year-old son, Cheikh, and her ten year-old cousin, Samoya.

She is also very deeply concerned about persons of African descent in the Diaspora (scattering) and indeed with all oppressed people, including Native Americans. An optimist by nature, she is also fascinated by what she describes as the tremendous possibilities of the New

Gathering of the Healers

World and the extent to which we can lead the world toward more racial harmony. As soon as I met her, I knew I had met a co-worker and friend for life.

We ordered lunch and I explained to her in greater detail what we were planning.

"I like this plan," she said. "The Bible says we must love our enemies and heap coals upon their heads."

"I'm not sure what that means," I said.

"It means you pray for them and bring them to knowledge. It means that you have to accept that they do wrong things," she continued, "and that they have to become 'at one' with God, which is to atone. The power of the African people is that the African knows how to love their enemies. We're not so good at loving ourselves. In fact, we've been taught to hate ourselves more."

"And that's why Africans will lead the world into forgiveness," I responded. "And even Nanny brought this message to her tribe. So basically the way we see it is we big-up the Jamaican people and then they will big-up the world."

"Yes. The spirit of our ancestors will carry this vibe," she said firmly, "and Nanny is this powerful African woman spirit which has held this nation together for a long time without recognition. When men don't act like fathers, the mothers do it alone. This is a spirit of service, of administering to the men's need. Every time a young man gets in trouble in this country, it is his female relatives that go to bat for him. Women have never used their strength against men in this country and men need not be afraid that we ever will because that's not who we are. We use our strength to support our men, to support our children. But you must know we are a strong people but we are also a very angry people. The basis for the anger is mature and it's real. But sometimes in our anger we destroy ourselves. I like your idea. Anything that promotes unity and working together is good for Jamaica."

"I'm glad you're joining us," I said. "I think now is the time we as the healers, as elders, must come forward and claim ourselves. It was really our experience Colonel Harris, the Maroon colonel from Moore Town, that showed us this."

Gathering of the Healers

"How you say?" she asked.

"Well, when Julia and I were in Moore Town last summer working on the first book," I said, "some of the Maroons up there said that Colonel Harris, who was the tribal leader and school teacher there for 30 years, had not carried on the spirit of the tribe because he stopped the tribal drumming, which had occurred every night in the village for over 250 years. They also said that as the schoolteacher for 30 years, he didn't teach the kids about Nanny or the Maroons. When we asked him about this he said that the elders wouldn't have chosen him to keep the spirit of the tribe alive. He didn't really know the Maroon history. He was the colonel and the schoolteacher. His job was education and administration not to keep the vision and spirit of the tribe alive. When he said that we realized that almost all political leaders are the administrators not the spiritual leaders. They can't teach the world One Love because they have not remembered it yet themselves. It's not their job to heal their societies with love. It's the job of the healers, the elders, and we must come forward now and teach the people love and forgiveness in place of revenge and counter-attack."

"My brother, I wish you were right," Antonnette responded. "My problem is I think as a reflex action, leaders will say 'I must punish my enemy.' Men—the culture of the male—is a retaliative culture, a punishing culture. The people in power don't understand the power of speaking and healing and feeling love. The emotional intelligence of the male animal leaves a lot to be desired. Men are into 'what makes you different from me' instead of 'what makes you like me.' And we have so much more that makes us one. Government in Jamaica must make a spiritual shift and call upon God."

"I agree. And it is hard for me to defend my gender. However, I think that has been in the past," I said. "I think it is shifting. Times are different now. In the past the choice was always between violence and non-violence. Now it's between violence and non-existence and this is beginning to make everyone see war differently. And the trump card, the infinite correcting mechanism, is that everyone on this planet, *everyone*, is looking for love. They might think they'll find it in sex or money or power or belonging or possessions but actually they're all looking for

137

Gathering of the Healers

love. So this One Love could start to spread very quickly across the planet because it's what everyone wants. You could start to reawaken that awareness like dominoes falling in a row. What we're playing in to is that every human being is looking for what we're trying to give them."

"Yes. It's like something that's contagious," she said, brightening. "It feels so good. And God is the connection because God is love. When I hold a child, a small child, I feel so good that I give a lot of that love to a lot of people as I walk through that day. So I know in my experience that love is a multiplying energy. Our nation needs this healing and my voice is not a voice of vengeance but a voice of healing."

After lunch, Scram, Antonnette and I drove over to the nearby downtown shopping district to get a copy of *The Story of the Jamaican People*, a book she said I needed to read. As we walked the busy downtown streets, almost everyone greeted her. Many people came up to her with words of encouragement and support. Though I knew she was on a tight schedule, she seemed to make time for everyone, giving them a few words of upliftment, reminding the young men to stay away from cocaine and take care of their children, telling the young girls to hold their heads high and don't let the boys pressure them, etc. She even stopped to wake up a homeless man sleeping in a doorway to see if he was okay, remarking enthusiastically after speaking with him, "That man's mind is as clear as yours or mine." She treated everyone kindly, almost motherly, with a quick and easy banter, often in patois. She is a country girl—one of the people.

As we walked along, she turned to me and said, "Jamaica doesn't need to be led so much as it needs to be loved." She was doing both.

After lunch, we headed back to Port Antonio driving the now-familiar coastal route. We stopped at Denroy Morgan's house to see Taliba, Tafire and Hyacinth and also stopped by Tasha's shop. As we were heading into Port Antonio, Scram and I began reflecting on the last two days.

Gathering of the Healers

"That was an incredible trip," I said. "I'm amazed how JAH brought us to Patterson and Seaga so easily."

"Ya know, you're administration makes me be a more Christian person," Scram said.

"In what way?" I asked.

"Well, all right," he continued, "becuz I nevah t'ought I would find meself in between all dese kind of people. In times like dis, to find myself between de world leaders, 'eads of my country, to go up dere an' talk wit dem, is a great light. It shows me to exercise more of dis One Love. Becuz it's pushing me right into dis level."

"But you've always treated people good," I said.

"Yeah, mon," he said. "Fe a long time but when me see it gettin' more power an' someone come to compel people about dis One Love, it make me a bettah Christian, a bettah Rastafari an' when we walked t'ru dat room ev'ryone was watching us. An' Seaga an' Patterson put down dere food to look to us. We go t'ru de heart of Babylon, Robbie, an' everyone was so calm an' surrendered like a lamb. De spirit of JAH say move an' we move. We got five birds wit' one stone."

"You've been saying all along that the heads of the country would read our book," I said, "but I just didn't know we would give it to them personally. And there are people of good will everywhere and some of these people in the government may read it and be changed by it. You know, Scram, it's becoming clear to me why God sent you and I together to do this. If it was just me, everyone could say that it was easy for me to offer forgiveness because I'm a white, middle-class American male and my life's been easy. But with you here they can't say that. But really your life's been pretty easy too, just not affluent. Even though you've lived in poverty, you haven't had a hard life."

"Becuz I call my worst poverty in my life, 'rich,' " Scram said. "When you cayn t'ink about dese t'ings an' you see yahself in a low stage an' still you cayn look upon yahself in a higher stage. An' de money is just one little piece."

"And you've never had the money like I did," I said, "but you've had the community life, the connectedness to your people. You don't have to be angry because Babylon won't give you more money. Babylon can't take people away or love away or JAH away so everyone can have joy if they only choose it."

"An' I 'ave JAH," Scram said. "JAH in place of me money an' dat made me rich. But still I know dat Babylon must treat de masses bettah."

"I agree," I said, "and yet so many of the institutions that were established to do this, like the IMF and the World Bank, seem only to be making thing worse."

Though at face value, it would appear that the rich industrial nations are moving more towards sharing their wealth with Third World countries, this may or may not be so. To many, it is just a masked form to further legally enslave these countries economically. Or as Cuban hero Jose Marti said, "You have to look for the hidden agenda in every meeting among nations."

Human beings of all colors and at all ends of the socio/economic strata have always indulged in exploitation when it benefited their own interests, even at great expense and misery of others. It is too early to tell if this vicious cycle is finally weakened by our species in general and leaders (both public and private) of the world powers in particular. We have moved from physical slavery, legal since the beginning of time until the last 150 years, to economic slavery. This does indicate that Babylon as a system is indeed getting much weaker but there is still a long way to go. As Luciano sings, perhaps we are approaching the time when "love will once again return to the hearts of men."

Obviously exploitation is always *by* the more powerful and *of* the less powerful. In the history of humanity, the more powerful were those that held the physical power, such as kings, warlords, and armies. However, now with this system weakening as humanity evolves to greater levels of consciousness, this power is shifting from physical to financial—still power that is used to exploit but at a lower level of power nonetheless. However, this financial power is immense. Consider the following:

Gathering of the Healers

*The top 200 multi-national corporations have almost twice the assets of the poorest four-fifths of humanity.

*The combined revenues of General Motors and Ford exceed the combined Gross Domestic Product for all of sub-Saharan Africa.

*The top 200 corporations' combined sales are more than the combined economies of 182 countries. That's all the countries of the world minus the largest nine imperialist countries.

*The 10 richest people in the world own wealth equivalent to the total production of the 50 poorest countries.

*The top 447 billionaires and mega-millionaires have fortunes greater than that of half of humanity or the 3 billion poorest people.

*The three richest capitalists in the United States—Bill Gates, Warren Buffet and Paul Allen—have wealth equal to the combined income and savings of the world's 600 million poorest people.

Given the complexity of the world economy and the fact that we have only the mass corporate-owned media to interpret the fast-moving changes in global finances, it is almost impossible to tell what economic movements are in the best interest in humanity and which ones are just being disguised as such. Media spin has been developed to an art by global powers. Though the U.S. presents itself as extremely generous in regards to helping struggling countries, in reality it has been a laggard in its development assistance, relative to the size of its economy. Its foreign aid at 0.10 per cent (less than 1%) of its gross national product is behind other developed countries.

In the end, we can only observe whether these changes have alleviat-

Gathering of the Healers

ed human poverty and misery to determine if these vast movements are benevolent or selfish, either unintentionally or by design. However, some indications are already troubling. When the IMF and World Bank made their loans to Jamaica (much of which went into the pockets of corrupt business and political leaders) it was only with the agreement that Jamaica's protective trade barriers be removed. Since then, farmers throughout Jamaica have been going bankrupt trying to compete with the flood of cheap U.S. products (all subsidized by the U.S. government) entering the island. In May of 2002, this situation got much worse, as reported by the *Gleaner*:

> The newly-passed U.S. farm bill (May 13), which is estimated to increase subsidies to the agriculture sector by 80 per cent to the tune of $US82 billion over the next decade has been received with widespread criticism from many quarters.
>
> According to news resources, the World Bank recently called it "a sad days for farmers."
>
> Argentine President Eduardo Duhalde said that the U.S. preaches free trade but engages in protectionism. Brazil criticized the bill for being detrimental to international trade, while Paraguay described the new farm legislation as a "big step backward" in meeting WTO targets. A top farm group official of the fourth member of the South American bloc, Uruguay, accused Washington of "telling two different stories" at international forums. The World Bank's data indicates that cotton exporters in West and Central Africa alone would gain further $US250 million in revenues per annum if the U.S., the world's biggest cotton producer, were to stop subsidizing domestic cotton production. Analysts however forewarn that the increase in U.S. farm support could further depress world commodity prices, making imports cheaper than local products in the developing world and ultimately forcing domestic farmers out of business.

Gathering of the Healers

This exploitation is nothing new. The following are comments by Dr. Osvaldo Martinez, chairman of the Parliamentary Economic Committee and Director of the Center for Research into the World Economy at the televised Round Table that analyzed the Free Trade Area of Americas (FTAA) on April 20, 2001:

> The FTAA is nothing more than a U.S. plan to establish a free trade agreement between the U.S. economy— in other words, the richest and most powerful on the planet—and the Latin American and Caribbean underdeveloped, deeply indebted, scattered economies whose Gross Domestic Products added together are ten times lower than that of the United States. We could say that, on the face of it, this is nothing other than integration between a shark and some sardines. Now, the reasons for the FTAA are not what the Caribbean or Latin Americans want nor are they the alleged advantages of economic integration for those countries. The reasons are, in fact, the U.S. strategic craving for domination over the region in the face of competition from its rivals in today's developed world.

Though it would appear that the March 2002 meeting of the UN International Conference on Financing for Development was a step to assist the poverty of the Third World, it may be a brilliant attempt to further impoverish it. Speaking at the conference was President Thabo Mbeki of South Africa who reminded everyone of the promise made at the Millennium summit to "making the right to development a reality for everyone and to freeing the entire human race from want. If the world continues on the current trajectory, the combined threats of underdevelopment, poverty, environmental degradation, ill health and disease, and conflicts over natural resources will undermine the prospects for political stability and prosperity across the globe."

It must be understood that exploitation of others is a species-wide

Gathering of the Healers

condition not only preserved for the rich and powerful. I have seen Jamaican shop owners exploit their two or three employees when they had the power to do so. Men have exploited women since the beginning—a condition that Gandhi called the "world's greatest evil." Exploitation is created by the illusion that power and money, not love, is what we are seeking. Until we understand that we will find what we are truly seeking not by getting, but by *giving*, we will exploit at all levels. Exploitation is simply not holding another's interests as equal to our own. It is a condition created by the illusion that what we seek is outside ourselves rather than the love within. We are all prone to it as long as we buy into this illusion. Vast power, such as that controlled by world leaders, exploits vast numbers. Small power, such as the shop owner, exploits small numbers. It is only love that can heal people's hearts, dissolve the illusion and remind us of why we are here and what we are seeking.

Sometimes this system of exploitation looks so vast and so entrenched that it seems only a miracle could correct it. In the end, it *will* take a miracle to correct this eons-old worldwide system of human exploitation. However, we are capable of miracles, individually and as a species. True "miracles" are any acts of unconditional love—One Love. These miracles always change people's hearts at all levels of the human hierarchy and then these systems will start to correct themselves toward more humanitarian expressions.

All expressions of real love are miraculous in the true sense. They reverse the physical laws by bringing more love to *both* the giver and the receiver. "Giving" and "getting" become the same. Miracles of love are teaching devices demonstrating it is as blessed to give as to receive. These miracles are natural, part of humanity's intrinsic Divine nature and when they are not occurring something has gone wrong, i.e., we have forgotten who we are. To correct what has gone wrong, we only need to remember our true nature as teachers of love—as miracle workers. When we have done this, even to a limited degree, we have joined with the most powerful force in the Universe—Love. From this joining, all manner of personal miracles—JAHincidents—flow.

"All of a sudden it hit me that you were talking to me personally—that I was one of the people that needed to forgive to help the island heal. It wasn't a matter of me sitting back and waiting to see what everyone else did. It was about me doing my part, not just for my country but for my own life."

—**Toni Foster,** manager of the Rockhouse Hotel

Chapter 10
January 21, 2002

Peaceful Retreats

By now I had lined up most of the healers for the press conference and in the two remaining weeks I needed to set up the logistics at the museum (food, chairs, audio and video crews, security, etc.). But more importantly I needed to be sure the Jamaican press knew about the event and covered it. I didn't think this would be especially hard, given the caliber of speakers, but I also didn't know whether they would take our efforts seriously.

I had been offered a cottage at the Rockhouse in Negril and decided that would be the perfect place to spend the next week handling these details and writing my speech for the press conference. I have done a lot of public speaking in my lifetime but have never written more than a few notes for any. However, I understood the importance of what we were doing and also I knew these speeches would be read by many more people in the newspaper, in this book, on our Website and through our e-mail list.

The Rockhouse is a small hotel stretching across the cliffs of Pristine Cove in Negril. Meandering along the cliffs are 28 architecturally-designed thatched-roofed cottages each with a private sun bathing deck nestled in tropical lush gardens. The resort includes a 60-foot cliff-top horizon pool and ladders and stairs carved into the rock that lead down to easy water access for swimming and snorkeling on the reef, where the water is crystal clear and 10 to 20 feet deep. There is also a restaurant on a balcony suspended directly over the water.

A day before driving to Negril I called Toni Foster, the manager of the Rockhouse, to confirm my reservation. I could tell by her voice on the phone that she was a very open-hearted person. We got into a quick conversation and she said she'd love to get a copy of my book when I get there.

"Toni, look down by your feet," I said. "There should be a box of books with my name on it. It was left by a guest that just left, Alex Holden, who brought them from my hometown."

"Your right," Toni replied. "They're right here. I'm almost standing on them."

I arrived late the next day and Toni was there to meet me. Toni, an attractive brown-skinned Jamaican in her thirties, is vivacious and caring, with the savvy of an efficient businesswoman. Her father, Maurice Foster, is a well-known Jamaican cricket player, coach and radio commentator. She had been raised in the upper-class society of Jamaica and lived most of her life in Kingston before moving to Negril to manage the hotel. She showed me to my cottage and we agreed to meet for dinner.

The cottage felt instantly at home, much more so than any other place I had stayed. It was one large room with a small loft. Downstairs was a large canopied bed, a desk and chair, a refrigerator, walk-in closet area and a bathroom including an open-air but walled-in private shower. The cottage was built on a 30-foot high peninsula-shaped extension of the cliffs with waves lapping (and sometimes crashing) on three sides. My windows and front balcony looked out to the sea and the adjoining cove. I knew I had made the right choice in coming here. This would be an excellent place to think through everything that I wanted to say to the Jamaican people. If ever there was an appropriate spot to write an inspirational speech, this was it.

After I settled in and went for a swim in the ocean, I met Toni for dinner. It was a warm, gentle evening and the restaurant was relaxed and quiet.

"You know, Toni," I said as we settled in, "I feel so close to you already. Like I've known you my whole life."

"Funny you should say that," she replied, thoughtfully. "I feel the same. I started reading your book and I really like it and what you are doing here with the press conference. Let me know if there is any way I can help."

"Well, right now, I'm trying to plan the public relations stage. I'm thinking it might be better if I hired a Kingston PR firm if I can afford it. They would have a lot easier time getting the press to come than an unknown like me."

"I can't believe you just said that!" she said. "Before coming here I worked for years at a PR firm in Kingston, TTP, and Angela Thane, the owner, is one of my best friends. She's got a really good heart and I know she'd love this project and would give you a good rate on handling your PR. In fact, Angela will be here in 10 days. I'm getting married February 1st and she's coming down for the wedding."

"I'm checking out in a week but my wife, Julia, and our daughter, Alicia, are flying in to Mobay January 31st" I said. "We all wanted to come back and stay here for two nights so I'll be here then."

"What else do you need?" she asked. "Maybe I can help you with other things."

"Well, I need to use a computer to write my speech," I said. "Also, I need someone to critique the speech and I need an inspired graphics artist to do a 'One Love-Make It Happen!' banner for the press conference."

"You can use my computer in the office," she relied. "Even if its closed, just tell the security guard to let you in and I'll be glad to critique it when you're finished. As far as the graphic person, William Watson works out of Angela's office. He's great and he loves Bob Marley. He'll be here for my wedding, too."

That week I contacted Angela and William, both of who agreed to handle these areas of the conference.

"Also, I have one more need but this is a long-shot. Do you know

147

Gathering of the Healers

anyone that knows Muta?" I asked. "I've been trying to get him to join us or at least cover the event on his program but I'm having no luck. I thought you might know someone who could approach him one more time."

"Incredible!" Toni said. "Yvonne Hope is my best friend. She used to be Muta's mate and they have two children. She'll be here for the wedding, too. You can talk to her yourself. They're separated but they're still very close and Muta listens to her."

We talked for hours. Toni was in a stage of extreme change in her life. A few months earlier, she met and fell in love with Ali, the front desk manager at the hotel. They were getting married in a few weeks and she was very excited. Unlike Toni, Ali was raised in the rural countryside in a modest but loving environment. In a country where race and class status are still very much important, it was a big move for a well-to-do, brown-skinned upper-class Jamaican woman to marry a dark-skinned man from the countryside. Yet, their differences appeared small in contrast to their love for each other. After I met Ali, I understood why. He is a gentle loving soul. Before parting that night, I gave her a copy of my book, *In The Spirit of Marriage*, as a wedding gift.

The next day, I went over to The Royal Kitchen, a small Ital restaurant run by Errol Chambers, a very peaceful elder Rasta. Julia and I had met Errol on a previous trip to Jamaica and loved him (and his food). It was also our meeting place to link up with Red (Maurice Lynch) and Bongo Roach (Joseph Roach), two of the Rastas featured in *Rasta Heart* who had also become our close friends. With the vitality of a teenager at 78, Red was considered the elder Ras of Negril. He had been quite well-off at one time, with cars and houses, when he left it all "feeling that the true spiritual life was at the bottom." His eyes have a twinkle and he is quick to laugh and always kind and concerned and surprisingly physically affectionate--rare for Jamaican men and even more so for Rastas. Bongo Roach, in his forties, is tall and lanky. He is a travelling roots man--selling herbal cures around the island. He has a serious but gentle and kind nature--very devoted to his faith and "de Almighty." By most economic standards, they are poor men but by all standards spiritually rich and totally fulfilled in their lives.

Gathering of the Healers

Red was at Errol's and over lunch I told them what we were doing, which they enthusiastically supported. I invited them to join us at the conference. I had decided that I would have a row of chairs directly behind the speakers' table that would be for the Rastas in the book, the "silent healers" at the conference. Red, perhaps more than any Rasta I have met on the island, truly lives the message of One Love. He is kind and generous to everyone, full of immense energy (at 78) and wise in both the ways of the world and the ways of God.

I gave them both copies of the book but was amazed to find out they, just like Scram, had seen it—twice!

"How is that possible? It just got it printed six weeks ago!" I asked, amazed.

"Well, this guy Alex came by wit' a copy," Errol said. "He said that he had brought you some books from the states an' left them at the Rockhouse for you. He read about us in the book and came by for lunch."

"Oh. That explains the first but how about the second?" I asked.

"Well, this woman, Sharon Brown, came by with her husband," Errol said. "She said she bought a copy of the book from you in Port Antonio a few weeks ago and read about the restaurant and came by with the book." Alicia and I had met Sharon one rainy day at the gift shop at the Dragon Bay Resort. She saw the book in my hand and asked to buy a copy. She and her husband, a dentist from Virginia, had made many trips to Jamaica, the last to arrange for a young Jamaican boy to have corrective surgery in the States.

After dinner at Errol's, I headed back to my cottage. That night Alicia called me rather upset, which is rare for my emotionally even-keeled daughter.

"Dad, sometimes I feel so alone here," she said. "I mean I have a lot of friends and everything and I've got a good social life but they seem so immature. A lot of times I can barely pay attention to their conversations. It's just not me and they don't know me. They think I'm still the same person I was before we started going to Jamaica and I'm not. I've changed so much but I can't share it with any of my friends. Can we think about moving to Jamaica?"

Gathering of the Healers

"I don't know," I said, understanding her dilemma. "I love it here but I don't know how it would work living here full time. You might have the same problem here and I don't know how good the schools are. Plus, I don't know how comfortable you and mom would be living here. A lot of the Jamaican men are still rather backwards in dealing with women."

"I guess you're right," she said. I could tell she felt better just venting. "Maybe you could ask around anyway. I could always home school like I did in third and fourth grade."

"We'll see," I said. "We'll talk about it when you get here next week."

Though I love Jamaicans and their culture, one of their most unconscious areas is that they remain a very macho society, making life for many Jamaican women, and holidays for many female tourists, very stressful. Men and women in Jamaica lead very separate lives, especially among the poor. A lot of the problems are due to the legacy of slavery, where both the mother's, and especially the father's, roll within the family was purposely undermined.

Men often desert the home and leave all child-rearing, including the financial responsibilities, to the mother, usually along with her female relatives. Because of this, most Jamaican women are independent, strong and industrious, which often brings men's insecurities to the surface when they interact with them. Women often do the housework, child-rearing, cooking and other menial tasks while the men chat at a rum bar.

However, because of their circumstances, Jamaican women due much better in school and comprise half of the workforce (though sadly in low paying jobs). More then three quarters of the students at the University of the West Indies are female.

Many female visitors to Jamaica are aghast at these "politically incorrect" attitudes by Jamaican men, not only toward their own women but toward tourists as well. Any woman traveling without a male companion, can plan on being propositioned often—sometimes gently, sometimes crassly. However, sex tourism is big in Jamaica, especially in Negril, where many women from the U.S. and the U.K. come and hook up with con artists or gigolos, often wearing dreads and posing as spiritually-minded Rastas. Many visitors think they have found true love on

150

the Seven Mile Beach of Negril only later, often after becoming pregnant, to find they were just getting hustled.

━━━━━━━━━━━━━━━━━━━━━━━━━━━━━━━━━━━

The next morning, still somewhat troubled by Alicia's call and wondering what life in Negril might be like for an American teenager, I stopped at The Royal Kitchen before heading up to Mayfield Falls. I wanted to give Ras Thomas, another Rasta in *Rasta Heart*, his copy of the book. Red was there and as we were talking a tall, young, white American teenager sauntered over and sat in his lap and started talking in Patois, which blew me away.

"Dis is Alec Grizzard," Red said. "'E is like a grandson to me. I've known 'im and 'is mudder and fadder since 'e was born. I 'ave known dis yout' since 'e was a lickle pickney."

"I'm glad you're here today, Alec," I said, "I wanted to talk to someone your age about living in Negril. My daughter Alicia just called last night to talk about living here. She'll be in town in a week. I'd like you to get together with her."

"I'd like that. I know Alicia. I've been reading the copy of your book that you gave Red. I know all of you real well and I'd love to meet Alicia."

"Great. I'm picking her up in Mobay a week from Friday. Why don't I stop by here and get you around seven for dinner. By the way, where do you live in the States?"

"We live in Blacksburg, a small village in the Blue Ridge Mountains of Virginia," he said with a grin on his face. "It's not far from where you live in the Blue Ridge."

As he was talking, Bongo Roach walked up. Bongo Roach is a traveling Rasta rootsman. Tall and lanky, with a broad face and widely-separated eyes, he is proud, gentle and serious with a mystical, almost monastic, quality about him. We all talked awhile and then I headed out to see Ras Thomas in Mayfield Falls, an hour and a half away. Bongo Roach decided to join me.

"Do you think many people will respond to our invitation?" I asked

Gathering of the Healers

Bongo Roach as we drove toward Mayfield Falls.

"It will not make much difference now," he said. "It cayn but de people's hearts, according to 'istory in de last years, are 'ard-hearted. Even de yout's. Dey no wanna work. Dat is what I see. But still you must do what de Almighty sent you to do."

"We don't need everybody to forgive," I said, "just enough to make a difference."

"It will make a difference to those who hear," he said. "You 'ave to do it an' not care. Many people will not change. Dere is a lot of evil in dere hearts but dos dat are good, 'ave to do good. You must do de vision dat you see and a few will overstand your message and many will not but still you must do dis."

This was a lesson that I needed to learn over and over again: to be unattached to the results. We were sending out a vibration of One Love into the world that day from some very powerful teachers. This vibration would increase the emanation of love on the planet no matter how many people came and no matter how many heard the actual words.

We arrived at The Original Mayfield Falls mid-day. The place looked better than before. (There are several other places calling themselves "Mayfield Falls" but this is the *original*—and the best.) Mayfield Falls spreads over a mile or so of a river that rushes through the Dolphin Head Mountains. It is a magical place, full of small waterfalls and 21 pools, all shaded by a bamboo rain forest. A guide takes you up the falls. Our guide the summer before had been Ras Thomas, a beautiful 30 year-old Ras, very wise and very serene. The resort is constructed like an African village, with thatched roofed buildings spread around an open field with beautiful shade trees creating a welcoming aura. It includes a restaurant, gift shop, changing rooms, picnic areas and a petting zoo. It is low-keyed with no hustling allowed. The owner, Sarah, was building a four-room hotel when I arrived.

This place has been her dream for most of her life—to provide a natural place of healing and peace for the visitors. Being raised in the area, she left when she was younger and became a successful business-woman, but the dream of developing Mayfield Falls stayed strongly with her. At one point it had almost been developed as an industrial site until all the heavy equipment they had brought in disappeared one night without a trace or clue. Sarah said it was the water goddess that lives nearby. Sarah and her husband finally bought the property in the mid-nineties and have developed it into one of the best natural attractions in Jamaica.

Ras Thomas was glad to see us. He had not seen the book or his picture in it but everyone else there had. Alex Holden had visited a week earlier but Ras Thomas was off that day. We all reasoned awhile and then I went to spend some time with Sarah while Ras Thomas and Bongo Roach got to know each other. It was great talking with Sarah. She is a very loving person who is fulfilled by working on her vision to help others. Her entire staff and complex reflects this.

My days at the Rockhouse drifted by slowly. The only intrusion was a large film crew that was shooting a commercial on the premises for two days but even that was fun to watch, especially the handsome young Jamaican man starring in the commercial. He seemed like a very old soul.

Mid-week, I got final confirmation by phone from Stephanie Marley that we could use the museum. This was a big piece in the puzzle and I was very grateful.

"Did you get the press release?" I asked Stephanie. "Can I go ahead and release it?"

"Yes. I did," she replied, "and I have no problems with it. In fact, it was after reading it that I decided this was something we should be a part of."

I had also heard back from Albert Ramsay, Abijah's manager, saying Abijah would attend. I had never heard of Abijah, a popular young gospel/reggae singer on the island, until the last few weeks when many people mentioned his name as a healer. Albert reminded me that Abijah was not a Rasta and I reminded him that this was "a One Love thing—not a Rasta thing." Ironically, or rather "JAHronically," I picked up the newspaper later that day and saw a big picture of Abijah. The accompa-

Gathering of the Healers

nying article went on to say that he had performed to a near riotous crowd.

I now had commitments from seven healers: Abijah, Denroy Morgan, Luciano, Tony Rebel, Antonnette Haughton, and Dennis Forsythe. Barry Chevannes had said he would try to attend but other commitments might make it impossible. I was still waiting to hear from four others: Mama B, Minister of Tourism Portia Simpson, Rev. Gregory of the Jamaican Council of Churches as well as Kymani Marley who still had not arrived in San San. In addition, I had heard nothing from Prime Minister Patterson or Edward Seaga.

Mid-week I stopped at the cyber cafe in Negril to check my e-mail. In my box was the following message from Edward Seaga's office:

"Dear Mr. Roskind,

As per your invitation to Mr. Seaga, he is unable to attend same function.

However, Mr. Allie McNab will be representing the Leader of Opposition and Mrs. Olivia "Babsy" Grange, Spokesperson on Information and Culture.

Many successes on staging your event.

Sincerely, Olivia "Babsy" Grange"

Also in my box was an e-mail from Rev. Gregory:

"Dear Ras Kind:

I regret that I will not be able to accept your invitation to be present for the news conference. I commend your effort in trying to mobilize various sections of the society towards reconciliation and healing and especially under the banner of Bob Marley, whose 'One Love' theme has touched the lives of persons all over the world.

Wishing you every success in this undertaking.

Sincerely yours, Howard Gregory."

The next day, I got a call from Portia Simpson's office and they said she was unable to attend but wished me her best. Also I got an e-mail

Gathering of the Healers

from Mama B's assistant declining, saying she would not be on the island that day. I was disappointed as I had hoped to have a member of Bob's family join us, but Kymani was still a possibility. I had asked Julian and Damian several times when I saw them at the museum but they would never give me a definite reply.

During my stay at the Rockhouse, I would get up before dawn and work on my speech in the office until the staff arrived at nine when I would get breakfast and go for a morning swim. Some mornings I would read my speech out loud to the ocean or to myself. It always had a calming effect on me. I hoped it would have the same effect on others.

During the day, I would call to make all the logistical arrangements for the press conference. At this point I was feeling great. I had worked through many of my fears that I would fail *and* my fears that I would succeed, which were just as powerful.

One of the details that I worked out was the actual physical logistics of the press conference. I decided that the conference should begin around 6:00 pm, when the traffic and heat dies down. Also I wanted everyone's schedule to be open without further commitments in their workday. I chose the back patio at the museum, with it's shade trees and waterfall as the best place, knowing that we could move into the theatre in the unlikely chance that it rained.

I decided to place the chairs in a circle to keep the tribal feel. I would place chairs in a semi-circle in front of the speakers' table, which would be set in a "U" shape. These chairs would be for the press and visitors. Behind the speakers' table and in front of the thirty-foot wide waterfall would be a single row of chairs in a half-circle to complete the circle. These would be for Julia, Alicia and the Rastas in the book and other healers who would be coming but not speaking.

Another decision that I wrestled with was how long I and the other healers should speak. Angela warned me not to go over an hour or we would lose the press, who would only use snippets anyway in the news-

Gathering of the Healers

paper articles or TV and radio programs. With seven healers plus myself and Scram talking that would give us seven minutes each. As I wrote my speech over the week, I timed it. By the time I was finished it was 30 minutes long, which would leave three minutes each for the others. One night toward the end of the week I passed Toni in the restaurant. I was still undecided on what to do, so I asked her to read my speech and give me advice. I gave her a copy and she said she would read it that night but already indicated that 30 minutes was too long.

The next night she joined me on the restaurant balcony to give me her report. I was rather nervous to hear from her as I had never gotten direct critique for my writing except from Julia and my editors and I had never written anything like this.

"You want the truth about what I think?" she said looking me sternly in the eye. Uh Oh!

"Well, I guess so. Go ahead," I responded, my stomach in knots.

"Well, the truth is when I started to read it I just knew I would have to slash it all up," she said slowly, letting the reality sink in. "It is just too long and as a PR person I could never recommend a speech this long to the Jamaican press. But when I finished I realized I wouldn't change or delete one word. It's perfect and just what the island needs to hear."

"You're kidding?" I said, incredibly relieved.

"But something else happened when I read your speech," Toni said, thoughtfully. "I've been talking to you all week about what you're doing and I've been sitting back thinking, *Let's just see what all these people here do. Let's see if they're ready to forgive.* But as I read the speech, it all of a sudden it hit me that you were talking to me personally—that I was one of the people that needed to forgive to help the island heal. It wasn't a matter of me sitting back and waiting to see what everyone else did. It was about me doing my part, not just for my country but for my own life."

That night I sat out on a ledge overlooking the ocean and decided that I couldn't shorten everyone's message to accommodate reporters' desires to go home. They would report only a few words in any case. I decided I would let each person speak as long as they wanted. I also suspected, rightly as it turned out, that since dealing with independent-

Gathering of the Healers

minded Jamaicans is like herding lions, few would keep to the allotted time anyway.

The next day, Toni took me out to meet Jackie Lewis. Jackie, who lives part of the year in New York City, operates Jackie's On The Reef, a holistic spa she built overlooking the ocean a few miles from the Rockhouse. Situated on a coral reef on one-and-a-half acres, this holistic retreat was created to help guests manage and reduce stress by getting in touch with nature.

Jackie, a tall woman in her fifties, greeted us and showed us around. The resort was peaceful and serene. I told her what we were doing and gave her a book. We agreed to have dinner together at the Rockhouse the following night. As we were getting ready to leave, she said something surprising.

"You know many of the Jamaicans have a black heart. What you are doing will not be so easy."

"What Jackie just said took me off guard," I said to Toni when we were back in the car. "I would have thought she would be more positive, more supportive."

"There is something that you need to know," Toni said. "A few months ago, someone killed her gardener in a personal feud. That has really affected her."

Once again I was reminded how hard it is to believe in the healing quality of One Love when we have experienced personal tragedies.

After leaving Jackie's, Toni and I drove a short distance down the road to visit two of her friends, Geo Gordon and Claudette Parson. Though they lived in Mobay, they kept a compound on the ocean nearby with two small homes with a pool and hot tub. Toni and Ali had rented it for their wedding the following weekend. They weren't there, but by now I was considering the reality of moving to Negril. Since the house was now vacant, I called and arranged to meet with them the next day to look over the property, just in case Julia, Alicia and I decided to move to Negril.

I arrived the next day around noon to find Geo and Claudette already there. As I got out of the car, Geo approached. With a full white beard and short locks, he looked thoughtful and wise. In his late-fifties, he

Gathering of the Healers

looked like he might have been an accomplished college professor on vacation. He later told me that 10 years earlier he got a message to stop shaving and cutting his hair and since then "no razor has come 'pon me." He was born poor, too poor to attend high school but had overcome the odds and become a successful engineer.

We chatted and I gave him a copy of *Rasta Heart* as we joined Claudette on the porch. Claudette is a handsome, Jamaican middle-aged woman, gracious and obviously well-educated. She carried herself with the confidence of a successful businesswoman, which she is.

"When I was informed of your interest in this plot of land," Geo said with an educated, almost-British accent, "there came a spiritual vibration that stimulated me to ponder, *Who is this person*? Before coming, I changed clothes three different times. A vibe said put on a yellow shirt, green pants and red underwear. And I had to do that. I had no idea you had anything to do with Rasta. I said to myself, *I can't be late.* I was so focused on you. I spoke with you as I drove along the highway coming here. When you got out of the car, I saw your vibration. I saw your spiritualism. I saw your power. It was there as a magic. And when you gave me that book, you didn't even know what you did because I have great writings and paintings of Bob Marley. If you look in my cell phone my introduction says 'Rasta.'

"Geo, do you consider yourself a Rasta?" I asked him.

"I search in the heavens, in the heights," he said, "to get the true knowledge of what life is because the signals from heaven is the truth and will be like oil on the water and never sinks and is there for you to behold. When I saw you, the first name that came to me was 'messenger.' And somehow that's you and that's the name the Almighty gave me to give to you because the Almighty God identifies Himself in unique places, through different people, different races, different cultures all over the world. He doesn't manifest in a particular race. That's why you've been given this duty to bring back the scattered sheep of the Almighty God because if you do not do that then the Almighty would rise up someone else to do that job."

"You got all that just since we met?" I said.

"I'm saying to you, Robert," he replied, "that the journey that you

Gathering of the Healers

have been elected and selected is to manifest for JAH, for God, as the term may be. Different cultures identify that same energy with different words. God manifests in many ways. One day, two years ago, I was walking down the street in Montego Bay and this old lady, a street lady, she must have been 75, called to me and said, 'Oh. You're still wise. Please don't forget that you must not trim or shave again or you shall surely die. Please remember that.' The friend I was with was in awe because I had just finished telling him why I never cut my hair or shave. God manifests Himself in various places. To my astonishment, about two weeks after that, I heard that they took up some street people from Montego Bay and took them to St. Elizabeth (a rural parish) to get rid of them. When I heard that, I saw the lady in my mind as they were picking her up and putting her in the truck."

"You mean they just picked up these people like stray dogs and dumped them in the country?" I asked.

"Yeah, mon," Geo said. "That's why you come here. This is one of the things you have to hear because the truth floats like oil. They had a big inquiry. The police were involved. The Parish Council was involved. The Parks and Market was involved. So when I heard that, I went to see this lady but I did not see her. You see every human being has a purpose on the earth and your duty is to bring love, identify love, generate love. To me love is a flower within God's garden. It is given to you by God. And what you are doing now, your journey, is bringing the people to that purity where we can live in harmony. Years ago, when I was 25, I got a message while I was alone, reading the Bible, Ezekiel 28. I saw myself kneeling down before a power with the hands of righteousness and compassion on my head, giving me instruction of how I should assist on this journey that you are talking about on earth."

"What do you mean by this journey that I am talking about?" I asked.

"This journey of love, purification of earth, getting earth purified. That was the instruction that was given to me. That is your journey. And when I had that vision, I asked God to give me a sign that this was He that had given me all these instructions and then I started to sing uncontrollably, to sing songs of joy and righteousness and happiness and here I am still singing those songs of joy."

Gathering of the Healers

Later that night Jackie, Geo and I had dinner at the Rockhouse. We talked for several hours. It was enjoyable but I could sense that Jackie, understandably, could not share my and Geo's optimism for the project. After she left, Geo and I sat until the early morning hours, alone on the now-closed restaurant veranda, talking. I felt like I had known him my whole life. At one point, I asked him to read my speech. When he finished, he looked me directly in the eye and said,

"This speech will be read for centuries."

After a week, I left the Rockhouse to move to The Roundhill about 20 miles west of Mobay. The Roundhill is one of the most expensive resorts in Jamaica but they, like many of the hotels where I stayed, had offered me complimentary accomodations, so off I went. The resort is on a 100-acre peninsula in Hanover Parish, overlooking the private beach and Round Hill Bay—a peaceful ambiance, perched on land that was once part of the century-old plantation. The property cascades past stately palms and tropical gardens down to its own pristine crescent beach.

The resort includes many private villas, most with their own pools, but my room was in The Pineapple House, a 36-room oceanfront hotel building overlooking the Caribbean Sea. All rooms have large louvered windows, almost 10 feet across, which fold back to take full advantage of the view. My room overlooked a fresh water swimming pool located right at the edge of the sea. In the distance, across the bay, were the coastal mountains.

With everything for the press conference now in place, I knew the last challenge was to be sure the press covered the event and got our message out to the people. I had pretty much handed this over to Angela at TTP but I was still worried that this last, and most important piece, might not be as effective as I hoped.

Late one night a few days before the press conference, I was watching "Gandhi" on my camcorder. There was one scene that really hit me. Gandhi was telling a crowd of Indians living in South Africa that South

160

Gathering of the Healers

Africa had just passed laws that invalidated all but Christian marriages and that allowed South African police to enter the home of any Indian without knocking or a search warrant. The crowd instantly got angry, with a few people saying they would attack, even kill, any policeman who dared violate their home even if it caused them their own life. The crowd angrily shouted their agreement.

"I pray for such courage," Gandhi told the enraged crowd. "I need such courage because in this cause I too am prepared to die. But, my friends, their is *no* cause for which I am prepared to kill. Whatever they do to us, we will attack no one, kill no one. They will imprison us. They will fight us. They will seize our possessions. But they cannot take away our self-respect if we do not give it to them. I am asking you to fight against their anger but not to provoke it. We will not strike a blow but we will receive them. We will make them see their injustice and it will hurt as all fighting hurts. But we cannot lose. They may torture my body, break my bones, even kill me. Then they will have my dead body—not my obedience."

The angry crowd instantly calmed and applauded. Gandhi's approach reminded me once again that people can be lead either into anger or love but will often chose love when both options are presented.

Later that night, I was sitting on a lounge chair by the beach contemplating the issue when I got an idea. IRIE!FM was the main vehicle for reggae music on the island. It played the songs of most of our planned speakers like Luciano, Morgan Heritage, Tony Rebel, Abijah, and Kymani Marley. Like the abeng, the horn the Maroons used in the 16th century to communicate with the tribe, IRIE!FM is the island's modern abeng. If I could get their full support to carry our message that would solve the problem. Muta's show is on the station and he was still being non-committal but if the station was willing to talk it up and then perhaps carry it live or rebroadcast it, we would effectively get our message out to the island.

Later in the morning, I called IRIE!FM and asked to talk to the owner, Karl Young.

"Karl, you don't know me but I have a message from JAH for you," I said laughing when he got on the phone. I explained who I was and

161

Gathering of the Healers

what we were doing. "Early this morning, I was on the beach at the Roundhill and I got an inspiration that if you would give this a lot of coverage this message would really get out. You've been sending out this message for years through the reggae music of all these healers. Were just asking you to let them talk directly to their audience."

He laughed and seemed vaguely interested but definitely not convinced that this was his personal destiny. He asked me to contact Brian Schmidt, his marketing manager in Kingston, but I could tell the overwhelming support I was hoping for was not to be. (Though I had several discussions with Brian before and after the event, IRIE!FM never gave us any coverage.)

I did, however, hear from Oliver Clarke, head of *The Jamaica Gleaner*, one of the two islandwide daily newspapers. I had e-mailed him info and he had his secretary call me and asked me to contact Garfield Grandison, the editor of the paper, who agreed to send a reporter.

I had contacted the offices of several business leaders on the island, including Butch Stewart, owner of Air Jamaica, and Chris Blackwell, who was opening a new tourist mall in Ocho Rios three days before our news conference. My hope was that they would not speak as healers but rather promote what we were doing in their own way. Even though Chris knew of me through my cousin Bobby, a business associate of his, I could never get a return phone call from either him or Butch after repeated attempts. While I was at the Roundhill, I also talked with Joseph Forstmayr, the director of the resort and president of the Jamaican Hotel Association and he politely declined participation. None of this really surprised me as I thought the business leaders were more likely to participate once we were better known. However, I wanted to send a message to them that all were welcome. This is not a "us" versus "them" thing. This is an "everybody is welcome" thing.

The days at the Roundhill were spent making last minute arrangements, calling for final commitments, typing up the contents for the press kits and generally getting ready for the press conference which was only several days away. On my last day, I decided to call Kymani Marley again. I had been calling Jon Baker at GeeJam Studios in San

Gathering of the Healers

San, where Kymani was recording a music video but Kymani had yet to arrive on the island so I had given up. I gave him one last call and much to my amazement Kymani answered the phone.

"Kymani," I said when he answered, "You don't know me but my name is Robert Roskind."

"Yeah, man. I know you," he answered in an American accent. "I was just looking through the book you left for me. It looks very interesting."

That's a good sign, I thought. I explained what we were doing and then personalized it to him.

"Before you decide whether you want to come or not," I said, knowing I had his interest, "let me tell you about the series of coincidences that have brought me to this phone call with you."

I then proceeded to tell him how the summer before, Jaime Delgado from The Bob Marley Experience had showed Julia, Alicia, my cousin Bobby and I a DVD of the Bob Marley Tribute, with him on a special track, filmed at Chris Blackwell's place in Oracabessa; how Bobby was at that concert and was a business associate of Chris and a good friend of Peter Shukkat, the Marley Family lawyer; how we had sent Peter a book to give Kymani the day before we came to Jamaica and how when we arrived at the San San Tropez we learned he would soon be in town.

"Man, you're blowing my mind," he said, enthusiastically. "I know you couldn't be making up that kind of story. I'll be there."

Kymani (or Ky-mani) was born in 1976, the son of Bob Marley and Anita Belnavis. He is often regarded as one of the most talented of the Marley children, blessed with an impressive voice that sounds very much like his father's. For awhile he sang with his siblings Stephen, Ziggy, Julian and Damian. His debut album *Like Father Like Son* was a collection of Bob Marley songs in showcase style. Perhaps his biggest breakthrough was his single "Dear Dad" in which he sings about the pain of never having known his father. He also is an actor, receiving roles in two upcoming movies, "One Love" and "Shottas."

Feeling good to have Kymani, Bob Marley's son, aboard, I sat out by the pool and read *The Gleaner*, only to see a big story on Kymani, headlined "Kymani Marley Comes of Age." In the same paper was an article showing a recent poll naming Portia Simpson as the best Minister in

163

Gathering of the Healers

the PNP administration. I turned the page to see a story of another poll saying that 18% of the people polled thought Antonnette Haughton would make a good prime minister compared to thirty-something percent for Patterson and Seaga. She was catching up.

―――――――――――

On the Friday before the Monday press conference, Julia and Alicia flew into Montego Bay from North Carolina. I sure was glad to see them. I had called home every few days and Julia had been my support system, my counselor, my advisor and my sounding board over the past six weeks. We decided to go back to Negril to spend Friday and Saturday night at the Rockhouse before returning to Kingston on Sunday to get ready for the Monday press conference. On the plane Julia sat next to a white American, Suzanne Gilbert-Finch, who was a close friend of Muta's and on her way to visit him. Suzanne worked with Nurses of Israel involved in the construction of a medical center in Shashemene, Ethiopia, the area of the country that Emperor Haile Selassie had granted to relocate displaced Africans.

"You look like Tom Hanks in 'Castaway,' " Julia said as we drove and we all laughed. I had not shaved or cut my hair in seven weeks.

"Are you ready for all this?" I asked Alicia.

"Ready for what?" she responded innocently.

"I don't know. I thought you might be a little nervous about meeting Luciano, Denroy Morgan, Kymani, people like that," I said. "Being in front of the media and at the center of a press conference in Jamaica is a long way from Watauga High School."

"Sure. What's there to be nervous about," she said non-chalantly.

As we drove outside of Mobay, my cell phone rang. It was Delano Franklin, Prime Minister Patterson's chief advisor.

"Mr. Roskind," Delano said in an upbeat voice, "the Prime Minister will not be attending or sending a representative but we wanted to tell you best of luck to you, my brother."

"Thank you for calling," I replied liking the fact that he had called me his "brother." "I hope I didn't make you uncomfortable with my invita-

Gathering of the Healers

tion." I didn't know if they resented my intrusion into the volatile Jamaican political scene.

"Not at all," he replied. "We are very comfortable with what you are doing. I just hope everyone who told you they were coming actually shows. I heard many of them are considering but not committed."

"Who said that?" I asked alarmed.

"Well, now, it's just what I heard. Best of luck to you," he said.

"Thank you, Delano," I said and we hung up.

Julia and I went over the list again to see who might not be showing. In the last week I had confirmed with almost everyone: Luciano, Tony Rebel, Abijah's manager, Antonnette Haughton, Dennis Forsythe, Kymani, and they all said they would be there. Denroy Morgan would not be back on the island until the day before the conference but his wife said he planned to attend. Barry Chevannes' wife said if he had to leave the island, he would send someone to deliver a message.

"I don't know what Delano was referring to when he said many are still considering," I said perplexed and concerned, my fear of failing emerging from its dark hole. "I hope this doesn't blow up in our face and almost nobody shows."

"It doesn't matter," Julia said, smiling. "If it's only the three of us and Scram that's okay, too. We're starting the pattern that night. It doesn't matter how many people come."

We checked back in to the Rockhouse and Alicia and I went over to pick up Alec, the fourteen year-old from Virginia who I had arranged to join us. As I thought, they hit it off immediately. While Julia and I dined at the Rockhouse, they wandered off on their own to hear a band on the beach.

The next morning, I got a call from a radio station wanting to interview me about the upcoming news conference. We set it up for two that afternoon. The producer told me I only had five minutes of the 15 minute program as they had already committed all the time to another guest. After lunch with Red and Bongo Roach at Errol's Royal Kitchen Julia and I headed back to the hotel to do the interview. Shortly before two, the radio station called our hotel room and as I was waiting to go on, I heard the host say, "Before we go to Ocho Rios where Chris

Gathering of the Healers

Blackwell, along with Prime Minister Patterson, are about to cut the ribbon on Chris's new tourist mall, let's hear from Robert Roskind, a man who wants to share his vision of Jamaica's future." My interview went on for ten minutes, giving Chris the last five.

We hung around the hotel all day where we met Angela from TTP and William Watson, the graphic artist who was doing our logo. They were there for Toni and Ali's wedding. After dinner that night as Julia and I were walking by the front desk, one of the staff who knew what we were doing said that Yvonne, Muta's ex-mate, was in the restaurant. We had heard nothing from Muta about joining us or covering the conference so we figured, *what the heck.*

Yvonne, an attractive, powerful woman dressed in African attire, was having drinks with two other women, all friends of Toni's down for the wedding. We asked if we could talk with her briefly and she invited us to join them. We talked for an hour or so at the end of which she said that if she talked to Muta before Monday, she would mention that she had met us and encourage him to support us. By now I was letting go of my attachment to getting the support of Muta and IRIE!FM. As Bongo Roach told me, "JAH calls but 'E does not beg."

"This is mystical! Historical! This One Love will go out into de world tonight. JAH! RASTAFARI!"

—Mortimo Planno

Chapter 11
February 3, 2002

Mortimo Planno

On Sunday morning Julia, Alicia and I drove five hours through the beautiful Jamaican countryside to Kingston. We stopped half way for a cold jelly coconut at a small stall along Bamboo Alley. It was run by a young Jamaican woman, very sweet and shy. We chatted with her. She had run the stand for years, buying coconuts from a man that cut them in the jungle for 20 Jamaican dollars each and reselling them for 40. Most of her customers were locals and friends. On a good day she could make a thousand Jamaican dollars, good money by Jamaican standards. She said she enjoyed her day and looked forward to coming out and talking with friends and a few strangers. She seemed quite contented, almost serene—something you seldom see in our American culture.

We checked into the Terra Nova Hotel around mid-day and relaxed around the pool before going to dinner. When we got back to the room, I called Denroy Morgan, as I had promised to do. Denroy had been off-island since I met with him a month earlier and I wanted to give him the details.

"Did you contact Mortimo Planno?" he asked after I filled him in on the logistics.

"No. I didn't even know he was still alive," I answered.

"Well, now," he said, "if you have done all your research and you haven't found Mortimo, something is wrong. If Mortimo doesn't come,

Gathering of the Healers

I cannot come either."

"I wish you had mentioned him when we met, Denroy" I answered. Once again my fears of everything unraveling started to creep out of the closet. "I thought you said you would speak. I didn't know it was predicated on anyone else being there. I've already put your name out to the press."

"No. That is not what I said," he replied. "I said I would come and support you in this. I did not say for sure I would speak. Mortimo is the elder Rasta. He is a national treasure and he should be there."

"This doesn't leave me much time," I said, frustrated. "The press conference is tomorrow but I'll see if I can find him in the morning and call you."

The potential of losing Denroy upset me. He and Luciano were the two people mentioned the most as healers.

"I know how bizarre it must seem to Denroy," I said to Julia after I hung up, "to have a white, short-haired American come down here and try to enroll him in this but I thought he was really solid."

"It's OK," Julia said, "Let's say a prayer to get us back in balance because what one person says or does is not intended to throw us off. It's just another point of view that someone is passionately going in one direction. We're all here forgetting and remembering love. The purpose of this press conference is to remember love. So tomorrow we get to have a press conference in the name of One Love. We get to have people come together in a circle with that intent, with that remembrance—so powerful. And I feel so grateful just knowing that it is going to happen. If two or more are gathered in One Love, JAH is there. This is not going to be a tsunami wave. This is going to be a slow groundswell. If Denroy doesn't come, it's alright. No matter whether he comes or not, he's made a big contribution to this. Whoever is meant to be there will be there. JAH's in charge of this. I'm glad Denroy's pushing for this. I'd like to meet Mortimo and ask him who started the One Love to begin with. I think he's holding the ancient information about the beginning of Rastafari. I feel honored that we get to go see him."

"I guess in a way this is perfect," I said feeling better after listening to Julia. "Having this happen so close to the event let's me once again

Gathering of the Healers

make peace with whoever comes tomorrow and whatever happens."

Mortimo Planno (his birth name is Mortimer Planner) was born in the ghettos of Kingston in 1920. He was one of the founding members of Kingston's first Rastafarian encampment in the Dungle area of Kingston. In 1939, as an early convert to Rastafari, he moved to Trench Town, a Kingston inner-city ghetto. In the sixties, he met Bob Marley and began instructing Bob on the truths of the faith. In essence, he converted Bob from a ghetto "rude boy" to a high-minded Rasta. Later, Planno, once a "rude boy" himself, would be Bob's manager, coordinating his career, arranging studio sessions, etc.

His devout studies of all matters connected with the faith, combined with his brilliant intellect, established Planner, or Brother Planno or Brother Cummie, as he is affectionately called, as one of the elders of Rastafari. To many he is not perceived as *an* elder Rasta but rather as *the* elder Rasta. He is attributed with being a major influence in the movement. Planno wrote quite a few songs for Marley including "This Train," "Payaka," "Chances Are," and "Haile Selassie Is the Chapel." An artist, psychologist, and a "thoughtists," as he would call himself, his "yard" at 18 Fifth Street was a mecca for Rastafarians from all over Jamaica. There they would gather, beating drums, chanting and reasoning. Planno served as a communicator in the 1960s between the Jamaican establishment and some of the Rastafarian community, asking the University of the West Indies to survey the Rastafari movement in 1959 in hopes of establishing a better relationship with the government and people of Jamaica. Arthur Lewis, then the Chancellor of UWI, completed the positive report which did help the relationship but only to a limited degree.

As the Research Institute for the Study of Man Website states:

> Planno has been one of the more charismatic adherents of Rastafari. Being intensely studious, an exceptional and eloquent orator, and harboring an abiding concern for the welfare of all Rastafari, he is known and respected among many Rastafari brethren worldwide. In 1961, Planno was selected to be a member of the

169

Gathering of the Healers

Jamaican delegation that traveled throughout Africa (Mission to Africa) to explore the possibilities of repatriation. On April 21, 1966, now known as Grounation Day (a Rastafari holy day), Planno was able to becalm a wildly enthusiastic and zealous mass of 100,000 Rastafari and other believers eagerly waiting to catch a glimpse of Haile Selassie I on his historic visit to Jamaica. This feat allowed the Emperor to make a more placid but still hurried de-planning to a waiting limousine. During Selassie's three day stay in Jamaica, Planno was among the selected Rastafari Elders who met with His Imperial Majesty (H.I.M.).

This latter fact and Planno's broad knowledge of, and adherence to, Rastafari beliefs and practices led Bob Marley, one or two years after Selassie's visit, to seek Planno out and "reason" with him in Trench Town. Planno passed on his knowledge of Rastafarian principles, rites and customs to Marley who eventually became an outspoken and internationally celebrated musician and dedicated adherent of the religion.

Mortimo now lectures at the University of the West Indies, Kingston, where the government, considering him a national treasure, has provided him a house for life on the campus.

I had read a little about Mortimo when I was researching Bob Marley's life while writing *Rasta Heart*. I was fascinated by the idea of meeting him but concerned that I could not pull this together in the few hours available before the press conference was to begin. I would have to meet with him in the morning and get to the museum by one o'clock to meet the people delivering the chairs and tables and meet with Mrs. Beharry, the manager of the Queen of Sheba Restaurant, about the catering. At nine in the morning, I called information but he was not listed. I called the University but hit a dead-end there, too.

"Denroy, do you have Mortimo's phone number?" I said, calling to tell him of my dilemma. "I've tried information and the University with

Gathering of the Healers

no luck."

"No. I do not know his phone number," he said, "but just drive up to the University and someone there can tell you how to get to his house."

Leaving Alicia by the pool, Julia and I headed out. Julia was very excited about meeting him.

"This feels very historical to me," she said as we drove toward UWI. "It's very mystical. Every since I've heard about him, I've wanted to meet him. As soon as Denroy said we must meet him, I felt very connected to him and blessed to be a part of this. I just feel that Mortimo is an essential part of what we're doing. Like he's the glue keeping everyone together."

We drove on the campus and asked the entrance guard if she knew where Mortimo lived and to our delight she gave us instructions to a small residential area of the campus. We drove through the campus and stopped at the guardhouse (security is a must in all parts of Kingston) and the guard there directed us to his house. The neighborhood was a large circle with 20 or so attractive, but small, concrete block homes set on the circle's outer rim. The yards were well kept and spacious, dotted with shade trees.

We parked in his driveway and approached a young Rasta, Nabbi, who was painting a colorful Rasta-colored sign on a work table in his front yard. He said Mortimo was resting in his bedroom but that we could go in. A young woman, Mortimo's nurse, greeted us warmly at the door and went to the adjoining bedroom to announce our presence before ushering us in to see Mortimo.

It is hard to describe Mortimo in words. He is more to be experienced than to be described. He was laying on his single bed in light blue pajamas with a coffee table in front of him filled with reading materials and medicine. He looked tired, like we had woken him up. But even at 82, and with heart problems, his personal power is obvious, almost overwhelming. He has two-foot long massive dreads and matted precepts, all jet-black, without a strand of gray. He is a large man, big-boned and solid. His eyes reflect kindness and sadness, like a man who has seen it all over his amazing life. He seems both infinitely wise and weary, like a laden prophet; and yet, at times a childlike glee seems to pop to the

171

Gathering of the Healers

surface.

His nurse brought in two chairs and we sat across from him as he remained prone in his bed, the coffee table between us.

"Mortimo, my name is Robert Roskind," I began.

"What's dat? Rascal?" he interrupted.

"No, RAS KIND!" Julia said forcefully, looking him directly in the eye.

"Oh, RAS KIND! I like dat!" Mortimo responded laughing, his powerful voice at full volume. He seemed to all of a sudden come alive where only seconds before he seemed sick and in pain.

I explained what we were doing and, given Denroy's feeling, why we were there. I couldn't really read him or sense whether he liked our efforts or whether we were just a noisy intrusion in his otherwise quiet morning.

"A lot of Rasta-hearted people are putting out this One Love vibration already," Julia said as we reasoned with him. "People don't quite understand that you're even here and how important it is for people to know you. We're just asking people to recognize what's already going on. Let's look at it and say it's a reality. One Love is a reality in Jamaica already."

"So what do you think?" I said. "Do you want to come tonight?"

"Yeah. Yeah," he relied. "Talking to Jamaican people is one t'ing but I would like to come tonight but not talk."

"That's fine," I said, delighted that he was coming. I explained the arrangement of the chairs in a circle with the elder Rastas in a semi-circle behind the healers. "I'd like to put you at the center of that semi-circle next to our fourteen year-old daughter, Alicia. Both of you would be directly behind the speakers, always in the camera's view. I think that would make a powerful image."

"You have a fourteen year-old daughter? Your daughter?" he said looking to Julia, his energy rising.

"Yes," Julia answered.

"Dat's good. I like dat part of it!" he said in an enthusiastic voice, a voice that comes from somewhere deep in his gut—powerful, booming. We all started laughing—the connection and friendship made.

172

Gathering of the Healers

"But I don't want to speak," he repeated.

"That's fine. You say volumes just by being there," I said.

"All this is mystic, historic, you know," he said, slowly, confidently. "Here, today. When you came, I had like a migraine but you came in wit' dis healer business and it come in like my healing process an' de pain is gone an my gift is to present to you this picture."

He then gave us a copy of the picture taken in 1966 with him standing next to Emperor Haile Selassie as he stepped off the plane on to the stair ramp in front of over 100,000 joyous Rastas, many throwing large cigar-sized spliffs at their feet. The picture is rather incredible. It shows Emperor, attired in a full-dress military uniform complete with medals and an officer's cap, standing safely behind a large soldier similarly attired on his right and Mortimo on his left. The then 46-year-old Mortimo, dressed in a white African-style, long-sleeved shirt and pants, with a large camera around his neck and a full head of dreadlocks, looks protective and concerned.

"This picture is also like a healing process. Every newspaper in de world almost 'ave dat picture. And these pictures are my paintings," he said, pointing to several brilliantly colored paintings on the wall. "An' I took one of these to give to His Majesty as a present at that time. A picture wherein I was showing His Majesty from the cross to the throne— Christ leaving the cross an' standin' dere at dat throne. An' he accept it an' I feel de way I'm feelin' wit' a lot of power comin' up to me."

"Before we leave, I'd love to really know," Julia said almost breathlessly, "how you felt when you were there with the Emperor."

"Muta asked me dat question on de radio," Mortimo replied loudly, coming into his full energy, "of 'ow I felt in de presence of His Majesty."

"I would like to know that," Julia said, looking Mortimo lovingly in the eye. These two had a very deep connection. "I want your full heart in your answer."

"You want my full heart," Mortimo said, chuckling. "You are my 'ealin' process. You are 'ealin' me right now, 'ealin' dis migraine."

"Yes. Because I set myself in the four corners," Julia replied, softly. "North, south, east and west where everything gets connected. You feel it in your head. Now I can feel it right here in my head. You feel that presence of JAH healing. It's a natural thing."

"Rastafari," Mortimo said, softly, slowly, gently.

"Rastafari," Julia repeated, softly, slowly, gently. "That JAH energy that was stuck is released now. It's over now and you're ready to release it. I want to share with you the feeling I have. I feel great fullness and then my heart responds in unison, in repeating the same pattern and then it becomes one connection, one link up of JAH. Then I express the love of JAH."

"Rastafari," Mortimo said again, softly, slowly, gently.

"And then I know I am in full receipt," Julia said, her eyes closed having entered some mystical heart space. "I have my great fullness in I. I am as JAH created I. I am creation. I am the light manifesting JAH love. Then I am inheriting. I have it. I give it in my expression. I receive it in great fullness and then I inherit the Earth, Mama Earth, livity. JAH-I!," she said breathing deeply. "So now tell me, Mortimo, what was it like to be with His Majesty?" she said after a peaceful silence.

"Can you imagine being in the presence of the great king, Haile Selassie I?" Mortimo said, an almost beatific smile coming across his broad face. "That's how I felt. I want you to use your imagination. Imagine yourself being in the presence of His Majesty, to get a look at him. It is mystic."

"That must have been wonderful," Julia said. "And you're there standing in front of him protecting him? It looks like you're protecting this grand treasure that comes on the island."

"He made me into a commander," Mortimo continued, chuckling. "Commanding the Truth. Make way for His Majesty."

"You brought today's miracle," Mortimo said as he walked us to our car. In the yard, I called Denroy on my cell phone to tell him Mortimo was joining us.

"JAH! RASTAFARI!" Denroy shouted back into the phone when he heard the news. "Now I will come to your conference." I then handed the phone to Mortimo.

"JAH! RASTAFARI! MY BELOVED!" Mortimo shouted in the phone at Denroy. They continued to talk awhile longer, mostly Denroy talking, punctuated with Mortimo saying, "Yes, I" every few seconds. They ended with a loud "JAH! RASTAFARI!"

"I hope that this is the beginnin' of dis 'ealin' process an' I want to get ready for tonight," Mortimo said, grasping our hands in his. "Dis One Love will go out into de world tonight. JAH! RASTAFARI!"

"You know that Bob wanted this," Julia said as we drove away. "It's incredible that I asked him the same question as Muta."

"You want to go see Muta now?" I asked. "We have enough time. We can give him one more invite."

"Yes. I feel like I'd like to go see him," Julia said.

We drove over to Muta's bookstore, Books About Us, near our hotel. We parked in front and walked in to find Muta in the book section, dressed in a handsome African gown and, as always, barefoot. I couldn't read whether he was glad, annoyed or disinterested in my unannounced visit. I introduced Julia and we instantly started talking about the press conference, now only hours away. We talked for almost an hour—a good reasoning between people with different viewpoints.

Muta felt that people talking about One Love would do little to solve the problems created by the system and leaders that were exploiting people everywhere. He felt having political leaders or their representatives there, even to listen, sent the wrong message. To him these were the people creating the problems in the first place. We had heard all the objections many times before from many people and we passionately offered him our responses that love could solve all these problems. In the end he remained unconvinced. He said he would attend but only as a spectator. He also agreed to interview me on his program the following month.

"I think Muta's tribe is to draw attention to the problem," I said as we drove back to the hotel. "Our tribe is to point to the solution. You need both tribes but sometimes we can get frustrated with the other's approach. There has to be those that fight injustice, environmental

Gathering of the Healers

degradation, exploitation *and* there has to be others who speak of love and forgiveness. Our different natures will lead us to different paths."

"Muta is a lone wolf, a warrior," Julia said. "A very powerful warrior. He must follow his spirit always."

Dropping Julia off to spend the rest of the afternoon with Alicia, I drove over to the museum to get everything ready. Scram and Bell were there to meet me as planned. It was great to be with Scram again, someone who was holding the vision as strongly as Julia and I. Kris Kristensen, a Dane who ran a small business assistance group in Port Antonio, had rented a car and had given them a ride. Kris, a very committed and open-hearted guy, had been featured in *Rasta Heart.*

The people from the chair rental company were also there and I showed them how to set everything up in the back courtyard before joining Scram and Bell in the front at the Queen of Sheba patio restaurant. As I was walking toward the restaurant, I was confronted by a middle-aged Rasta.

"Are you Ras Kind?" he asked. He seemed to have an attitude.

"Yes. That's me," I answered, already defensive.

"I'm Ras Witter. Denroy Morgan said I should talk with you. I am a representative of de Nyabinghi House of Rastafari. Also I painted de murals 'ere at de museum," he said pointing to the brilliant murals on the inside of the front wall.

"Look, Ras Witter, I don't want to be disrespectful but I've got a lot on my hands right now," I said. I was already feeling rushed to get everything in place and I wanted to connect with Scram. "Can this wait until after I eat. My friends are waiting for me over there and they've come all the way from Portland."

"No," he said abruptly. "I want to be sure that you're not one of those white authors that comes down here and writes on Rastas and then never give any money to us. Do you plan to give any money to the Twelve Tribes, to de Nyabinghi, to de Bobos? I want to know more about what you are doing tonight." I really didn't want this vibe right now.

"I don't know what Denroy said to you," I said. "I just talked to him an hour ago from Mortimo Planno's house and he's supporting us and coming. I give half of the book royalties to the Rastas in the book. In

Gathering of the Healers

fact, I've already advanced everyone a lot of money up front so I am returning funds to the people whose wisdom I'm sharing in the book. Look, I'm going to go eat with my friends and I'll be glad to talk with you later," I said and walked over to Scram and Bell.

Scram, Bell and I ate lunch and talked with Mrs. Beharry about the catering. The Queen of Sheba makes excellent dishes, healthy and tasty and very reasonably priced, and I knew she would give us her best. Before heading back to the hotel, we checked to be sure the tables and chairs were set up like I planned.

I checked Scram and Bell in to their room and Scram joined Julia, Alicia and I out by the pool while Bell went off to visit friends in Kingston. It was good to be all together. We had come a long way and gone through many experiences and lessons together. We were all different people since we met—clearer, more confident, more directed. We had all joined together to help love grow and JAH had taken us on this incredible journey together—the book and that night would be the tangible results of our joint vision. We joked, talked and played around the pool and then retreated into our rooms to get ready—physically, psychologically and spiritually.

"The purpose of this press conference is to remember love. So we get to have a press conference in the name of One Love. We get to have people come together in a circle with that intent, with that remembrance—so powerful."

—Julia Roskind

Chapter 12
February 4, 2002

The Gathering of the Healers: The Healing of the Nation

S hortly before six, Julia, Alicia, Scram, Bell and I drove around the corner to the museum. Traffic was starting to die down and it was a warm Jamaican evening. Everyone was in great spirits but I must admit to my usual tension. Worries, greatly reduced but still there, raced through my mind. *Would the speakers show as agreed? Would the press come and carry the story? Would the photographer and the audio and video crews come on time? Would I do a good job with my speech? Would the small crowd be supportive?*

We parked inside the walled compound and went to check everything out. The museum was closed and appeared strangely deserted as I had always been there during business hours. Much to my delight, and relief, I noticed Luciano in a corner with a few of the local Rastas playing his guitar. Much of my worry lifted. I really wanted Luciano to show. He was such a clear voice for One Love and though I had talked

Gathering of the Healers

to Denica a few days before and she said he was excited about coming, you never know. We all went over and after introductions we left him to his music. He said he was in the midst of composing a song he felt inspired to write for the event.

The Queen of Sheba restaurant had set out a beautiful buffet of mostly Ital food and fresh juices. Several people had started gathering there, talking and laughing. We wandered around to the back, pleased to find the photographer and both the audio and video crews had arrived and the TV-J, the Jamaican network, crew as well—another good sign. Denica was there with Sonja. They both looked beautiful in full African gowns and scarves. As I chatted with our photographer, Trevor Grouch, telling him what I wanted, Mortimo showed, looking regal in a pure white cotton outfit with a black scarf accented with green, yellow and red.

Mortimo sat in the back of the rows of chairs and was instantly joined by Ras Witter who was still there. I wandered up front to check on the catering but Julia stayed around only to hear Ras Witter express all his problems about what we were doing, encouraging Mortimo to reconsider his involvement.

"I like Ras Kind's movements," Mortimo said, cutting him off, slowly moving his outstretched arm over the circle of chairs under the trees, the waterfall in the background.

By now both Antonnette Haughton and Dennis Forsythe had arrived. Also Frank Lumsden, the Maroon leader from Charles Town I had talked with a few months earlier, was there. We all chatted awhile as others arrived. By 6:45 Denroy and his wife, Hyacinth, had arrived with their adult son, Steve. Errol, Bongo Roach, Red, and our teenage friend, Alec Grizzard, had all driven up together from Negril. Kris was there along with Albert Ramsay, Abijah's manager, who said Abijah was driving in from Mobay but would be there soon.

Basil Walters, also known as Ras Bas, a reporter from *The Jamaica Observer*, and Anthea McGibbon from *The Daily Gleaner* arrived shortly before the conference was to begin. None of the radio stations we contacted sent a crew, nor did CVM, the other island TV station. Also three speakers never showed including Kymani Marley, Tony Rebel and

179

Gathering of the Healers

Barry Chevannes.

I was disappointed that the radio stations hadn't come. Radio talk shows in Jamaica are very big and I was hoping a station might carry the conference live, especially IRIE!FM but I knew we could get them audio tapes of the conference for future rebroadcasting. As we walked to the back courtyard, with Luciano rehearsing his new song in front of Bob's statute (a memorable and appropriate scene), I felt pleased with the turn out. In addition to the press and speakers, there were 30 or so other guests, including Barrington Laing, the manager of the museum, Djamalia, the artist we had met there a few days before, a few of the local Rases, Angela and a few of her staff from TTP, my PR firm. Muta came late and sat in the back row. There were maybe 40 people in all—a good, supportive group.

The setting was perfect—a pleasant Jamaican evening, under the trees in Bob Marley's backyard, surrounded by Ras Witter's beautiful murals, the waterfall gently splashing in the background. We all took our seats, the speakers at the "U" shaped tables with the empty speaker's chair in the middle; the guests and press in the rows of chairs in front of us; the Rastas from my book in the single semi-circle of chairs behind us along with Julia, seated next to Denroy Mortimo, and Alicia, seated next to Mortimo, in the center. I sat next to the empty speaker's chair with Luciano, Dennis Forsythe and Antonnette Haughton to my right. To my left, on the other side of the speaker's chair was Scram and to his left Abijah, who arrived a few minutes after we began. (Mike Henry, who spoke not as a healer but as my local publisher, was seated next to Abijah.)

Feeling very solid and relaxed, my worries about who would show now over, I began the press conference.

"I want to thank everyone here for coming," I began, "especially the guests and speakers and Barrington Laing and the Marley family for allowing us to use Bob's home tonight. I know Bob is smiling on our gathering. Before we begin, I want to ask my brother, Luciano, to start our conference with a song. I was most excited to come here and ask Luciano to join us. My family has listened to his music almost exclu-

Gathering of the Healers

sively for the last four months and I felt that he was one of the clearest and loudest voices for One Love in the country."

At this point, Luciano, dressed in a beige long-sleeved shirt, vest, and pants with a matching jungle helmet, came forward with his guitar and sat in the speaker's chair next to me.

"Greetings. A very blessed good evening to you all," he began, his voice soft and melodious. "Greetings in the name of the Emperor Haile Selassie, King of Kings and Lord of Lords, Conquering Lion of the Crown of Judah, Earth's Rightful Ruler. Greetings in the name a Yashuah, in the name of Yahwah, I am that I am. I greet you in the name of righteousness and love.

Seeing that our theme for this evening is One Love, I want to sing a little piece of vibration that I just got while I was standing by outside this wonderful house of the great honorable king, Robert Nesta Marley. I could never sing without lifting my hat to all the patriarchs (he lifts his hat to the Rastas behind him) and all those great people who have fought and defended I and I through all these rough times. I and I give thanks for those who have proven that love *is* the answer. We have love *and* justice that go together. This song is asking where is the brotherly love and where is the sisterly love."

Strumming on his acoustic guitar, in a beseeching and powerful voice he sang:

I say, where is the brotherly love?
And where is the sisterly love?
And I say where is the brotherly love?
And where is the sisterly love?
Although they move away the Berlin Wall,
that didn't solve the problem at all
cuz west man dey still have big wall
and east man didn't get better at all.
What are we fighting for?
What's the meaning of this tribal war?
Together we are stronger.

Gathering of the Healers

Come on, let's pull together.
 I say where is the brotherly love?
And where is the sisterly love?
Where is the brotherly love?
And where is the sisterly love?
When JAH made man
it was for us to live as one.
Together we are strong upon this creation.
Now, respect to the foundation
and respect to man and man.
Respect to everyone in creation, OH, JAH.
I say, where is the brotherly love?
And where is the sisterly love?
Where is the brotherly love?
And where is the sisterly love?
Though man thinks that he is civilized
all we do is brutalize, victimize and criticize
and dash the old people aside.
It's not right, no, in JAH's sight.
Let's all live up and unite, yeah,
whether black or white
it's enough in JAH JAH's sight.
I say where is the brotherly love?
And where is the sisterly love?
Where is the brotherly love?
And where is the sisterly love?"

Robert Roskind's Remarks

"Thank you, my brethren," I said, as the applause died down and I took the speaker's chair in the center. "I want to officially welcome everyone to the 'Gathering of the Healers: The Healing of the Nation' press conference. For the benefit of the radio audience let me tell you who is assembled here as national healers. The people joining me here to address the Jamaican people include: Luciano, Denroy Morgan of

Gathering of the Healers

Morgan Heritage, Abijah, Dr. Dennis Forsythe, and Antonnette Haughton. Behind us in a tribal semi-circle are the Rastas featured in my book and our special guest, Rasta leader, Mortimo Planno, who was Bob Marley's mentor and the man who welcomed Emperor Haile Selassie off his plane when he visited Jamaica in 1966. In the audience are the press as well as friends and supporters. Also joining me here is my wife, Julia, JAH I as she is called, my daughter, Alicia, my friend and brother, Thomas Anderson, Scram, as he is affectionately known, and myself. My name is Robert Roskind and my Jamaican friends also call me Ras Kind or Robbie.

It is a very joyous moment for us to find ourselves here with all of you. It is a dream—a vision—come true. This vision is of great importance to your country and the world, for we are joining together to see if a society can heal itself through the love of its people. It is the first time such an experiment has been attempted. It is appropriate that we gather at the home of one of the great teachers of love, Bob Marley, who has been sending this message into the hearts and minds of Jamaicans, and the rest of the world, for over three decades. The planet is ready and we will start here.

Before we hear from everyone else, let me take a few minutes to explain the genesis of this event. I am an American author and just as many of the musicians joining me here use their music to get out their message of love, I use my books. My books *In the Spirit of Business* and *In the Spirit of Marriage* teach love in these important areas of our lives. A year ago October, my family went on a vacation to Ocho Rios, our first visit to the island. While we were there we met a few Rastas working at our hotel and were greatly impressed by their kindness, dignity and calm. On the last day of our vacation, as Julia and I floated on a raft down the Rio Grande River, I decided to return to Jamaica and write a book on the wisdom of the Rastas, Bob Marley and Jamaica. I returned a year ago today to begin.

We made several trips to the island to work on this new book, *Rasta Heart: A Journey into One Love*. Many wonderful and moving things, all chronicled in the book, happened as we wandered around the island meeting the Rastas that really knew this One Love—not the dreads, the

Gathering of the Healers

"wolves in sheep's clothing" as they are called, but the real heart Rastas. Scram was one of these Rastas, as were these gentlemen sitting behind me.

As Julia, Scram and I worked on the book, we all wanted to find a way to make the book more real, to show a more tangible form of this One Love. Many visions and inspirations occurred to us. The first vision related to the book's introduction and to this event today. We decided to release the book during Bob Marley's birthday week and in doing so to invite the Jamaican people this year to begin to not just listen to and sing Bob Marley's songs but to live his words by exercising greater forgiveness in their personal relationships. In essence, to *be* his songs. I arrived back here shortly before Christmas to prepare for this launch, which I assumed would be modest and entail me talking with a few members of the local press. During this time, I realized that this message could have a much greater impact if we were to invite well known Jamaicans who were already teaching this One Love, the 'healers' as we now refer to them, to join us.

During January, Scram and I traveled across the island to talk with the people who, through their work, lives and reputations, were considered teachers of love by many of the Jamaican people. Some of these healers you see assembled before you. We invited them to join us in a spiritual experiment to see if this much-troubled island could be healed by the love of its people. As you can see, many here are singers. As Bob Marley demonstrated, this wave of Love emanating out from your island is carried not only by many of your people but by your music. These messengers of Love are the planet's tribal drummers.

One love, unconditional love for all humanity, is probably best described in Corinthians chapter 13 as follows:

Love is patient;
Love is kind and envies no one.
Love is never boastful;
Nor conceited, nor rude;
Never selfish;
Not quick to take offense.
Love keeps no score of wrongs;

Gathering of the Healers

Does not gloat over another's sins,
But delights in the truth.
There is nothing love cannot face;
There is no limit to its faith, its hope and its endurance.
In a word, there are three things that last forever:
Faith, hope and love;
But the greatest of them all is Love.

To exercise One Love does not mean that you like a person, seek out their company, or allow unloving or abusive treatment by them. It does not mean that you forego justice or reparations for past wrongs committed, for it is only through making amends that our soul is cleansed. You would still 'Getup! Stand up! Stand up for your rights!' One Love simply means that in your heart you understand that everyone you hold bitterly is a child of God who may have temporarily forgotten who they are and gone astray and you wish the best for them. You understand that, like you, they were sent here by their Creator to remember their own Divinity by learning and teaching love. All the great teachers of love in the last century—Mandela, Tutu, King, Gandhi, Kofi Annan, Anwar Sadat—all men of color, understood this and, while passionately confronting oppression, led their people into love.

This One Love was best revealed in an ancient mystery we uncovered while writing this book. The mystery involved one of your national heroes, Nanny, the powerful African chieftress of the Windward Maroons, the escaped slaves who fled the British and lived free in the Blue Mountains. She led her tribe to freedom in 1738 when England, being unable to subdue them, granted all Maroons liberty, the first Africans to be freed in the Western Hemisphere.

During our travels around Jamaica, Julia and I began to feel there was some connection between Nanny and the Rastas, even though there was a 200 year span between the two. Nanny led her people to physical freedom. The true Rastas are leading people to emotional, spiritual and mental freedom. We asked many people, both Rastas and Maroons, if they knew of such a connection. No one did until we asked Roy Scotte, a Maroon leader in Flagstaff in the parish of St. James.

Gathering of the Healers

When asked if he knew of any connection between the Maroons and the Rastas, Roy told us that when Nanny made the 'Great Trek' where she marched with several hundred warriors from the Blue Mountains in Portland to Gun Hill in Flagstaff where we were then sitting, it was not for the reason that the history books said. The books said that Nanny marched for several months, avoiding capture by the British, to tell her brother, Cudjoe, the leader of the Leeward Maroons, not to sign the peace treaty offered by the British.

Mr. Scotte told us that this is not what he was told by the tribal healers. He said that his foreparents were told by their foreparents that the reason Nanny, who never left her mountain hideaway, marched across the island, at the risk of being captured and killed, was to deliver one message to her tribal members in the West. When we asked him what was her message, he said, 'Nanny came here to teach us One Love. She said that we must never hate the English or this hate would weaken our tribe. She told us we must love them even if we must fight them to keep our freedom.'

Mr. George Sterling, the oldest living Maroon, later confirmed this fact. It was then that we understood how deeply this concept of One Love and forgiveness was rooted in the Jamaican soil.

What is forgiveness? *True* forgiveness, forgiveness that heals, is the crucial element of One Love. True forgiveness is not our pardoning some one we feel has unjustly attacked or injured us. It is not thinking I, being the better of the two, will forgive you in my magnanimity. This is 'forgiving-to-destroy.' It only reinforces the person's sense of shame and unworthiness.

True forgiveness is understanding that every so-called 'attack' is in reality an appeal, a call for healing and help. It is an asking for love, regardless of the form it takes. And if we answer their call with our love, we remind the other person of their Divine perfection, instilled in them by their Creator. Our forgiveness is a wake up call to someone who has fallen asleep. This is 'forgiving-to-heal.' This is what Christ was asking us to do when he said 'love your enemies' and why on the cross he said, 'Forgive them father for they know not what they do.'

And by exercising this true forgiveness, by reminding our 'transgres-

Gathering of the Healers

sors' of their true Divine nature, we remind ourselves of our own.

What do we mean by a 'healer?' In Biblical terms they would be called 'peacemakers' and in tribal terms 'elders.' A healer or elder, regardless of their physical age, is anyone who exercises this love and true forgiveness and thereby teaches it to others, and in doing so leads God's children back to Him. Every one of us is potentially a healer. We need only to open our hearts and minds to love. And to me a healer is a true Christian and a true Jew and a true Muslim and a true Rasta.

Again it was a Maroon who clarified to us the importance of the healers to the tribe. When we were in the Maroon village of Moore Town in Portland Parish we met with Colonel C.L.G. Harris who was the Maroon colonel and school teacher there for over thirty years. When we told him that some Maroons felt he did not fully carry the spirit of the tribe because he stopped the tribal drumming in the village—drumming that had occurred every night for over 250 years—he said, 'The elders would not have chosen me to keep the spirit of the tribe alive. I knew little of the Maroon history. I was the colonel, the administrative leader.'

As we walked away from his house, we began to understand the impact of his words. We realized that now is the time for the healers of the tribe, the one's who know and teach love in all societies, to come forward and teach the people. We cannot wait for our political and business leaders to lead us into peace and love. They do not know how. It is not their tribe. They are the colonels, the administrative leaders.

And there are tens of thousands of other Jamaicans who could justly join us up here as healers but God has led us to these people. You may or may not agree with our choices but I would like to ask you to suspend judgment, as much as you can. When Bob Marley was criticized after releasing his gentle Kaya album he said simply, 'My music is my music.' I would say to you, 'Our vision is our vision.'

And our vision is simply this: We believe that it is possible for the Jamaican people to heal their country and redirect it to the honor, peace and prosperity it deserves. We believe they can do this by doing one simple thing. We are inviting all Jamaicans to forgive, as much as they are presently able, everyone they are holding bitterly in their hearts. We are inviting you to transform your past, often ancient, hatreds into pres-

Gathering of the Healers

ent loves, for the holiest place on earth is not a religious shrine or tomb but rather anywhere an ancient hatred has become a present love. And these hatreds can be one day old or centuries old, toward one specific individual or an entire race or nation of people.

We understand that not everyone will immediately accept our invitation to join us in this love because as my brother Scram reminds me, 'Is not every heart ready to cherish this One Love.' But we believe, we know, that as enough people on this beautiful, powerful island of Jamaica accept our invitation to forgive others it will heal this country and your crime rate will go down, your divorce rate and accident rate will go down, your tourism and economy will increase, even the health of your people will improve. And what is even more important is that you will teach other societies all over the world that they too can heal their countries with love and you will have fulfilled your National Pledge and Jamaica will "play her part in advancing the welfare of the whole human race" and you can rightly claim your national motto, 'Out Of Many-One People.'

I have heard many objections as to why our goal is unobtainable. Cynicism and a sense of hopelessness pervade our world in general and this island in particular. This must be dissolved and not passed on to the next generation.

Many have said it is too naive, too idealistic, an oversimplification, that love could never solve all manmade problems like war, corruption, cruelty, betrayal. To them I would say the lack of love has created these problems and therefore the infusion of love will correct them. If you will look at the people in front of you, over 20 of us with over 800 years of life experience combined, Rastas and reggae stars, politicians and businesspeople, white and black, I think you would agree that though we are idealistic, we are neither naive nor foolish.

Some said it is easy for me as a white, middle-class American, and even for these other successful and secure people joining me, to speak of love and forgiveness, but this is much harder for the poor and oppressed. Soon you will hear from Scram, a man who has always known poverty, 'quashee' as you would say. A man who still goes in the middle of the night to spend six hours cleaning the market place in Port

Gathering of the Healers

Antonio for 10 U.S. dollars a day. And all of the other Rastas sitting behind us who speak through our book live in similar conditions—poor in material terms but spiritually rich and *never* the victim. Their message is the same as ours.

Others said that the political system is too corrupt and can never change. To them we would say that your political leaders, and yes even the gunmen and the dons, are also seeking this love, though they may not understand this as yet. Like all of us, their hearts too can be transformed and healed.

And to these gunmen who have hurt or killed their fellow human beings, and to the dons who have instructed or encouraged these men to do so, your life too is redeemable. In God's eye all his children are welcomed back to Him and all are capable of claiming their place as healers—no matter what crimes they have committed. Your redemption lies in finding youths that are going astray down paths similar to yours and leading them back to love.

Others said we were asking too much, that it is too hard to forgive when you have been badly mistreated, enslaved, exploited, betrayed. To them we would say, 'You are right. It is hard to forgive. It is the second hardest thing in the world. The only thing harder is to *not* forgive because, as a friend once told me, 'Resentment' does more damage to the vessel in which it is stored than the object on which it is poured.' As Nanny knew, to hate is to weaken yourself and your tribe. Whether we believe it is fair or just, God has created our world so that our personal happiness is directly linked to our forgiving ourselves and others. We cannot be happy with a bitter heart. This is His design, not mine.

And finally, someone said a press conference was a good idea but how do you sustain the concept. We are asking you, everyone here today, especially the press, and everyone listening to or reading these words, whether you are in the slums of Trench Town, the small shops in the Blue Mountains or in the fine homes overlooking Montego Bay to join us. We are asking every Jamaican willing enough—brave enough—to accept our invitation, to sustain this belief in your hearts and minds, in your everyday relationships and conversations, in your treatment of everyone that you encounter. We are asking you to join us in a sustain-

189

Gathering of the Healers

able effort to heal this island, an effort whose rallying call is 'ONE LOVE-MAKE IT HAPPEN!'

One might ask, 'Why Jamaica to lead the world into this One Love vibration? Why this small island for such a magnificent destiny?' It is clear this vibration cannot emanate from the world capitals of Washington, Moscow or London, or even from the religious capitals of Jerusalem, Rome or Mecca. But why Jamaica?

Few, if any, countries in the world have known the suffering of Jamaica. For over 500 years, since Columbus first set foot at Discovery Bay, foreign powers, have dominated Jamaican life and seldom with the concern for the happiness and well-being of its people. Within two decades of Columbus' arrival, all 60,000 indigenous Arawak Indians were dead. Then began over 300 years of the most brutal slavery imaginable, where the average slave worked 18 hours a day and was dead after seven years. After Emancipation in 1838 and up to today, the Jamaican people have continued to be exploited by both local and foreign powers. If Jamaica, with its great 'sufferation,' as the Rastas would say, can heal itself through love and forgiveness, after all it has been through, it will have the moral authority to look to the world and say, 'You, too, can heal your nation with the love in the hearts of your people.'

And the centuries of suffering will then be understood for its spiritual value. Just as pressure on a piece of coal makes a diamond, so has the pressure of this suffering created a diamond here. This diamond is the Jamaican people in general and, the heart Rastas in particular. For when you take away from people the chance to enjoy the material comforts of life, the clearest thinking of the tribe will say, 'Where can I find happiness and peace?' And they find their joy, their 'livity' as Rastas would call it, in what God has given free to all His children: His love, the love of others and nature.

Many Rastas, especially the older Rastas, have held this reality clearly in their hearts and minds despite decades of prejudice, mistreatment and indignation. They were often the 'poorest of the poor,' oppressed *by* the oppressed. But they held their heads high, with dreadlocks flowing, and never played the victim or gave in to bitterness and despair. Christ

Gathering of the Healers

and His disciples would feel quite at home among them.

Jamaicans are already some of the most loving people in the world, perhaps the most loving. Any Jamaican that has traveled abroad, and any foreigner who has come to know your people as we have, can testify to this. Even Dr. Martin Luther King, Jr. saw this. A few weeks ago, in an article in *The Gleaner*, Martin Henry wrote, 'In a supreme compliment, (Dr. King) declared that Jamaica was the place he felt most like a human being. He was free here—everywhere the genuine warmth and love of Jamaicans renewed his strength to love his enemies as his Lord.' When God gave out geographic assignments, Jamaicans got the bonus. In the U.S., we have the things but things do not make people happy. Here you have the heart vibes and that *does* make people happy.

Jamaica has the most fertile soil for One Love to grow. This was made clear to me a few days before Christmas. As Alicia, my teenage daughter, and I drove through the crowded streets of Port Maria, with everyone spilling out into the street, laughing and talking, I noticed her eyes welling up in tears. When I asked her what was the matter, she said, 'I just love it, Dad. It's so easy for people to be together here. This is how I want to live.'

Though Jamaica presently has one of the highest murder rates per capita in the world, everyone here knows that this dishonor does not reflect the true nature of this magical island but rather the aberrant behavior of a few people misguided by anger, greed or hate. We are only asking Jamaicans to do more of what they already do so well—love and forgive each other and to do so with such commitment and passion that your love solves your country's seemingly unsolvable problems. Do not wait for the PNP, the JLP, the UPP, the NDM or the IMF, to solve them.

As Caribbean writer George Lamming wrote: 'If we could ever succeed in planting in people, not only the idea but the fact, in their consciousness, that they are the makers of history, then you alter the relationship between them and those who hold them in their hands.'

We have all gathered here today to plant this one concept in your mind: that you, the people of Jamaica, at every level—rich and poor, Rasta, Christian, Jew, Muslim and atheist, black, brown, yellow and white, rural and urban, young and old—control your own destiny and

Gathering of the Healers

the ability to heal yourself and this island is within your hands and your hearts.

To use a wonderful Jamaican phrase, we are here to 'big you up,' to ask you to join us in claiming your destiny as teachers of love to the world. And we are here also to 'big up' your political leaders, to tell Prime Minister Patterson and Opposition Leader Seaga and all Jamaican politicians, that they are indeed men of destiny but in a much greater sense than they know.

Your politicians can answer this call by seeking peace above votes and publicly exhibiting their personal friendship and doing everything in their power to see that their followers do the same. It must not just be photo ops but a true expression of love and respect. If Mr. Patterson and Mr. Seaga and your other politicians can do this now, they will have taught politicians everywhere how to put their people first and their own desires second. This will be their legacy *together*, a legacy much greater than winning the next election.

Over two decades ago at the One Love Peace concert in 1978, Bob Marley asked Mr. Seaga and Michael Manley to do the same when he brought them on stage and had them join hands with him. What followed in the months ahead was some of the worst political violence in Jamaica's history.

However, things are different now. The people are ready to claim their power and they no longer can wait on their political leaders. Even if Prime Minister Patterson and Mr. Seaga and other political leaders should not decide to accept their Divine calling as teachers of love, this time the people will heal their nation. Victor Hugo once wrote, 'There is nothing more powerful than an idea whose time has come.' And as Nanny led her tribe away from the old system of slavery, we are leading you away from the old system of mental slavery because until you forgive, you are never truly free. Or as Bob Marley sang, 'Emancipate yourself from mental slavery. None but ourselves can free our minds.'

As Nelson Mandela once said: 'We ask ourselves, who am I to be brilliant, gorgeous, talented and fabulous? Actually, who are you not to be? You are a child of God. You're playing small doesn't help the world. There's nothing enlightening about shrinking down so someone won't

Gathering of the Healers

feel insecure around you. We were born to make man into the glory of God that is within us. It's not just in some of us, it's in *everyone*.'

Prayer alone is not enough. Our forgiveness and our love must be added to our prayers for God helps those that help themselves. We are God's ambassadors on earth. He loves us *through* each other. Will enough people accept our offer to successfully and visibly heal this country? Has humanity evolved far enough to heal its societies through love? Given the times we live in, it is essential that efforts like this be implemented and pursued until they are successful. For as my brother Bushman sings, 'Tribal war won't stop the problem. Only love of the heart can stop it.'

Let's begin here, now. And for every person accepting our invitation to step forward into love and forgiveness, your own personal success is instantly certain. Your own life will become healed. And with each step—each act of true love and forgiveness—it will feel so good in your heart that you will take the next and the next—all the way Home, for this is what everyone is seeking.

We are asking today that healers in all communities throughout Jamaica, from St. Thomas-in-the East to Westmoreland, from Kingston to Montego Bay, from every city and town, from every village and hamlet, to step forward and accept our invitation and claim your place along with us. You know who you are and your people know who you are. Continue to teach love in your communities but now do so more publicly. And we are asking all Jamaicans to join them as healers by not just complaining about the present state of your country but also asking yourself, 'Am I adding to its problems by holding anyone bitterly in my heart?' Or as one of your citizens, Martin Schade, wrote in *The Gleaner* recently, 'To stop violence in our country, let us first look at our hearts and stop the violence there.'

Our next vision will manifest in four months. As today's event is called, 'The Gathering of the Healers: The Healing of the Nation,' the next one we are calling 'The Fires of Forgiveness: The Healing of the Nations.' In mid-June the 'Americas' Tall Ships,' the masted schooners of old, similar to the slave ships that brought your foreparents to this island, will be in Port Antonio and Montego Bay. In the hills above

Gathering of the Healers

these two ports live the Maroons, direct descendants of these slaves. We have asked the Tall Ship committee and the Maroons, and we plan to ask the honorary Tall Ship Chairman President Jimmy Carter, to join together at the waterfront for an international healing ceremony. With the ships in the background, we will light a huge bonfire, a fire of forgiveness, and ask the world that four hundred years of African slavery be forgiven, but never forgotten. This forgiveness should begin in Jamaica, which was once the most brutal slave colony in the history of the world.

And at the exact moment that these bonfires are lit, we are asking individuals, villages, neighborhoods and communities all over the island to light their own 'fire of forgiveness' so that Jamaica will be ablaze—ablaze with forgiveness. And we will light special fires where troubled ghetto youths can go and meet with healers and turn their lives around and leave their guns behind. And we want to ask that everyone here, the press, the entertainers, the politicians, the business people, join with us in keeping this message in front of your people on an ongoing daily basis until critical mass is reached. Four months from now when the tall ships come and the fires of forgiveness are lit, these results can be visible to all.

To members of the press we make a special request. Comment on our vision, this is necessary in a democracy but also let your people hear our words directly by printing and rebroadcasting them in your media. You are the national Abeng, the tribal horn that the Maroons used to communicate with each other.

In closing, we are asking each of you to pour out your love and forgiveness, especially between now and June. Go past the pain of it and give it all you've got. In Sir Richard Attenborough's documentary on Mother Teresa, he said: 'There is a light in this world. A healing spirit more powerful than any darkness we may encounter. We sometimes lose sight of this force because there is suffering, too much pain. Then suddenly, the spirit will emerge through the lives of ordinary people who hear the call and answer in extraordinary ways.'

We are all ordinary people who God can use to do extraordinary things. Hear this call and let this spirit emerge through your life. If you

Gathering of the Healers

will do your part, we will do ours by riveting the world's attention on Jamaica on June 14th for the Fires of Forgiveness. And when the entire world wants to know why Jamaica is ablaze that night, the success of our efforts together over the next few months can be told through reduced crime and murder rates, a recovering economy and even more smiles on Jamaican faces. Once this 'Miracle in Jamaica' is seen, people all over the world will come here just to be in your vibes. Finally, One Love will truly have become Jamaica's message to the world. Thank you."

Thomas Anderson's (Scram) Remarks

"Next I would like Scram to return to the mike and share with you his thoughts on One Love," I said as I finished my speech and vacated the speaker's chair.

"Ladies and gentleman, once more now that we have heard everything that Robert has said and we want to congratulate the Roskind family to pull up this message from so far away and to come our way. And tonight it's not we alone, all of us that are here. We are the messengers, now. So we wouldn't have anyone over there or behind me to question what this One Love meant because deeply inside of us we know what the One Love is. To the people that came tonight, we certainly know if they did not know what this One Love is they would never be here. So we come as true soldiers tonight and to send this message to the four corners of the earth, especially the leaders.

Now this message, leaving Jamaica to the four corners of the earth, it is not only we sending it, not only we over here, not Mr. Roskind alone, nor his wife, not Scram alone, but everyone in this audience tonight. The responsibility is set before us. And when this thing happened, don't say it is we alone do it but every heart inside here tonight. We want to know that we have a meditation inside of us because sending this One Love out there, it's going to individuals, every individual. We want them to reconcile within their own self what this love means to them.

195

Gathering of the Healers

So when I look around and see bredren and sistren came and all de bredren that don't arrive yet tonight, I know that they are still sending the message because Tony (Tony Rebel) has been sending the message and Luci (Luciano) for years. We want each and everyone here just to have a firm belief in themselves sending this message. We don't want to know that the message just go by I and Robert and his wife and daughter. We want to know that everyone here tonight is sending the message across the world. Everyone agree with that? Yes.

When I was small, I heard people speaking about love and I been checking that sound into my hearing all the way until today and to see that love is the key for the door of truth. Some people say 'love' to pull up a little closer, to grab a shoe, or to grab something off the line but we want to skip over that type of a love. Now we are getting down into that genuine part of it. The one that teach us the way around, the one that can teach the heads of government to deal with the lower class of people the proper way. That is the love we need and that is the love I believe that brother Luci always sends through.

But right now to me, the people, they hear about the love and they sing it and they dance it a lot, but they don't sit down and get right back into themselves and to say, 'This love is so real that I shouldn't even hurt the man a hundred miles away from me. I should never speak anything so downgrading on someone instead of calling him over and you both sit down and discuss all the things the way that you believe that love, true love, would teach you. That is the kind of feeling that I ever felt that could carry the world through. And when Bob had faith to move into such a region and to leave it in our way, the way we have it, I believe that something is there. Something in the love is so special that people want to know and to feel within themselves.

And that is the type of love that we want to send. Because right now when I look and consider and see what's taking place in the far out distance and I knew that Rastafari is the one that always try to talk these things and try to be against all these corruptions and now Rastafari finishing up the work, now, as a last call to the nation. Pay attention to yourself. Get this love up to date in you because it *is* the last call. Now is the last call—*final movement*. And it is dedicated by all who are

196

inside here this night, sending the message to the world, to the greatest world leaders, the mightiest world leaders. Rastafari from Jamaica sending this One Love to hit the heart of them, to know the right movement and the way of life that they are supposed to deal with. And that is where we want them to reconcile within themselves and say, 'You know that I am sorry.' Just that. 'I'm sorry for what I have done to you people.' And that they can get their forgiveness in time and then we know that we are in a better shape.

Now for what is really taking place in our midst in Jamaica island now, innocent people going down. You just hear that someone in their bed and get shot, in their bed, in their bed, man. To I view these things, its the worst thing among human and our heart is aching to know that all these things taking place and we ask the elder, that is elder than I, to mediate on these things daily that we can have immediate change on the island because I am looking for some cooling down of even the gunshots. To my prayer I am looking for this peace and love to arise. If it is from the depth of the earth, I am looking for it to rise. And if it is in the elements, I looking for it to pour down. The peace and happiness that we all can enjoy. And I will leave these few words into the hearts of everyone that is here tonight that we can meditate together, in the name of his majesty, Emperor Haile Selassie I."

Luciano's Remarks

"Thank you, Scram, me brethren," I said as Scram finished. "Now, I'd like to ask Luciano to return for more of his thoughts."

"I do give thanks for this opportunity and I do give thanks for the gathering, for the wonderful people that have gathered here who have one focus, one purpose—to bring about love and peace in our community. It's a very good topic. When Brother Robert brought it forward to I and I, I thought it would be important that I, as an ambassador of love, to come forward and say a few words. I do agree in many circumstances and in many cases as Brother Robert has said, that we all need to for-

197

Gathering of the Healers

give and we all need forgiveness in order to have a free heart to allow the power and the flow of God's love to manifest in us.

But in my analysis of the situation and observing what is going on, I realize that this is an achievement that we all dream and aspire to and have a great vision for, which can only come about when we have made justified those who have been unjustified. And I do agree that there can be no love at all without justice and this basis and premise I will make my comments.

I have been singing for many years and I have tried to apply my little knowledge of God, knowledge of humanity, knowledge of love itself, in my own way. I put together words, positive words, that encourage people to think positively and creatively and I think this is the purpose of love. Love is a positive energy which, when applied, it will activate people of all different walks of life. If you have done a wrong in your life, or in your expression, once you receive this love, this love energy, it will energize you to do something with what you have. If it's land, you will want to share it. If its wealth, you will want to share it. If it's inspiration, you will want to share it. And wanting to share, it means that you will want to care about those that are in need, those that have been ill-treated, even by your own hand. For you to be forgiven, it seems to me that you, who have been forgiven, must find some way of making an amends. And this is the true balance of the equation.

I could honestly say that Jamaicans are forgiving people. There is no doubt that we Jamaicans are forgiving people. We say Jamaica is made out of many different people. So we say people who have come here from all different nationalities, all different walks of life, all different races and creeds, they have come here and become one within this tradition, this vibration of people growing out of a struggle. But if we should look around, we will realize that there are some people who have suffered more than others and it is true. For example, the body, the physical body, has skeleton. It has backbone. It has cartilage and all. But if you realize the backbone stands a lot of weight and when you lose the backbone, you know what happens.

What I am saying is we, the black people, let us say the Africans, we have suffered a lot. We have gone through a lot of victimization, geno-

198

cide. I do not want to sound bitter in myself because I'm not. What I seek now is justice. And in my own knowledge of love, serving love, it means that I must see that the justice is administrated from the heads of governments straight unto the little man out there in the street (applause). Thank you.

We all need to make amends to our wrongs. I say every time we find ourselves in a situation, whether it is good or bad, we have something to do about it. And sometimes because of stubbornness we find ourselves in situations in which we ought not to be. And in this case, I say we all need to make amends to wrongs that we all have done. As the good saying says 'We must forgive those who trespass against us that we can be forgiven for our trespasses.'

Now when Brother Rob came into the office and mentioned this wonderful plan, I said to myself, *This is a great idea.* As a matter of fact, I must be honest with you, we need this kind of forum. We need this kind of gathering, this kind of dialogue, and people to reason from all walks of life. We need the press, photographers. We need people to come and write about these things because here we are soliciting for love and in the same breath we have to solicit for justice. I say what you see happening in this Jamaica here even though we are so loving, we are caring, we have gone the extra mile. Many of us are suffering from amnesia (applause and laughter).

But there is a little saying that I always remember, an elderly lady said to me. 'My son, you must forgive but always remember because if people don't remember, it might happen again.' And we must be frank, and outspoken and truthful about this. Now, when Brother Rob brought this wonderful plan to me, I want to give thanks to all members here. Excuse my bad manners but I have been so heated, wanting to go into the depth of the matter. When Brother Rob brought this very great plan to me, I said, 'This is a very good idea, Brother Robert, and I'm willing to work along with you,' but, I know he remembers this, I said to him, 'But Brother, for us to just forgive and forget, it's not going to be that easy.' I tell you honestly, because what we have really gone through. We need to address these matters. Children living in the ghettos, like where you see zinc, barbed-wire, like a concrete jungle. This kind of vibration

Gathering of the Healers

has brought out a kind of vindictiveness, a bitterness in the people. And I know that the environment has a lot to do with it.

Now here we are, a group of people that were taken out of the motherland and brought out here in the Western Hemisphere to gratify the needs and the desires of entrepreneurs, backa masters (overseers on plantations), who just want to build their empires and their colonies. To me we have done so. We have built these empires. We have built these colonies. We have established these things. We have been the backbone of the workforce. Now we need love *and* we need justice. There can be no love without justice and this is why I say as a messenger, I would have to be here to represent as an ambassador of love *and* justice. Some people they call me 'justice' sometimes. It is a topic that I treat tenderly.

So when Brother Robert brought me this plan of the 'Fires of Forgiveness,' it is like sending a message across that we want to rekindle that spirit of fire, to rekindle—love inside of us. But how much can we light up when we know deep in our heart that our youth, our children, are going through rough times. Our people are faced with different problems, economical stress, joblessness. They can't get food. They have been driven off land, gone to different places. And I will tell you something more. I visited in Manchester an area where the bauxite company is digging away dirt and they almost dig underneath the place where the people live and they told them to get out but the people couldn't leave just like that. For some people they feel so connected to their little homeland. And you know what, the dust from the quarry sweep over the people and place and they get bronchitis and everything.

I went there and the people said to me, 'Luci, do something about this.' So I write a song and you know what, they banned the music. They put it on a black list and said it must not be played. Honestly. And what we have to go through to even leave the island as a band, it is a disgrace sometime, Brother Robert. So this is why I speak of justice. So I'm willing to work along with this plan but the first issue that I am going to raise is the matter of reparations. Honestly, we Jamaicans have gone through the mill. As brother Robbie say, they have found the love amongst us. But right now we are crying out. We don't really want to

Gathering of the Healers

bring it to the level where Nanny and Sam Sharpe (leaders of armed rebellions) and all these great heroes have taken it. We are crying out now with the music and the love and the word and saying 'Please, give us some justice. We need reparations, restoration.'

We are willing to continue to love and forgive but I am saying that we need at the same time for our people to realize what wrongs they have done because you see it's our people still. We are all out of one source. God Almighty is the one source. So for those who have wealth, who have found themselves if their fathers or mothers have left them with a lot of wealth and land and machines, to give unto us, give unto I and I the free emancipation that I and I can really take this machinery to Africa. So those that are skillful can get work. To me this is one way that we can bring about the love, the true love upon creation and especially in our communities.

For example now, they have brought about some laws, I'm talking about the leaders, which we know have forced us against the wall. Brother Marcus Garvey, a great prophet and messiah, thought that it is only when our backs are against the wall that we move. Right now I see that our backs are against the wall and it is the right time to rise with the love. We need to see that love being extended from our leaders, from so-called politicians who come and have claimed the wealth of the people to use it to the benefit of the people. Now we have been so good administrating towards them. We have shown love. We have been so hospitable and I do agree that most of the wealth that is being made from tourism has been brought back out of this island. It's not been spent in the communities. It is horrendous and this is the truth. We must face the truth of life and what is happening around us.

So I say 'love *and* justice.' We need love from everyone. Love from those who see themselves as leaders. Love from those who are defenders of oppressors and people who have beaten and taken away the wealth of other people, to bring forward. Because to bring a balance for example you have a scale. It's as if some of the weights have been taken over to one side. We need this wealth over to the other side to balance it. We are not saying that we want everything that they have. We need enough so that we can restore ourselves and repair ourselves (applause).

201

Gathering of the Healers

So with this in mind, we focus. Be forgiving. Be willing to forgive. But also we're looking and waiting patiently to see the willingness of the people to make amends of wrongs. So I give thanks for a brother whose been very bold. To me I've been looking for a messenger. I see and I wait and I pray and I say that I know that somehow the message of and the work of I and I must reach to the level and when the great Gong (Bob Marley) said 'One Love,' he looked straight and say 'Are you ready to save us from Armageddon so when the man come there will be no more doom and all those things.'

What we need to have is a oneness of spirit for being with one another in love and sharing the wealth of the earth. Blessed. So now Brother Rob mentioned about the ships coming and he says these ships represent the same colonial ships of I and I people and bring I and I out here, so these ships represent the same empires that have really brought I and I out here so I am saying, when these ships come, I want to send a request right now, that some of these very ships that are boasting these empires should be used to transport I and I people for a pilgrimage to the motherland because sometimes the plane fare to Africa is too much (applause).

This is a very good start because after tonight and the lighting of the fires this summer, we have to take into action this machinery that we are cranking up. The JAH-Messen-JAH Ministry is more than willing, the Rastafari, the Twelve Tribes, the Nyabinghi, and all those that represent righteousness here, whatever denomination, whatever religion. I give thanks for everyone who has turned up this evening, speaking for love in our community. So with these things in mind, let us focus on justice *and* love. They go together. Blessed. Give thanks."

Dr. Dennis Forsythe's Remarks

"Thank you, my brother, Luciano. Next we'll hear from Dennis Forsythe," I said after Luciano had finished and the applause had died down. "I met Dennis through his book, *Rastafari: For the Healing of the Nations*. Most of you know Dennis. He was a past professor at the

202

Gathering of the Healers

University of the West Indies and a practicing attorney when he became a Rasta and became a lightening rod for many Jamaicans who felt that wasn't appropriate for one of their leading citizens to do. That has manifested by his losing custody of his own child because he had been arrested for one spliff. He represents the individual pain that has come down on the heads of many people who chose this path."

"Thank you, my brother," Dennis said in a clear strong voice. "Greeting brothers and sisters. Greetings from the plain clothes Rastaman (applause). I give thanks to the Marley heritage for the theme and the inspiration for this gathering. I also give thanks to brother Mortimo Planno, to Morgan Heritage, my brother Denroy Morgan, and to all the brothers here, to Luciano, the mighty ambassador of love. I give thanks to all my brethren and sistren here. One Love! JAH Rastafari!

I pay particular and special tribute to my brother, Bob Ras Kind, and to his family for the energy and the inspiration for this gathering and also for his message. I see brother Bob as the twenty-first century wise man from America who has followed the light and the vibration of Brother Bob Marley's music to Jamaica to inquire into the tremendous transcending power and the source of Robert Nesta Marley's universal message. And from his journeys and travels, Brother Bob Ras Kind has written this penetrating book which I regard as describing the essence of Rastafari. The book is really showing that Rastafari exudes and embraces One Love in a truly holistic way and Brother Bob is also saying that this is the message which the world at large needs today and what Jamaica needs today. I give thanks to Brother Bob Ras Kind for that particular message. He is indeed a messenger (applause).

I share Brother Bob's vision because I myself have trod the particular pathway of Rastafari since I returned to Jamaica in 1977 and wrote my book, *Rastafari: For the Healing of the Nations* in 1984. Since then I have kept on traveling. I have kept on trodding and my unwritten book will be called *Trodding to Zion* because this untold story is a story of following the light of Rastafari into meditation, into self-analytic thinking, into self-application and applying those aspects of Rastafarian theory and practice which I see most plausible. And it also involves the Babylon reaction to my movements toward Zion.

I find that there is a remarkable convergence of ideas between Brother Ras Kind's findings and those of myself as contained in my book. Both of us followed the same kind of methodology, a methodology of reasoning with the brothers. And from our reasonings, I find that Brother Bob and myself have come out with a similar definition of Rastafari because he sees, and I see, in Brother Bob Marley the essence of Rastafari. He embodies the consciousness of Rastafari. Brother Bob has risen up to embody the ideals of this movement and I wish to impart the definition of Rastafari which has propelled me over the years. It is a definition of Rastafari which I see evidence in the findings of Brother Bob Ras Kind's book and I want I and I to penetrate this definition of Rastafari from the Marley heights so to speak. This is a definition of Rastafari from the Marley heights of consciousness. From his songs, from his life story, his life history, and from the lives of other Rastafarian brothers and sisters, I see Rastafari as multi-dimensional. It is a mystical, herbal, Biblical pathway leading one from one state, Babylon, to a higher state called Zion (applause).

It is a movement. It is a pathway to a higher level. That level is embodied in the mystical tradition of His Imperial Majesty, Selassie I, Rastafari. It includes Marcus Garvey and it includes all of the ancient mystics, great religious mystics, who have journeyed before us and shown us that life involves a movement from the lower to the higher levels of consciousness. Others call this the movement to the seventh level of consciousness. Any man or any woman who trods this particular pathway can never be an apostle of violence.

It's a movement inwards. It is a movement involving the use of herbs, not just ganja, herbs of all kinds. It is a movement in which one journeys inward in order to integrate mind, body and soul. It is a movement which is compelling in its own right. I wrote my book, *Rastafari: For the Healing of the Nations,* because I was overcome. I was caught by a spirit, the spirit of truth, to tell the story. I have discovered that by the use of the words of JAH as contained in the Bible, by the use of herbs of all different kinds, I was able to journey inwards. I was able to spend

Gathering of the Healers

hours and years journeying inwards as a way to link up with the Divine source of power within and I have no regrets (applause).

All of those elements are vital to comprehending the power of Robert Nesta Marley and of other Rastafarian elders and prophets. The mystic, herbal, Biblical pathway from one state, Babylon, to a higher state, Zion. That is the overriding definition, the power of Rastafari, that has propelled myself. However, because time does not permit, I need only to focus on one particular aspect, the herbal aspect because I find that in my movements and travels that is one of the most important elements within Rastafari and I see Brother Ras Kind's book picks up on that particular element.

Ganja is indeed a symbol of peace and love for Rastafari and also for the universal mystic church. There is a universal mystic church which ganja plays a preeminent role. Ganja is vitally important to heal the body, mind and soul. I personally have championed the cause of ganja legalization because of the role ganja has played in my life. I returned from being abroad in 1977 and I was a sick person in my mind, body and soul. Because of my lessons from Rastafari, today I'm a far cry from that marginalized and broken down individual that I was. I have mentally decolonized myself to a large extent through Bible teachings and the holistic effect of herbs on myself. For those people who see ganja in a negative way, I can say to them that you are misguided and you are backwards in your thinking. I say that you must stop using the process, the due process of law, to mash up people's lives and to kill the lamb.

I say to the people of Jamaica from this particular perspective of One Love, I say to you, 'Shame. Shame on you for harassing, criminalizing the young people and the older people of this country for personal usage of ganja.' I cry 'Shame!' from this Rasta perspective of One Love that the Jamaican authorities could have dealt such a shameful contempt toward me. For what reason? I can only say that the Establishment does not like the Rasta vibration in myself, within my movements. I have broken away from sterile academia. As a result they do not like the way in which my body exudes a new spirit, a new movement of love. That is why they were able to send the police to my house to arrest me for a

Gathering of the Healers

small portion of ganja, just a spliff. They arrested me. After reading my book, they then convicted me and labeled me a criminal and then I was pronounced in a high court action, the supreme court of Jamaica, pronounced an 'unrepentant drug addict.' Since then, for the last five years they have held this against me saying that I would not be a suitable parent for my child because I couldn't tell my child not to smoke ganja. As a result, I am not a fit and suitable father. This is a disgrace. This has denied me the right to apply righteous precepts to the upbringing of my own son. So I denounce Jamaica for being hypocritical.

The Honorable Robert Nesta Marley is our mentor, our hero, and to have ganja presently against the law and people denounced as criminals and treated in contempt, that is a situation that can no longer persist. So let me in conclusion take this opportunity again to thank my brethren, everyone here, one and all, for your presence and for your energy in adding a little element to the fire—the fire that needs to be ablaze and that is already ablaze through the songs particularly and to other like Brother Ras Kind. I say to you, 'One Love,' and I share my brethren's view of love.

Antonnette Haughton's Remarks

"Thank you, Dennis. As always I find your thinking inspiring," I said. "You know when you go out and talk to individuals or groups and say, 'I want to see if we can heal Jamaica with One Love,' you get a lot of reactions. One of the best experiences we had was when Scram and I started driving around the island from the Rebel Salute to Nine Mile to Kingston meeting with healers, was when we went to the UPP (United People's Party, a new Jamaican political party) office. I knew little about the UPP. We met with Grace, Horace, Betsy and other staff members and after explaining why we were there, much to our amazement it was the most enthusiastic welcome we had.

What you find out is that if people have been wondering their entire life how they could get love to expand on this planet, like many of us here have, if you go to that person and say, 'We've got a plan,' they

Gathering of the Healers

instantly respond positively. If they've given up the hope for it, you see that in their faces. If they've never even considered it, you see that in their faces. You quickly find out where they're at about whether One Love can work on the planet when you ask these kind of questions. We left the UPP offices feeling wonderful. They knew that Antonnette would accept our invitation. We then met with Antonnette a few days later and she did agree and after our meeting we took a walk through the streets of Kingston with her. We saw tremendous amount of love coming towards her from the people there and it was clear to me why so many Jamaicans had named her as a teacher of love. So with that in mind, Antonnette."

"I want to say to the elders, Kris, Mortimo Planno, that I grew up with Mortimo Planno as an elder and it really is an honor to just hail up the elders. My brother, Luciano, you powerful energy, speaking words of truth and wisdom and righteousness in our nation. I want to hail up brother my brother Ras Kind, his wife, family, that saw what I know of my people—that we are a very special people. We are a blessed people but I never thought of it as pressure creating diamonds before but I will remember that. I'll remember that because we really are a very special people and we are about reminding Jamaica that we are a very special people.

I carry to this process a female energy. An energy of healing, an energy of nurturing that women have been raised in from that time. I want to say that I feel particularly honored to be here. I'd just like to start with what the Father taught us how to pray as was said before, 'Forgive us our trespasses as we forgive those who trespass against us.' Our forgiveness is contingent upon our capacity to forgive and those of us who seek justice, must do justice. For God so loved the world that he offered all of us everlasting life.

You know, Nelson Mandela said it is not our darkness that we fear but rather our light—that we make our light so shine that we give permission to other people for their light to shine, too. That is such a powerful wisdom in this One Love energy that my brother has spoken. As my brother Luci said to him, I also said to him—we cannot seek forgiveness

Gathering of the Healers

or forgive those that ask for forgiveness with their lips. That we must do forgiveness because for me God is not a noun. God is a *verb*. God is a doing word. It's what we *do*. That's what counts. So that as Luci said, 'What walks with forgiveness is a need to atone.' 'Atone' comes from the concept of being 'at-one' with God. So as we seek forgiveness and as we give forgiveness, those who have done wrong must atone to seek that oneness with God (applause).

The Bible says 'Blessed are the peacemakers for they shall be called the children of God. Blessed are the poor in spirit for theirs is the kingdom of heaven.' We must come to the process with a broken and humble spirit. We must know that we really are not worthy. We are only worthy through God's grace, through God's infinite forgiveness, through God's infinite power. We, the people of Jamaica, know this. It is our life. Rastafari will present that life. I remember as a child, because I'm a country girl, so I come to town for Christmas, so I'm walking with my mother around parade and for some reason my mother always gets the place by the elder dreads and it was always, 'Peace and love, sister.' I remember this vividly. I was four and five and that is my first and vivid memory of Rastafari—men with beards and peaceful faces sitting in the park hailing 'Peace and love, sister.' So we repeat, 'Blessed are the peacemakers for they shall be called the children of JAH.'

Our nation needs to make a spiritual shift because today we fight against principalities and rulers of darkness. We have to put on the whole armor of God so we can be able to stand in these days. We must understand that this death and this worshipping of death, this mayhem, this bloodletting, is a part of the war against God's people. We must call One Love. We must know that every man and woman is capable of redemption. St. Paul was a murderer when God struck him down and blinded him to come and preach God's word. Moses was also a murderer when he was called to lead God's people. God is infinitely wise and offers all salvation. And true greatness is our capacity to forgive our enemies. *True greatness lies in our capacity to forgive our enemies* and to demand justice on behalf of the poor.

I want to stand behind this mike and just remind all of us because many of us have reached a place where we believe that government is

208

Gathering of the Healers

an evil thing. It is the devil's work. I want to just remind us that God called David to rule Israel when he was a boy and smelled of goats and he said, 'Me?' and God said, 'Yes.' God anointed David to rule Israel. And he spoke of righteous government. Righteous government takes care of the poor. Righteous government takes care of the widows and orphans. Righteous government is compassionate and caring government. Governance is not the devil's work. Do not let them fool us. When the children of Israel turned their backs on the teaching of their God, then Josiah became king and Josiah opened back the temples and started to read the scriptures, prosperity came to Israel. So we know what is right. We know in our hearts that there is righteous government. Our nation needs to make a spiritual shift. Our people need to remember that God gave us, every single last one of us, the power. He gave us the power to change our world. He gave us the power to change our lives. He gave us the power for healing. Jamaica does not need to be led as much as it needs to be loved. *Our nation needs to be loved.* Our people need to feel the power of love coming from those who they choose to lead them. We need to stop believing that government means evil. I ask tonight that we ask for reparations and we ask for justice and we give justice by being the best selves that we can be and the best selves we can be is the self that forgives, the self that heals, the self that serves, the self that Jesus taught us. Forgive your enemies. Do good to those that hate you and despitefully use you and abuse you. Pray for them. Your prayer, honestly given from your heart, asking to heal them, is the most powerful weapon in this war against principalities, power and the rulers of darkness.

I want to honor my brother. He came from elsewhere and he saw what we have forgotten—that we are an extraordinary, special and powerful and mystic people. The people who produced Bob Marley, the people who produced Robert Nesta Marley. We are an amazing people. That love that we have, we now need to turn inwards to heal the broken-hearted, the gunman, the terrorists, those that have never known love because many of the terrorists in our nation are terrorists because they have never been hugged. They have never been loved. They have never been valued and they don't know how. Let us teach them how to love by our lives.

This is not a voice of vengeance. This voice is to heal. On behalf of all the sisters in this country who raised their children against the odds and who loved their children and who loved their men, all the sisters that have stood up for their sons and their husbands, we, the women of this country, have never used our strength *against* our men. We've always used our strength in support of our men. I want to remind them that we love always our sons, always our men. We ask that we, our sisters, step up and be part of that powerful healing of this nation. That we continue to do what we always have done—to love and to support and to heal.

Ras Kind, this is a new time. This is a new energy. My nation is a giant that is just about to stretch and honor, as we honor our ancestors and our elders. Remember if we don't, we cannot leave a decent world for our descendents. So we stand on the shoulders of our ancestors and reach for a better way of life. We call the hypocrisy what it is. We commit ourselves to truth. Speak the truth and shame the devil. Let us not be afraid of the truth because God loved the truth and we, His people, must love and speak the truth too. 'If My people who are called by My name will humble themselves and seek My face, I will heal your nation.' We must humble ourselves because unless God builds the house we labor in vain.

I want to honor Rastafari. They are the manhood of my nation. I want to honor Howell and Pinnacle and every man that ever stood up in the face of being trimmed in the sixties—humiliated, abused. I want to say they represent the best of us. I want to say that we need to honor those that remain humble and righteous, that My people that are called by My name will humble themselves and seek My face, I will heal thy nation.

This nation is waiting to be healed. The ball, my brothers and sisters, is in our court. We need to stretch our hand. We need to call forth to the Almighty God because He makes no promises He does not keep (applause). It is One Love, One Heart, One Aim, One God, One Destiny (applause).

Gathering of the Healers

Abijah's Remarks

"Thank you, my sister. One thing that struck me as Antonnette was talking," I said after Antonnette finished, "was that we are not a large group but we are a powerful group. What we are saying tonight here will go out unto the world. When I started asking people who they felt love from in this culture, many names I recognized—Luciano, Tony Rebel, Morgan Heritage, Antonnette Haughton—but all of a sudden a new name came up that I had never heard before. That was Abijah (applause). And I heard it over and over again to the point I couldn't ignore it so I called his manager, Albert Ramsay, a very open-hearted individual, and during our conversation at one point he said, 'You know, Abijah is not a Rasta.' And I said, 'Well, he's a teacher of love isn't he?' and Albert said, 'Yes' and I said, 'Then to me he's a Rasta. This is about One Love.' Abijah, I'm delighted that you've accepted our invitation. You're the youngest person up here tonight. I think you can speak best to your generation. Thank you for coming."

"It is a privilege for me to be here tonight," Abijah said taking the speaker's chair. "I want to say 'Respect to the elders, much respect.' It is an honor for me to be up here and represent things that I know that we need to hear. The fact is, I know that we're from different religions but we are one. The Almighty is one and he expects us to be one. He is not divided (applause). He expects us to be one.

Last night I was thinking just what I could say about love and I remember a situation came up a couple of years ago, a few days after Hurricane Gilbert. I was living with my father then. My father plays with the Mystic Revelation of Rastafari Band but he had an accident and he couldn't move around that well and Gilbert made us feel very rough. We were very, very poor—living in zinc house, real ghetto stuff and everything blown down, you know. I remember we didn't hear from anybody at all. Nobody call us until one day I saw he got a letter from a far friend that was all the way in Germany that had seen him perform there with the band. The letter said, 'How is it, Brother Winston? I heard that Gilbert struck and I hope that you are fine.' It was the first time I ever saw my father cry. It real shook me that much that I run out of the room where he was. I stayed outside and peeped in because I thought, *man no cry*. That not supposed to happen—especially if it's your father. And then I realized how much giving is important.

Love is not just words. Love is action and I wrote four simple points this evening. L.O.V.E., a four letter word, that is often misinterpreted or misunderstood. I start with 'L' because we should learn the way of life, not thinking love is found in a sexual relationship only or that love is a type of feeling. But rather love is more action than words that captivate the heart of every living being in JAH's creation.

And I go to 'O' and I say, 'OH,' this will be a revelation,' (Applause, laughter. This is the opening words from his popular song, 'Revelation.') 'O' for overstanding, you know. If we don't wake up and realize that this misinterpretation of love is affecting our children and our environment. You see, often times we think that it's to our convenience when we point a finger, we blame, and be ashamed of things we think we could have done better. You know, I say this because I have a two-year-old daughter. Sometimes I think, *What if I couldn't bring home something for her to eat*. But yet I would love upon her and throw her up in the air. Would I still be loving her? I think, no, because I should go out and find a way to provide for her. So it's really out of *action* that we can demonstrate love rather than sitting down. I'm not saying you don't feel the love for her even if you can't provide, a lot of people are in that circumstance where they can't. Guess what. You have to do something.

And I go to 'V,' which stands for 'victory.' It's found in ways of those who search for it, those who work toward goals, toward unity, embracing goals that were given to us by our forefathers, great legends such as Bob Marley, Marcus Garvey, and the list goes on because victory is found with love.

And 'E' is enjoying and appreciating everything that the Father has given to us; not taking anything for granted but rather seeing that we need each other to be a winner. We should look and learn from the things around us such as the birds, the ants and the plants. They have one thing in common—they all work together. You know, at my house I have a lot of pets. I grew up with pets. I raised rabbits, guinea pigs.

Gathering of the Healers

Right now I have some turtles, you know (laughter). I just got some new creatures and the other day a sister came and she said, 'I just saw something under the corner of your house, man. It was a rat.' And I say, 'No, man, those were hamsters and gerbils,' (laughter). But I appreciate them. You know why? I sit and learn from them. I sit and learn from the animals because I've never seen them fight against one another.

Sometimes I feel like we have so much that we can take for granted, you know. We can see, smell, hear, taste, be creative, write good songs and sometimes we turn those good songs into negative songs and our children become a product of it. So that's why I believe that we have a great responsibility on our shoulders to lead our people to victory with the things that we say, the things that we do. The other day I was standing in the line downtown and some people say, 'Abijah, we like your music and we like Luciano and we like Morgan Heritage but we just can't listen to the radio any more. Because every time I turn on the radio I hear about bumping on de woman and this and that.'

It's sad. It's sad but it's true. It is true and each of us have to take responsibility because sometimes we come across people who write these songs and we can say something. We don't have to be negative or discouraging because it's all talent. It's just how they use it and sometimes the way we grow up can affect us and we can become products of society. So if you can just say one thing that is positive to each other it can make a difference in this world of disorder. It can make a difference in that entertainer's life, you know.

My wife always complains about me playing loud music in the morning. This one song I put on repeat, repeat, repeat from the New Day album, 'No Nights in Zion.' To me it's a song that can make me meditate, a song that fills me up and makes me feel closer to JAH—closer to the Almighty. People search in different ways and I can strongly say that it is sad to see so much church in Jamaica and there is so much crime. But also it is sad to see so much Rastas, so much different religions, and there's still crime. That means that everyone of us will have to stand and take responsibility and make a difference. We are not here to point fingers. We're here to talk about love, where to find solutions. And the only way we can do that is to look within ourselves.

213

Gathering of the Healers

Whether you're a Christian, you're a Rastaman, you're a Buddhist, I don't really know them. Sorry. Whatever. I believe that we should take responsibility within ourselves as our brother Luciano said earlier and learn from the things around us. Learn from the ants. Learn from them. Check it. Check their level. Don't you think that there's so much birds in the world that they could just peck us and kill us off but they're not doing that. They're living love. They're living harmony. They're living together. They fly together. Even the fish. I watch Discovery Channel and even the fish change course together. That's unity. That's why they're strong so when a predator come on them they can win. You see there is no miracle greater than love. It is God's most precious gift to us. It is not a feeling. It is a daily decision. JAH bless (applause)."

Denroy Morgan's Remarks

"Thank you, Abijah," I said. "I can certainly see why I heard your name so often. Now let's hear from our final speaker Denroy Morgan. Denroy is the founder of Morgan Heritage, an internationally acclaimed reggae group, formed with five of his 29 children. It's appropriate that Denroy was last as he was the first of our speakers to agree to join us. I've met several of his children and it's also clear to me why people have mentioned him repeatedly as a teacher of love."

"First I would like to say, Greetings in the Lord and Savior Jesus the Christ and Emperor Haile Selassie I, the first. Without doubt, he's the King of all Kings. He's the Lord of all Lords and he is the Conquering Lion of the Tribe of Judah and he says that with faith and courage and a just cause and this day David will slay Goliath (applause).

I am not here to big up any one. I am here to strengthen the calling of the ancient Israelite, of the true Christ-like people and the *real* Rastafarian. The time has come for the Messianic fulfillment to manifest in the earth. What we are here presenting to the world is something that for thousands of years has not seemed humanly possible: that we can achieve justice and equality for all by the way of love. Because

Gathering of the Healers

when we study our history as Israelites, we have always had to fight with people for our rights. We had to fight the Amarites, the Cannonites, the Jephesites, the Havites, the parasites and all the other 'ites.'

And when the Ark of the Covenant was with us, we beat them all. The Ark of the Covenant represents the presence of the living god of Abraham, Issac and Israel. And we as a people, I'm referencing to the Rastafarian community, need to take a look within ourselves and see how many of us can say that God is with us and we are with him. A lot of times I find where I see the action of our people indicates that God is with us but we were with ourselves.

Now we need to understand that the time has come for us to live that sacrificial life—the life that prepares us for the kingdom of God on earth. Thy kingdom come on earth as it is on heaven. The kingdom of God on earth will be ruled by man in the *flesh*. The kingdom in heaven will be ruled by the Almighty and the celestial beings. We understand that the Rasta community has appeared divided to the people of the world but I can testify to you that we are *not* divided. We are *united*. We are united around the divinity of His Imperial Majesty, Emperor Haile Selassie I, the First.

We could be hypocritical and be like the churches and come together in our differences for one purpose: to not pay taxes to our government and to act like we are united and we are so divided. We come as Baptist and Presbyterian and Anglican and the minute we finish what we are about, that day we go back in our own shell. Well, I am appealing to the Bobo Shanti. I'm appealing to the Twelve Tribes of Israel. I'm appealing to the House of the Nyabinghi and I am appealing to the Ethiopian World Federation and the Ethiopian Orthodox Coptic Church of North and South America, to put away our differences and let the love begin from within our house.

Charity begins at home and you cannot give anything to anyone that you do not have unless you are a thief (applause). So for sure the word 'One Love' came from the mouth of a Rastaman. We are proud to say he was a Jamaican but he defended Ethiopia, the home of the true Christian teachings. We cannot allow time to run out on us where we are waiting to let the word of Rastafari present to the world by articulate

215

Gathering of the Healers

people, people who are educated and it may come from the Roman Empire and they will be ready to accept it.

I want to recognize a couple of elders in the house tonight that may not have been mentioned. From the Nyabinghi house, Anthony Ras Witter. He's here with us (applause). He's the artist that did this work on the wall over here. JAH Rastafari! He also has a testimony. It may not come in a book but it is in his heart. I want to recognize our beloved elder, Brother Mortimo Planner (applause). And had Brother Planner not been here tonight, my presence would not have been here but I spoke to Brother Robert and he listened to the voice. I say, 'You come to St. Thomas to see *me*, all the way from Kingston and Brother Planner is at the University and you haven't gone to see *him*.' I said, 'Do you know who he is?' He said, 'Yes. I read about him. I read about him in the history.' I said, 'You read about him and you have not sought him out for this mission that you are on here in Jamaica?' and I said, 'Well, I'm asking you if you want my presence go and seek him and don't call him on the telephone.'

Robert called me this morning and said, 'Can you give me Planner's number?' and I said, 'You are in Kingston. He is in Kingston. Drive and see him and then you can call and tell me what happened.' Next call I got from him, he was with Brother Planner. I spoke to Brother Planner and the elder told me to be here and I heard the voice of the living God. So I'm here (applause, shouts of 'JAH Rastafari!').

A lot of the young brothers and sisters here may not know that Brother Planner is the Rastaman that His Imperial Majesty Haile Selassie spoke to directly and asked him to speak to the people of Jamaica. The Jamaican government *knows* why Planner is at the University. JAH Rastafari!! The government of Jamaica *knows* the oppression that has been on the face of the Rastaman over the years. It's about time we ease up and bring about the freedom that we can have economical strength in this country; that we can be a symbol of the Royal Black House of David, showing the world that we are here to restore the tabernacle of David by the way of the Solomonic Dynasty upon that covenant that the Almighty made with David, that as long as there is a sun and a moon there must be one in the flesh to rule upon the

Gathering of the Healers

throne of David, which is the ruling kingdom of this planet in the universe (applause).

For sure the leaders of religion may not like what I have to say but I don't care about that. The truth shall set us free and I know a lot of them know the truth. When they read about the Lion of Judah in Revelations, they make it seem like they're talking about Jesus Christ in His first advent. Revelations is a prophesy that was written *after* the crucifixion so how could the prophesy become history? His Majesty Emperor Haile Selassie I, is the redeeming force in the earth. He *is* the Messiah—without doubt and apology of the time. He has called so many people from different walks of life. From different nations and he has never had to go out as statesman, as a politician, or as a priest or as a prophet to solicit anyone to his divinity. JAH Rastafari!

Many people want to know what is the magic of Bob Marley? Emperor Haile Selassie I the first, the vibration of Ras Tafari is cleaving to the vibration of the Rastaman—the positive vibration (applause). There are only two vibes on the earth, positive and negative. It is assured that the true vibration of the Rastaman is a positive vibration. It has to be from the oath of the Almighty God of Israel. JAH Rastafari!

I am not ashamed to be a Rastaman. Neither am I ashamed to be a Christ-like man. I am not ashamed of being an ancient Israelite. How is that so? The time has come when the children of the lamb must be united with the children of the lion. The children of the lamb are those that are called by the Messianic calling, by the way of Yashuah the Messiah, who has been presented to the world as the name Jesus Christ and the language of English as it traveled though the journey from Hebrew to Greek and Latin to English. We accept it and we understand that word remained one and the same—the power of the living God. The manifestation of God is in flesh, JAH Rastafari! And we understand that God is not a name for the Almighty. It is a title and we who are like unto him wear that title. JAH Rastafari!

I want to thank Brother Robert. I know that I was supposed to be a five-minute thing (laughter). I would like to say more but I just want to thank you for coming and strengthening the inspiration of the Rastaman. Many dreadlock Rastas oppose Morgan Heritage for the

217

Gathering of the Healers

light that came through them that 'you don't have to dread to be Rasta' and I have seen where many man without hair on the head has been ridiculed and for sure you're a baldhead Jew (laughter). Blessed art thou, my brother. You brought a message to me at my home in St. Thomas. I know that you know the Torah and know you may also know the Kabbala, and since you are a former hippie, I know you know the power of love and I see dread on you even though you have none on (laughter). You said to me that the teaching is that in the days to come, which is now, every man should be his own messiah and that was what God put in you to give to me. I believe that God could have sent a dove to feed Elijah but he chose to send a raven and I did not look at you by your hair. I looked at you by your vibration. It was positive. JAH Rastafari! So I thank you for that.

The Messiah is one who redeems us from our sinful, natural ways to the ways of God— the ways that will uplift our souls and allow us to live a life that will shine a light that man will seek and glorify the Almighty Creator of the Universe. As we are here to strengthen the work of the Rastaman, the work of Bob Marley, the words of the Rastaman, the word 'One Love,' and we believe that if every man possessed that One Love, I'm not talking about hypocritical love. I'm not talking about carnal love. I'm not talking about partial love. *I'm talking about Divine love.* JAH Rastafari! The sacrificial one. Glory to the Almighty. If we possess that, then we'll be able to give that and share that and if we can share that Divine love, one unto another, we'll definitely bring about a healing to the nation.

And the healing of the nation is not just a Jamaican thing, it's a *world* thing because the entire world is in turmoil today. We talk about crime in Jamaica. Crime is in Israel. People are getting killed while they're having a good time in Israel. Jerusalem is supposed to be the land of holiness. We're talking about what's happening in Jamaica, look at what's happening in Sudan, what's happening in Palestine, in Afghanistan. They're trying to set India and Pakistan to war over nuclear power. JAH Rastafari!

Brothers and sisters, take a look around. Take a look into yourself, find your own love and share it with your neighbor. For these few

Gathering of the Healers

words, I give thanks.

The press conference took almost three hours, with the day slowly and gently turning to night. After Denroy's address, Red asked me if he could close with one of his songs. I had known Red for a year, heard his songs and knew he would take us to a good place so I invited him up to sing. Red was a perfect close to an amazing evening. His song, accompanied by Luciano on the guitar, was lively and upbeat and he sang it with such passion that soon everyone was on their feet singing and clapping with him, even the press and audio/video people. We had all just listened to hours of reasoning from people who had devoted much of their life to expanding love on the planet. There was little ego from the speakers and no sense of competition with everyone having a sincere respect for each other and feeling unified in a common goal. The healers had shared their individual views of One Love, and when combined together, like facets of a diamond, created a precious gem.

The feelings were intense and joyous. Something special had just occurred, some vibration had begun that *would* go out into the world and we all could sense it. A number of people had tears in their eyes. I felt almost overcome with a mixture of satisfaction, gratitude, hope and relief. At that point I really didn't care what happened next in regards to visible results. We had all come together and invited the island, the world, to join us in One Love. That act stood alone—complete and perfect.

Not wanting to leave the energy, everyone stayed around for an hour afterwards until the people from the museum said they needed to close. We took pictures together, talked, hugged and generally just enjoyed the vibes. Muta came out from his back-row seat and warmly greeted everyone, most of whom were longtime friends. With hugs and thanks to everyone, Julia, Alicia, Scram, Bell and I headed back to the Terra Nova.

"Every morning we get up an war wit' de animals an' try to murder dem an' eat dem. You are eatin' de pets of de eart'. You cayn't put your knife and fork in my flesh an' tell me dat you love me."
—Anthony Ras Witter

Chapter 13
February 4, 2002

Reasoning into the Night

B ack at the hotel a group of us gathered around the deserted pool area. It was now about eleven and everyone was still in great moods. Scram, Julia, Bell and I were together at one end of the table with Ras Witter (who had warmed to us after the conference), a friend of his and the cook from the Queen of Sheba next to him. At the other end was Errol, Red, Bongo Roach, and Panner, a friend of theirs from Negril. We sat together reasoning for hours.

"Tell me how this whole Rastafari thing started back in the 1930s," I asked Red, who in his late seventies was a Rasta elder and knew many of the original Rastas. "Were they preaching in churches, writing books, preaching on street corners?"

"When I was a yout'," Red said, "if a Rastamon was preaching when de cops are comin' you bettah leave like a bullet. You couldn't preach about Rasta when I was a yout'. Rasta was an outcast in dos days. Dere was nowhere to live. No one employ you. You doan't 'ave a womon. You doan't 'ave no family. But dat 'as changed now."

"De first Rasta daughter dat exist amongst de Rastas," Ras Witter

Gathering of the Healers

added, "was a womon named Sis. She lived in Back-A-Wall (an area of the Kingston ghetto). She lived dere for quite awhile before other daughters came around."

"I'd love to know her story," Julia said. "Is she alive? Does anyone know her story?"

"She died in 1995," Ras Witter said. "But I knew her personally."

"Did she have a strong love of JAH?" Julia asked.

"She 'ad de original knowledge of de King of Kings," Red answered. "She and Sister Ivy and Sister Miriam. Dey were all empresses, daughters of Zion, trodding t'ru de Nyabinghi order. Dat was in de beginnin' when Rasta preached from sidewalk wit' a little box an' t'ing. Babylon would come an' mash all dos boxes and t'ings, you know. Dese daughters will tell de bredren when de police come."

By now everyone is cracking up at full Jamaican volume.

"Hear me now," Ras Witter said taking the floor back, "Politics is a mortal game come to mortal people. It take a lot of blood, dis game. De most blood runnin' is in dese times. Dese are de times of de endin' of dese evil forces."

"Yes. Babylon is very weak now," I added. "Twenty years ago if Rastas were sitting around this pool at this hotel smoking a spliff, you'd be in jail."

"We'd be *dead*," Red said.

"What we are enjoyin' 'ere now is a fraction of what we 'ave already won," Ras Witter said. "Our ganja is still leavin' de island. It moves on high level, medium level and low level. Medium level an' low level, de police an' coast guard dey stop dat. High level never stop becuz dey pay de police and politicians. You 'ave an airbase in Jamaica, private airbase, dat take ganja and fly away. An' de wharves are under de private sector and 80 ships come every month. An' dey bring in de cocaine and guns an' take out de ganja. Dat is why dere is so much killin' in Jamaica. Dey come wit' cocaine an' leave wit' ganja. All de yout' are gettin' hooked on cocaine. De cocaine an' de meat eatin' toget'er attack de body an' de brain—two evils." (It is believed that most of the guns and cocaine are coming from the U.S.)

"And they never get busted?" I asked.

221

Gathering of the Healers

"Who would bust dem is de ones dat protect dem," Ras Witter replied. "Dey are untouchable. Mission impossible. De best herb in Jamaica, we cayn't get it. It all goes to America. When I am in New York, I cayn get it. One seed sell fe three 'undred Jamaican."

"When I was a hippie, everyone wanted Jamaican weed," I said.

"An when de hippies came to Negril in de seventies," Red said, "even if dey didn't 'ave no money, my mudder would feed dem an' let dem sleep in our yard. It was like a big family den. Dere was no 'otels, only a few restaurants. It was a small fishin' village."

"And de government said dat de Rastas were evil," Ras Witter said. "De philosophy got mixed up so bad dat dey say de Rasta was a hater. But if we represent Christ, we are de immortal sons of de Almighty who come to set a principle between right and wrong an' spread dat gospel of love. Our duty is to get people to prepare for de shift. Love is de name of de constitution dat dis creation run upon—made by de Fat'er. Evert'ing abide in love. It is like a womon. Anyt'ing dat you cayn do, she cayn do more becuz she 'as de power to multiply. Love or 'ate, she cayn multiply. A mon must 'ave dat blueprint of life in 'is house, de woman an' de children, or 'e's not balanced. An' some pets in de 'ouse, too. An' de center you provide around dese three t'ings, is you should make dem love you. Dat is de basic blueprint of de entirety of love. Love is cut short becuz it fail to engulf de universal familyhood of nature."

"Yes, I," Red said in agreement.

"How did the idea of not eating meat come into the movement?" I asked.

"The idea of an Ital life came t'ru de Bible," Ras Witter responded, "De study of Genesis bring man to what is Ital. All herb shall be for food, for everyone, even de animals."

Ras Witter's Biblical reference is correct. In Genesis 1:29, the first thing God said after creating the universe, the earth and Eve and Adam was: "I give you every seed-bearing plant on the face of the whole earth and every tree that has fruit with seed in it. They will be yours for food. And to all the beasts of the earth and to all the birds of the air and all the creatures that move on the ground—everything that has breath of life in

222

Gathering of the Healers

it—I give every green plant for food."

"So as the early Rastafarians closely studied the Bible and were willing to live by what it said, they naturally became vegetarians?" I asked.

"Yes," Ras Witter continued. "De ancient Rastamon would nah kill a goat, a chicken, a pig. Automatically your eatin' 'abits changed. Everyt'ing about you changed. Noah did nah eat meat. De Fat'er dat choose Noah chose a vegetarian or dey would 'ave eaten all de animals on de ark," he said and we all cracked up laughing.

"De Fat'er put a vegetarian amongst de animals," Ras Witter continued. "Every morning we nah get up an war wit' de animals an' try to murder dem an' eat dem. No mon should steal any blood to get a meal. You are eatin' de pets of de eart'. You cayn't put your knife and fork in my flesh an' tell me dat you love me. You kill de goat and call it mutton. You kill de baby calf an' call it veal. You kill de chicken an' call it fowl. You kill de cow an' call 'im beef. De meat is attackin' de lower bowels an' now dey put pork in everyt'ing as a preservative, even in candy, cakes. De crime dat is on de earth right now is all caused by de murdering of de animals becuz de animals give praises to de Most 'Igh. But de pastors in churches dey doan't say not'ing 'bout dat."

"De churches nah say not'ing 'bout de killin' of de animals," Red interjected. "De Ten Commandments say 'Thou shall not kill.' It does not say, 'Thou shall not kill *humans.*' It means thou shall not kill any animal—not cow, not goat, not fish, not shrimp, not pig.

"Man only took 'imself out of dat commandment and it backlash on us becuz we keep breakin' de commandment. Dis is de order of love," Ras Witter said. "When de Fat'er say we 'ave dominion over de animals, it is not to kill de dumb animal. Not so. Each animal is linked to a certain cycle in de universe, like people linked to plants. When we disturb dese cycles, you disturb de whole universal concept of love becuz love is de preservation of de creation. Simple. De way you preserve it is to make everyt'ing to 'ave a chance to live. An' when you eat de animal, de carcass, dere are a lot of side effects dat come in, a different level of energy. Dis is 'simple murder,' when you kill de animals. An' when people start to fight wit' each o'ter, it's becuz of de blood dat dem eat. De blood dat you eat causing de fight becuz you are mixin' your spirit wit' de animal's in your temple, in your body. De butcher shop 'ave a lot of hate expressing becuz you are goin' dere to buy a carcass of a dead animal to keep you on your diet. All de t'ings dat you get out of meat, you cayn get out of plants, de same vitamins an' protein. So if you want to get dis from de bush an' de grains dat de cow eat, you eat dem an' not de cow. Each an' every living t'ing 'ave a life span. Babylon tell you dat eatin' meat, you will live to three score and ten—70 years. Dat is why dey call it a 'diet' becuz it makes you die. You see Babylon doan't 'ide anyt'ing from you. But you cayn live much longer den dat as a vegetarian. Dat is why de Fat'er make the plants first so dat man and animal would 'ave dem to eat."

"I once read," I said, "that all animals were once vegetarians until humans started killing and eating them and that put out the vibration of killing on the planet."

"Is true, mon," Ras Witter replied. "And de alligator is de worst. Dat is why Babylon put de alligator on Jamaica's national coat of arms. You cayn't 'ave peace an' an alligator. De alligator 'as no mercy an' it is a merciless government dat rulin' Jamaica right now. Babylon doan't 'ide not'ing. An' dere is a mon and a womon on de coat or arms, naked. An' de mon 'as no spear, he 'as a bow but no arrows. Dere are no arrows in 'is arrow pouch—empty. An' de womon 'as a basket of food an' de alligator is over dis basket. So de mon caynnot protect de womon or 'imself an' dat is de way it is in Jamaica even until today. Babylon make it so dat our mon caynnot protect 'imself or 'is family. A coat of arms supposed to show you 'ow well your country protect you but not 'ere. It shows you 'ow weak we are. An' it says 'Out of Many-One People.' It should say, 'Out of One People-Many.' An' dere are five pineapples on the coat of arms becuz de people get de rough skin on de outside and de politicians get de sweet fruit on de inside."

"You dig your grave with your fork," Red said.

Eating Ital

Eating ital is important for our health, for our mind and spirit, for the animals and for the future of the planet. Also, I can testify to this, in the

Gathering of the Healers

first nine months that Julia and I ate a meatless mostly Ital diet we lost more than 60 pounds combined. I have reduced my blood pressure medicine to 30 percent if its previous dose. All my previous lower back pain and occasional hip pain are gone. We feel and look much better.

To put our "normal" western diets in perspective we must view our present attitudes concerning eating meat, eggs and dairy products in the same way we must view our previous attitudes regarding alcohol and ganja. Just as the powerful alcohol and tobacco industries have spent billions of dollars convincing the public, and millions more lobbying politicians, that their products are the wise alternatives to marijuana, so has the meat, egg and dairy industries, the "saturated fat industry," spent billions "educating" us that their products are safe, healthy and a must in every diet. In many countries, the saturated fat industry has become the nation's de facto nutrition educator. In the U.S., the dairy, egg and meat industries supply million of "educational pamphlets" to the nation's public schools convincing us at a very young age that eating their products is essential for good health. Almost no scientific evidence now supports this core assumption and most evidence refutes it.

Many people believe that humans are natural carnivores (meat eaters), not herbivores (vegetarians). Let's look at the facts. Carnivores have several things in common. All have claws, sharp front teeth for tearing with no flat molars for grinding. They have no skin pores and perspire through their tongues. Also, carnivores have short, relatively smooth intestinal tracks (three times their body length) so that rapidly decaying meat can pass through quickly. Humans have none of these. Our greatly convoluted and textured intestinal tracts are 10 to 12 times our body lengths with infinite cavities where meat can lodge and putrefy. Our stomach acid is 20 times weaker than meat eaters causing incomplete digestion of animal products. Unlike carnivores, we have salivary glands in our mouths that pre-digest grains and fruits and we have an alkaline saliva with ptyalin to predigest grains. Carnivores have acidic saliva with no ptyalin.

The American Dietetic Association (ADA) states "most of mankind for most of human history has lived on vegetarian or near-vegetarian diets." Today both the ADA and the U.S. Department of Agriculture

Gathering of the Healers

(among many others) strongly encourage a vegetarian diet. Quite simply, the human body was not designed to be carnivorous and eating animal products makes us unhealthy.

In addition to the toxic property of meat, eggs and dairy products themselves, we also ingest tremendous amounts of hormones, tranquilizers, antibiotics, pesticides and dangerous chemicals that are injected directly into the animals or added to their feed. Recent studies show that almost 90 percent of all toxic chemical residues in the American diet come from meat, fish, dairy products and eggs. This is even true of shellfish, such as oysters, clams, muscles, scallops and other mollusks, that filter polluted water. The American Medical Association (AMA) recently passed a resolution opposing the feeding of medically important antibiotics to livestock because it poses a serious human health threat by creating resistant bacteria.

The United States, home of the most sophisticated medical technology and best-trained doctors in the world, also has one of the lowest life expectancies of the industrialized nations. It is also one of the highest consumers of meat and animal products in the world. Only a handful of the world's medical schools give our future doctors much information in nutrition and the effect on diet and health. Most give almost none.

We have been so brainwashed as consumers that the first thing that comes to mind when we consider being a vegetarian is, *How will I get the needed protein without animal products?* Almost every food contains protein and meat is only a mediocre source of protein at best. The average American consumes eight times the amount of protein needed. Only 2.5 to 10 percent of the calories consumed by the average human need to be in the form of protein. Unless you eat almost all junk food, it is almost impossible not to get the protein you need. There is no nutritional need for humans to eat any animal products. All of our dietary needs, even as infants and children, are best supplied by an animal-free diet.

Let's take a scientific look at the statistics linking the consumption of animal products to our health. Meat eaters are 60 percent more likely to die of cancer, twice as likely to die from heart disease and 30 percent more likely to die of other diseases. Studies have shown that vegetarians have stronger immune systems than meat eaters. We have become convinced that strokes, heart disease and heart attacks are almost an inevitable byproduct of growing old. They are not. For every one percent increase in the amount of cholesterol in your blood, there is a two percent increase in your risk of having a heart attack. Every one percent reduction reduces risk two percent. Elevated cholesterol, anything over 150, promotes atherosclerosis, the buildup of cholesterol, fat, and cells in the arteries that feed the heart muscles.

In 1984, the United States Federal Government released the results of the broadest and most expensive research project in medical history to date. It concluded that the research "... strongly indicates that the more you lower cholesterol and fat in your diet, the more you reduce the risk of heart disease."

According to *The Journal of the American Medical Association*, a vegetarian diet can prevent 97 percent of coronary occlusions. One of the largest studies of lifestyle and health found the heart disease mortality rates for lacto-ovo vegetarians (those eating egg and dairy products) to be only one-third that of meat eaters; for vegans (those eating no animal products), the figure was one-tenth. Studies show that over 90 percent of former meat eaters that switch to a vegetarian diet report that it increases their energy, vitality and overall feeling of well-being.

Another myth is that as people age, they need greater amounts of calcium to ward off osteoporosis, a condition that causes one out of four women to lose up to half their bone density by age 65. The dairy industry would have us believe that the obvious solution to this problem is to eat more dairy products which are high in calcium. What they do not say is that this added intake of dairy products actually worsens osteoporosis by leaving a negative calcium balance. High-protein foods, such as meat, eggs, and dairy products, leach calcium from the body as excess protein is processed by the liver and passed through the kidneys, making the kidneys work harder and causing the loss of minerals such as calcium.

The good news is that switching to a vegetarian diet can often reverse health problems created by years of meat-eating. The famous diet and health expert, Dr. Dean Ornish, author of the bestselling *Dr. Dean*

227

Gathering of the Healers

Ornish's Program for Reversing Heart Disease: The Only System Scientifically Proven to Reverse Heart Disease Without Drugs or Surgery, demonstrated that this process can be reversed in his 1990 study of patients with advanced heart disease. The plaque that had been growing in their hearts for decades actually started to dissolve within one year of adhering to a low-fat diet.

The link between meat-eating and cancer is also scientifically proven. There is not a single population in the world with a high meat intake which does not also have a high rate of colon cancer. The meat is literally putrefying and decaying in your colon. Meat, eggs and dairy products also have no fiber, which acts like a broom in your intestines sweeping things along. The high fiber content of a vegetarian diet also helps "wash away" excess cholesterol in your digestive tract. Even the digestion of meat itself produces strong carcinogenic substances in the colon as well as extensive bile acids.

It takes only three or four hours to digest vegetables, fruit and grains but 18 to 24 to digest meat. So if you even eat meat once a day your body's digestive system is always working. If you've been eating meat your whole life your body probably has been continuously digesting since you were weaned. Your body has never rested and it can only really heal when it's resting. When it doesn't rest properly, we get sick.

It is also now known that breast cancer is directly related to fat intake. The National Cancer Research Institute in Tokyo monitored 122,000 people for decades. The results of this study were that those who consume meat daily face an almost four times greater risk of breast cancer than those who ate little or no meat. Similarly, the more eggs, butter and cheese consumed, the greater the risk of breast cancer.

Even diabetes, which is reaching epidemic proportions in the U.S. where 16 million people or 6 percent of the population now suffer with this disease, is tied to meat, dairy and egg consumption. It is even worse in Finland which has both the highest rate of diabetes in the world and the highest rate of milk and cheese consumption. In 1992 the New England Journal Of Medicine reported, "Studies in animals have suggested that bovine serum albumin is the milk protein responsible for the onset of diabetes." Recently, *Preventive Medicine* reported that blood

228

sugar levels declined on a vegan diet, "despite decreased medication use."

Another health problem that is reaching epidemic proportions in industrialized countries is allergies, especially asthma. Over 3 percent of all Americans now have asthma, many of them children under 10. Many children are having to get their ears surgically drained for mucous buildup. Millions more suffer from periodic sinus problems. One cause for allergies being so prevalent in children is that their bodies have not yet adapted to assimilating the poisons in their environment and especially in their diets.

Almost all research on the causes of allergies now points to animal protein as playing a major role. Milk especially is known to be a common pathogen for asthma. For instance, many babies break out in painful eczema if they ingest cow's milk as their bodies use the skin as an organ of elimination. Like many allergies, their condition clears up if animal products, especially dairy products, are removed from their diets. Even chronic asthma sufferers have been cured by switching to a pure vegetarian diet.

Early onset puberty is now linked to the intake of meat, dairy and egg products. The average American now consumes 666 pounds of dairy products per year. These products are laced with bioactive hormones (59 in cow's milk alone) such as pop estrogen, progesterone and prolactin. These hormones work on a nanomolecular level, which means that it takes only a billionth of a gram to produce a powerful biological effect.

In addition to this evidence, there is now conclusive scientific evidence that eating meat, eggs and dairy products causes or contributes to a host of other diseases and ailments. These include cancer of the cervix, uterus, ovaries and prostate, hypoglycemia, multiple sclerosis, ulcers, constipation and other intestinal problems, hemorrhoids, obesity, arthritis, gout, kidney stones, gallstones, high blood pressure, and anemia.

In addition to the problems associated with too much fat, cholesterol, and protein, consumers of animal products take in far greater amounts of residual agricultural chemicals, industrial pollutants, antibiotics and hormones than do vegetarians. The absorption of antibiotics through meat-eating results in antibiotic-resistant strains of pneumonia, childhood meningitis, gonorrhea, salmonella, and other serious illnesses. Dairy products are also the leading cause of food allergies and have been implicated in neonatal tetany, tonsil enlargement, ulcerative colitis, Hodgkin's disease, and respiratory, skin, gastrointestinal and behavioral problems.

Approximately 9,000 Americans die annually from food-borne illness and an estimated 80 million others fall ill. Meat contains 14 times as much pesticide residue as plant foods; dairy products, more than five times as many. Fish is another source of dangerous residues. The EPA estimates that fish can accumulate up to nine million times the level of cancer-causing polychlorinated biphenals (PCBs) found in the water in which they live. Ninety-five percent of human exposure to dioxin, a "probable" cause of cancer and other health risks, comes through meat, fish, and dairy consumption.

Around one in the morning the reasoning ended. The last image was an endearing one. Alec, Bongo Roach, Errol, Panner and Red (the Negril contingent) all decided to get a few hours sleep on the floor of Scram and Bell's (the Port Antonio contingent) hotel room. The next morning Scram said they all laid together talking in the dark for several hours—six Rasta elders and a fourteen year-old kid from Virginia. I only wished I could have recorded those conversations.

Everyone woke up late the next morning and by the time we all met around the pool, the Negril group had already headed back. Julia, Alicia, Scram, Bell and I went over to the New Chinatown for lunch. We were all in great moods and after lunch we planned to take Scram and Bell to the Kingston bus station to catch the bus back to Port Antonio.

"Mom and Dad," Alicia said to us as we were eating, "what would you think if I went back to Port Antonio with Scram. I could stay at the San San Tropez and I could meet you on Thursday when Scram comes to Mobay to do the talks (Jaime Delgado had arranged for us to do a series of talks at the Wyndham and Half Moon Bay Resorts). I'd be safe traveling with Scram and safe at the San San with everyone there. They're like family and always watch out for me. You guys are going to be running around Kingston the next three days and it's kind of a drag for me."

"That sounds good to me," Julia said. "I love the idea of you're traveling on the public bus system with your Rasta grandfathers. I think you'll have a lot of fun."

"Sounds like an adventure you'll remember your whole life," I concurred, "Much better than hanging around the pool at the Terra Nova. Let me call Fabio and arrange a room."

We took everyone back to the hotel so Alicia could pack and then dropped them off at the bus station. I was so proud of our daughter at that moment—standing on the curb with Scram and Bell, happily hugging us goodbye, ready to ride five hours on Jamaican public transportation and loving it. She had continued to grow into every new situation that our Jamaican adventure had placed her in since it began 16 months before. She had matured immensely, letting go of things that weren't important and understanding and incorporating things that were. She was relaxed with each new situation we placed her in, whether it was visiting the small, humble shop of a Rasta in the remote countryside of Jamaica, talking with a reggae star, or Bob Marley's 82 year-old mentor, Mortimo Planno, with whom she developed a special bond.

"The respect I had for Bob was more than just that of a wife. It was because of what I saw him doing for the world. And in himself not even knowing how powerful he was becoming."
—Rita Marley

Chapter 14
February 5, 2002

The Kingston Kids

The next morning, Julia and I woke up early and drove around the corner to appear on TV-J's "Smile, Jamaica," the top morning talk show hosted by Simon Crosskill and Neville Bell. This show reached hundreds of thousands of Jamaicans and I was excited about addressing the island directly. I would have 15 to 20 minutes, a long time for TV, so I didn't feel rushed in getting my message across. But I had no idea how the hosts would receive me. Would they be hostile? Mocking? Supportive?

Before going on, I was ushered into a waiting room where an attractive Jamaican woman calmly started to put on my makeup. As we talked, Julia and I were amazed to find out she was Denroy Morgan's daughter-in-law, Charis, married to his son Graham.

Neville and Simon, two attractive, well-dressed young Jamaican men with crisp English accents, greeted me warmly and I knew by their vibes this would go well. Neville began the show by reading from a copy of my speech that Angela, my PR person, had supplied him. For the first ten minutes, I explained our overall vision.

"You gotta get to some pretty tough people," Simon said as I finished my explanation.

"We know that," I said, "and we're not naive enough to believe everyone will join us. In the beginning, we'll get to the more open-hearted people and the others will come in later. We know that not every heart is ready to cherish this One Love. Will it be successful at a national level? We'll see. But for everyone joining us, it will be successful for them in their lives."

"Is this just some misplaced idealism?" Simon continued. His tone was questioning, not cynical. "Are we really capable of that sort of unselfishness as to go through our daily lives allowing people to do certain things and just turning the other cheek?"

"Only if you think Jesus was a misplaced idealist. One Love doesn't mean we don't have personal boundaries," I replied, glad to hear this question that I knew would be on the minds of many of their viewers. "One Love means you have those boundaries and you don't allow people to abuse you but in your heart you remember that they, too, are a child of God sent here by their Creator to teach love and they have temporarily gone astray, as we all are prone to do. Are humans ready for this? We better get ready. We need to move to love as quick as we can."

"Are you a Christian?" Neville asked.

"I'm a Christian. I'm a Jew. I'm a Rasta. I'm it all," I answered.

"Why did you choose Rasta to write about? Why Jamaica?" he continued.

"I didn't choose this, God chose me," I answered. "I just came here on a family vacation and got the inspiration to write a book on the Rasta expression of One Love and it grew from there. The press conference came about because we were looking for a way to encourage people not to just read the book but *be* the book as we were attempting to do."

"Are you at that stage where you find it easy to forgive and then you heal yourself quickly?" Simon asked sincerely.

"Yes," I answered, "but then when I'm attacked I have to go through my own process to find that equanimity again."

"What do you expect from people reading your book?" Neville asked.

"I don't care if everyone reads the book," I said. "I'm more interested in people hearing our message of forgiveness."

After the usual thanks, they followed with a beautiful Gospel song,

Gathering of the Healers

delivered by a local singer. Julia and I headed back to the hotel where I was scheduled to do a radio interview on a popular rush-hour talk show with Ronnie Thwaites. Ronnie was Scram's old friend that we saw at the prayer breakfast. He is also a Jamaican senator and has a popular radio show. Like the TV show, this interview went very well with Ronnie interested in determining if I really thought this was doable.

After the interview, I was scheduled to talk to several hundred Kingston high school musicians at an open-air amphitheatre near the Bob Marley Museum. I had been contacted by Marjorie Leyden-Vernon from the Jamaican Cultural Development Council (JCDC). She had been looking for speakers to talk to the students during Bob Marley's Birthday week and had gotten my name from Jaime Delgado. I had agreed to give a twenty-minute presentation. Marjorie had come by The Rockhouse with her two children for lunch when I was there a week earlier and I liked her very much—a real Rasta-hearted woman.

After some searching, Julia and I finally located the theater and was pleased to find Rita Marley there as she too was speaking to the students. She was with her daughter, Sharon Marley Prendergast, and two of Rita's friends, Sister Minnie (also called Nana) and Eleanor. We introduced ourselves and she said she knew of us and had heard that our press conference had been incredible. Also appearing with us was Michael Bennet, a Jamaican recording producer and Tony Laing, from Intellectual Property Service Centre, to discuss intellectual property rights.

We all chatted awhile before we went on. They all seemed as delighted to meet us as we were to meet them. Rita is an attractive, proud woman with a young girl quality about her that instantly endears you to her. She was dressed in a distinctive long African gown and turban, reflecting her new home, Ghana. We gave them all copies of our book and Rita invited us to a party later that night at the museum, which we instantly accepted.

Rita was born Alpherita Constantia Anderson. Her father, Leroy Anderson, was a carpenter and a musician. Her mother, Cynthia "Bada" Jarrett, was from Cuba, where Rita was born, staying there until the family moved to Jamaica when she was three months old. At eight, Rita

234

Gathering of the Healers

and her five brothers and four sisters were left to live with relatives so her parents could migrate to England. They were never reunited. Rita lived with her Aunt Viola until she met, and soon married, Bob.

Always hardworking, she was a nurse and Sunday school teacher before pursuing her musical career as a ska singer, singing with a group called the Soulettes. At 17, she had her first child, Sharon, and soon dropped out of high school. She met Bob as their musical paths crossed in Trench Town. They fell in love and married on February 10, 1966. The next day, Bob left to find work in the U.S., living with his mother, Mama B, in Wilmington, Delaware. Rita appeared on many of Bob's early recordings with the Wailers, and when the Wailers broke up in 1974, Rita became part of the female singing trio, the I Threes, along with Marcia Griffiths and Judy Mowat. Rita, Judy and Marcia recorded and toured with Bob during his solo career.

After Bob's death in 1981, Rita continued her singing career which included a solo hit "One Draw." Recently, her interests have been elsewhere including developing the careers of her children (Ziggy Marley and the Melody Makers, Rita and Bob's four children) and managing many Marley family enterprises, including the Bob Marley Foundation.

As I looked out at the eager faces of the teenagers I couldn't help but be struck by the irony of the scene. Only a few years before, and to some degree still, the Rastas were the pariahs of the Jamaican society. Now the government was paying to bus their "brightest and best" to hear from the wife of a Rasta and a man who had written a book on Rastafari. Times have definitely changed.

Rita spoke first, getting a rousing hand of applause from the crowd.

"Thank you. You all look like brothers and sisters to me," she began. "I greet you in the name of His Imperial Majesty Emperor Haile Selassie The First, the Lord of Lords, the Conquering Lion of the Tribe of Judah, The Elect of God Himself. And I greet you in the name of One Love because One Love represents us all. As Brother Bob says, 'One Love, One Heart. Let's get together and we'll be alright.' And remember Bob was not about being successful. He was about being heard. Bob was singing these words about our lives. Because Bob is for real and I would not say 'was' because Bob still 'is' and he always will be. We'll

Gathering of the Healers

always have Bob Marley like we always have music."

She chatted warmly with the teenagers, kidding them about their quiet singing of the National Anthem and seriously suggested they might have sung louder if they change the anthem to Bob's song "One Love," which drew more applause. She then invited everyone to sing "Happy Birthday" to Bob and to come by the museum that night for the party.

After Rita spoke, Sharon addressed the audience with words of guidance and encouragement. Attractive and sophisticated, Sharon, like most Marleys, is musically gifted, performing with the Melody Makers along with her siblings, Cedella, Ziggy and Stephen. She is also an actress, appearing, along with sister Cedella, and Denzel Washington in *The Mighty Quinn.*

I was next. My 20 minute talk went well, my best yet. I was becoming more comfortable talking in front of groups, especially about this subject. I have done a lot of public speaking in my life and for 10 years ran a school in the San Francisco Bay Area that taught people how to build and remodel their own homes where I taught adults four nights a week. However, in the last few years I had been living the life of a reclusive author so I was a little rusty.

"Although he came on a vacation," Marjorie said as I took my seat, "it was some divine destiny. It is a Rasta Heart he came and investigated and something happened somewhere out there. You know when we say we plant a seed and it starts to grow and it flourishes and you reap. I think we are reaping the benefits of what we have inherited in the life and work of Bob Marley," she finished and pointed to me.

When she finished, Marjorie asked for questions from the audience. The first question came from Justin Whyte, a reporter with the *Jamaica Observer.*

"Mr. Roskind, what I want to understand or what I am asking," he began, "is who do you represent and what do you hope to achieve from this project you have undertaken? And who will it benefit?"

"Good question," I replied. "The answer to that is I represent JAH, God, and no company or sponsor. Bob Marley once said, 'By and By JAH shows everyman his hand and JAH has shown I mine.' And God has shown I mine. I am just an ordinary person who has asked God to use him and his family. That has been the prayer for my family for years and I am amazed to be here. I've lived the life of a reclusive author. My books have been moderately well received. We came here to do a small launch and JAH had other things in mind. The concept is to begin an experiment to see if the human species has evolved enough to heal ourselves through One Love. Who will benefit? Everyone who agrees to join us and hopefully the country, and the world, as a whole. So the question is not will we heal Jamaica, but rather are you ready to join us and heal your own life and relationships? Did that answer your question?"

"Yes. But considering the magnitude of what you are doing," Justin continued, "I know that you got permission from the Marleys to write the book, are you in partnership with the government, the Minister of Culture? Do they know about this project?"

"They know about it," I said. "We don't accept any sponsorship. We're just individuals. We don't work with the government. We invited Prime Minister Patterson and Mr. Seaga to come and hear from their healers. They declined. We came here because the JCDC asked us to but we are not working for the government or any corporation. We want to stay outside of that."

"But let's clarify that we didn't get permission to write our book from anyone but God," Julia interjected from her seat on the front row.

After the JCDC meeting, Julia and I returned to the hotel for the afternoon. Basil Walters (Ras Bas) another reporter from *The Jamaica Observer*, joined us for lunch. He brought us a copy of the day's paper that included an excellent article he wrote on our press conference. The article was in the special Bob Marley Birthday section and was wrapped around a huge color layout of Bob with, "One Love—Jamaica's Message to the World" in large type. It was a very positive article that covered all the essentials. Though *The Daily Gleaner* would do another positive article the following Sunday by reporter Anthea McGibbon,

Gathering of the Healers

this was our first print coverage.

Before returning to The Bob Marley Museum for the party, I did another 15 minute interview on the radio with two popular talk show hosts, Cliff and Carol. Feeling rather expansive from the last few days events, I was talking with them enthusiastically about the beauty of the Jamaican culture and how some of the Rastas we met found joy without many material possessions.

"I have read some of your book," Carol said in a stern voice, "and frankly I see a lot of inaccuracies."

"I'm not sure what you're referring to," I answered. "There might be some inaccuracies in the scientific facts, like the rate of cancer in meat eaters versus vegetarians or something like that. I'm not a scientific researcher. I got those facts from other books."

"No. It's not that," she countered. "I think you have over romanticized the Rastas."

"Well, that's possible," I replied. "I have a tendency in that direction but all I can tell you is the people look and live like I described, I transcribed their words verbatim and my evaluation of the joy, clarity and health they seem to exhibit was my true feelings, so in that way it's not really inaccurate."

"Well, thank you for being on the show, Mr. Roskind," Carol said in a clipped tone and hung up. There was still five minutes left of the 15 minute interview.

After the interview, Julia and I headed over to spend some time with Mortimo, stopping to get him a few sacks of Ital groceries on the way.

"Mortimo," Julia said as we got up to leave after an hour of reasoning with him, "there is something in you that you must tell the world. Rastas here and everywhere need to know what you know."

"Yes, I," Mortimo answered with a knowing grin, taking Julia's hand gently in both of his and looking her directly in her eyes. "You have inspired me."

After visiting with Mortimo, we drove to the museum for the party. We were in great moods. At the museum there were a few hundred peo-

Gathering of the Healers

ple around, listening to singers (including Abijah), eating birthday cake, dancing, and otherwise having a good time celebrating Bob's life and their own. Jamaicans at all levels of society love a party.

As soon as we walked in Ras Witter was waiting to tell us that Rita wanted us to join her in a private building off to one side. The building, next to the Queen of Sheba restaurant, was small with comfortable pillows all over the floor and beautiful artwork all over the walls, including an amazing portrait of the Queen of Sheba painted by Djamalia, the artist that was at the press conference.

Rita was sitting on the floor with Sister Minnie. We were delighted as we had really liked Nana's vibes. Nana is a powerful articulate woman, who moves with grace and confidence. Tony Laing, who was on the panel with Rita and me, was also there along with 10 or so other people pleasantly lounging around the floor talking softly. We gently melded onto cushions by Nana and Rita and started to chat with them.

"I understand you and Rita are living in Ghana," I said to Nana as Rita got up to greet other friends. "Do you live in the city there?"

"No. We live in small villages," Nana answered. "Rita and I live in different villages. In my village there are maybe 10,000 people."

"Why Ghana?" I asked, amazed that such worldly women would choose a Third World country.

"Ghana is a wonderful place," she answered, enthusiastically. "The people there are wonderful. Let me tell you about this woman in my village. She is a local healer and what she does in Ghana is very normal there but if she ever came to the States she would be a millionaire. People come to her and tell her what is wrong with them or wrong with a loved one. Maybe they are physically sick or having emotional or mental problems. Then she goes out into the forest. I have been with her there. She sits and she meditates and prays about that person. Soon in the forest around her a few plants will start to visibly vibrate. Not everywhere like there was a breeze or something but just a few isolated plants. Then she gets up and picks leaves from those plants, thanks them and then she puts the leaves in a small bag with the person's name. They use them and get well. No one there considers this unusual or in any way out of the ordinary. Healers all over Ghana do this."

239

Gathering of the Healers

"That's incredible!" I said. "What is it like to be around people who are that tuned into the forces of nature that they can do that?"

"I'll tell you what it's like," Nana said, her eyes glowing with intensity. "You could never find it here. You have never seen queens and kings living in mud huts!"

"Now I understand why you live there," I said and we all laughed. "That means that when we are our true selves, living naturally, we are royalty, God's masterpieces, no matter what our social or financial level."

"Exactly! They know nothing about cars or a big 'ouse. Dey doan't know dos kinda t'ings," Nana said flipping into a little Patois, something most Jamaicans love to do. "In time, they know plenty. All they need to know is about the water an' the farmin'. And all they know is about de farm an' then dey grow plenty. In time if dey doan't get enough food dey want to know, 'What did we do wrong? Why dis time you doan't give us enough food.' But dere's always plenty of yams an' dey 'ave a yam festival an' there are yams everywhere. An' they perform the yam ceremony an' throw yams on de road and everyone gets up and jumps and shouts and the next dey in de marketplace dere are yams up to de roof. Ya 'ave a festival at de river an' dere is a priestess at de river that knows the spirit of de river. Dat river could 'ave a 'undred crocodiles an' snakes an' nobody dare go in dat river an' only dat priestess when she call on dat spirit, she crawl in dat river an' she swim wit' dos crocodiles an' dos snakes just like she's part of dem an' no one else dares get in dat river. This is what I want to bring to my people here."

"Her name is Mother," Nana continued, "and when you are with her you are in the Motherland, not the Fatherland, because you are not always sure of your father but always your mother. She is the kingmaker. She has more power than the king or chief."

"Nana, do the women there tell a creation story about Mother Earth?" Julia asked.

"I am she," Nana replied with confidence and calm.

"Yes. I know that to be true for me too," Julia replied. "When women tell each other their stories about being Earth Mother, we claim it for ourselves, too, because we are mothers walking upon this earth giving

240

Gathering of the Healers

birth to our children and multiplying the creation story, the continuum. She's living her story. Women know peace. They want their families to have peace. They don't know war."

"That's what makes women have children, not men," Djamalia added, joining our reasoning. "I'm glad you can see that the answer for a lot of things is for women to claim their power."

After awhile, we joined the festivities outside. Abijah had just finished singing. I chatted with him until his fans started to gather and we agreed to meet the next day at The Terra Nova. A group of Nyabinghi drummers were playing "Fly away Home to Zion" and everyone was moving rhythmically to the music. The night was warm and pleasant. The setting, Bob Marley's home, was perfect. The crowd—Rastas, women, children and tourists—was very mellow, very roots.

"You see there is no miracle greater than love. It is God's most precious gift to us. It is not a feeling. It is a daily decision."
—Abijah

Chapter 15
February 7, 2002

Abijah

The next morning Abijah joined us at the Terra Nova. We had not met him until the press conference and wanted to spend more time connecting with him. Accompanying him was a young Jamaican man who was teaching him to drive. Also, Dawn Sagely, an attractive Jamaican healer working with herbs, bio-radiant energy and bio-therapy, joined us with her Italian husband, Frank, and her 28-year-old son, Keno, who looked a lot like Bob Marley. They had lived in Italy until moving back to Jamaica, Dawn's homeland, five years earlier. She had contacted me after seeing me on TV-J and wanted to get together.

Abijah is in his late twenties, with a handsome, clean-shaven face surrounded by pencil-thick jet-black dreads hanging shoulder-length. Though physically young, he exudes the peace, wisdom and confidence of a very old soul. He has a constant pleasant smile on his face as if he's thinking, *This is some planet I landed on.* One critic writes that Abijah's music "is provocative and mysterious, lending an honest depiction of the ethos of the modern world."

Abijah, Hebrew for "My Father is Jehovah," was born Andrew Smith to Cynthia Wingo, a devout Christian, and Winston Smith, a devout Rastafarian, on June 9, 1972. His father was a drummer with the well-known reggae group the Mystic Revelation of Rastafari and from an early age Abijah hung around the group, often playing the drums. A

Gathering of the Healers

Michael Jackson fan, he began imitating the singer, rehearsing and choreographing his performance to imitate his hero. However, from a very early age he said he knew that he wanted to find "what God wanted him to do." By 6, he knew that was to sing His praises and bring unity to his native Jamaicans in part by bridging the gap between Christians and Rastas.

Since 1999, he has taken his homeland of Jamaica by storm, drawing large crowds entranced by his energetic stage presence and often capturing the show when appearing with other artists. He is starting to branch out, appearing on neighboring islands of Trinidad and Grand Cayman and at most Jamaican reggae concerts. He was heading for concerts in the U.S. and Japan later that year.

His popular single "Revelation" did well on the island and his first album by the same name was soon to be released. "Revelation," which talks about spiritual solutions for social problems, has been hailed as an "instant classic" by the *Jamaica Observer* which wrote, "if ever there was a list of singers that forces one to stop and listen, then Abijah would be high on that list. His 'Revelation' is on the lips of many a fan, and his spectacular stagemanship is captivating...Abijah is one of the bright sparks on the recording scene and given the confidence that he exudes, in time he will mature into his own inimitable self."

In a 2002 interview, Abijah explained his worldview: "The greatest gift a man could ever have and the biggest weapon is love and forgiveness. A man can come with 50 of the biggest guns, and the most money, but if he does not have love and forgiveness, he's not powerful yet."

Before converting to Christianity in 1994, Abijah was pursuing a career as a deejay but gave it up because it lacked a spiritual environment. "It was my personal decision," he recalls. "I gave it up because I knew it would hinder me."

Now married with a daughter and a son, he is a pillar in JamM, the Kingston church's ministry for artists and musicians. His goal is to use his music to reach a wide cross-section of the population and spread virtue and love among Jamaica's music industry. He hopes to affect many of the young artists and deejays who have veered into violence, sex and anger.

243

Gathering of the Healers

He struggles to keep his ever-growing success in perspective. "Sometimes a little ego gets in there," he says. "But whenever I feel it coming on I just pray, because that's the time when you have to get back in touch with yourself and remember that God is doing this thing and not you."

We settled back in comfortable chairs in a private conversation area in the lobby. It was a warm sunny morning and the hotel lobby was quiet and uncrowded—perfect for reasoning together.

"Am I late?" Abijah asked.

"Not by Jamaican time. That means you showed today," I said and everyone laughed.

"I was taking a driving lesson. You know, I never really trusted driving," he said, in a sweet, gentle English with a Patois lilt, "but now I must learn to drive because of my immediate family. It's scary out there," he said and we all laughed. Abijah is relaxed with himself and quickly puts people at ease.

"I find it scary when I'm *not* driving. Everyone in this country seems to have some sort of perverse death wish," I said. "Tell me, Abijah, what's your personal history? Were you born here?"

"Yeah, mon," he replied. "I was born here in Kingston. We were poor, very poor. I grew up in the ghetto. My father played with the Mystic Revelations. They've been all over the world. It's still going and getting bigger. So I grew up with reggae music, with Rasta music like Bob Marley. My mother was a Christian, a churchgoer, and my dad was a Rastaman but they lived together happily. There was the usual conflicts because, you know, men are from Mars and women are from Venus. But it is good. They're still together up to this day and that tells me with different religions, we can still live together."

"So God has assigned you to be a bridge between those two faiths," I ventured.

"Most definitely," Abijah replied. "I was inspired by my father's band to be a part of the whole thing but most of my relatives are musicians. My auntie, Constance Marley, is Bob Marley's sister. But with my dad and the Mystic Revelation, they did not get paid what they should have so I grew up in a struggle to survive. After leaving school at 17, I started my first job, working as a janitor at a pharmaceutical plant but my heart was in my music. That's where I met my manager, Albert Ramsay. He was the general manager there."

"I talked with him," I said. "He has a good heart. He instantly agreed that you would like what we were doing."

"Yes. He is a good man," he said. "When I worked at the plant, I used to say to him, 'Mr. Ramsay, good morning. How you doing?' Even though I was the janitor and he was the manager. Everybody feared him because he was the big guy but I would always tell him, 'I do music, you know,' and he would say, 'What type of music do you do?' And I would say, 'I'm a singer.' And he would say, 'I don't have any time now.' "

"Because everyone in Jamaica is a singer," I said and he laughed.

"Yeah. Everyone," he continued. "Until one day he came to one of my performances at a church. At that time I was impersonating Michael Jackson. It was a big Christmas concert and he was there. And the next day he said, 'I saw you on stage last night. You were good.' So I said, 'You wanna manage me?' I knew he didn't come from a musical background but I knew he was a man of integrity and a man who handles business very well. At the time I was probably saying it as a joke."

"How sure were you that you had what it takes to break out?" I asked.

"I was very positive," he answered, "if I got the right breaks. At the time there was a lot of competition. And I kept pushing on Mr. Ramsay to quit his job and manage me."

"How long after he saw you did he agree to quit and manage you?" I asked.

"Well, now, it was two years after he saw me sing," Abijah answered. "He started to get some advice from friends, from his wife's brother. After awhile the company closed down and he would come to the church from time to time. He said he wanted to have a meeting with me. By then we had become very close as friends. The manager and janitor thing had broken down. But I always see people as equal anyway. He finally decided to go into the entertainment business and do a number of things. So I was like a guinea pig. I was bald-headed at the time, three or four years ago. Then I went to music school to learn the guitar but always I was writing my own music. Since I was a young kid, I was always writing music. But still I had to keep working after he started to manage me."

"So you didn't quit your day job?" I said kiddingly.

"No. I didn't quit yet," he answered, "but then things started to happen very fast. After one month at the guitar school the teacher called Mr. Ramsay and said that I had learned everything that there was to learn. I would get one class for one hour a day and I would practice the whole rest of the day. So in one month I practically mastered the teacher's level of playing. He had me demonstrate to the whole school. Which to me was shocking because I thought that everybody did that, you know? And that made Mr. Ramsay have more confidence. From then we started to record. The first song that I recorded went right to the top."

"When was this?" I asked.

"That was two years ago when I recorded 'Revelation.' It went on the charts for several months and is still there to this day."

"What did that mean to you to have a hit here in Jamaica?" I asked. "Did that mean you could quit your job?"

"Not at first. I was making ice cream and people at work would kid me because they would hear me at a concert and see me at work the next day. But I quit two years ago because I started to earn a little better," Abijah replied. "Still then we had to take my music to the radio stations. Some would play it; some wouldn't. But then they started playing it more and more because people starting listening to the lyrics. But also I quit because I wanted to spend more time with my family. I wanted to balance. But when I quit, it was still a risk. So I quit with the faith that this would work. It has been good."

"Is Albert working with you full time?" I asked.

"No. Not now but I know one day he will," he said laughing. "Now I am popular with the younger generation. The other day I was at the JCDC meeting (shortly after my talk there) with the high school kids and I had to run to my car. They all chased me like I was the Beatles. That was very special. Another thing happened to me that was special was when my daughter, Azziza, was born. I believe she is blessed. She was claimed to be the 'six billionth baby' in the world on the UN

Gathering of the Healers

Population Day."

"So that happened two years ago about the same time your career started to take off," I said.

"Yes. And that helped me," he said, "because people worldwide wanted to know who was the father of this child. It was on CNN, ABC, everything. The Prime Minister sent us congratulations. They were looking for a boy and a girl. The boy was born in Africa and the girl was born in Jamaica and it was mine. Her education is paid up all the way through college. To me that's a blessing—a touch from the Almighty Himself. She was born in a very poor hospital here and when she was born, I got a phone call because they don't let the father in, only the mother. I mean, of course, the mother," and we all laughed.

"So I was at home waiting for the call," he continued, "and the doctor called and said 'Come down with your family and your camera right away.' So I thought that he was just excited that everything was OK. And I asked him was it a boy or a girl and he wouldn't tell me. So I went to the hospital and there was a large crowd and I asked somebody why there was a crowd and they said the six billionth baby was just born. And I said, 'That's cool. Who was it?' And then the nurses said, 'There's the dad,' and pointing at me. And then the media people started taking pictures and moving me through the place. And then I reach up to the room and saw the baby. Everybody was there. They had the Minister of Education, some members of Parliament, some media people. And my wife was just freaking out but freaking out in a good way. I was like numb. When I reached back home, the phone was ringing. And even now if something is happening with the government we might get invited. I would love for her to meet the boy."

"Maybe they'll get married in about twenty years," I said.

"Away from that another special thing happened to me," he said. "The other day the Jamaican Tourist Board wanted somebody to sing 'One Love' for their new One Love commercial and I was called to be part of the audition. Everyone was there, famous and infamous. Mostly younger singers in my age group. But they wanted someone just to do the song and they wanted to get an actor to do the rest. And I got the job for the singing *and* for the acting and this is going out worldwide."

Gathering of the Healers

"Did you shoot that commercial at The Rockhouse in Negril a few weeks ago?" I asked.

"Yes. That is where we shot it," Abijah answered.

"That's kind of amazing. I was staying there then. You guys were filming right outside my cottage."

"Yes. That was me. Incredible," he said. "Let me say that what you are doing now is very strange to the world, strange to Jamaica. You have started out on a good foot but it can get rough because it can hurt people that want to fight that love down because what you are doing is bridging the gap—bridging the gap between white and black, with love, which they don't like. Africans don't like it and white people don't like it."

"Some don't but not all," I said. "We thought we would encounter a lot more of that negativity than we have. I've encountered a lot of resistance and people's cynicism and skepticism but I've encountered none of the anger I thought I'd get."

"Yes. Some don't like it," he said. "And really and truly each person should stop and look within their selves and see just what it is they can change to bring us together."

"Abijah, I'm glad your name came up," I said. "When I contacted Albert he told me that you were not a Rasta and I told him this wasn't about Rasta. This was about One Love, which to me was the same."

"It is not everybody that understands about this," he replied. "There are different levels in the spiritual world. This Rasta thing and this Christian thing, I try to bridge the gap. A lot of time I get in trouble from the Christians and from the Rastas. The Christians say, 'Abijah, you're going to go to hell!' And I just say, 'OK. Thank You.' And to the youths, I'm not just a singer. I'm a leader to them. I do a lot of interviews and I tell them these things even if it steps on a lot of people's toes. And it doesn't matter to me if you're black, white, Chinese or whatever. It's what you do that's important. I studied the Rasta movement because I wanted to know more and I learned that Emperor Selassie was a follower of Jesus. You can't tell some Rastas that. I believe JAH, the Almighty, can use anyone of us and He can use Selassie, which He did. He used Bob Marley, too. We are instruments—tools—every one of us, but we must be careful not to use our power for our own selfish needs. So I see Selassie as my brother, not my God."

"That was our conclusion in our book, too," Julia said. "We are really not promoting the Rasta thing but the One Love thing. That's something everyone can agree on. If you veer at all from that, you get arguments."

By now it was mid-day and Abijah had to head out and Julia and I needed to drive to Mobay where we were meeting Scram and Alicia. Scram and I were booked to do a presentation that night at the Wyndham Rose Hotel. Abijah walked out to our car and I gave him a copy of *Rasta Heart*.

"I will cherish this book my whole life," he said. This is a very fine human being.

We drove four hours across the island and met Scram and Alicia at the Richmond Hill Hotel, a quaint hotel with a beautiful view from the pool and restaurant of Mobay and its harbor. We arrived late that afternoon and Julia, Scram and I ate by the pool while Alicia swam. Alicia was excited about her travels with Scram and Bell on the public bus system, reporting that she had a great time. She said one time while Scram and Bell were sleeping, a guy came up to talk to her and Scram slowly opened one eye and waving a warning finger at the guy, said, "Our princess" and the guy instantly retreated.

"Yesterday I did an interview with your friend Ronnie Thwaites," I said to Scram as we ate. "He said that it often takes someone from outside the culture to appreciate certain aspects of it, like Rastafari. We've been trying to make it clear in our interviews that we are not about just Rasta but One Love. Let's be sure we do that tonight."

"If dey are gonna distinguish dis love an' call it Rasta love," Scram added, "I doan't see why we cayn't say, 'Yes.' Becuz from de day dat Rastafari originate on dis island dey give dere howdy-do in 'One Love.' Like when dey meet you early in de mornin', de first t'ing dey gonna hail to you, dey say 'One Love, mon.' An' people ignore dem. Dese

Gathering of the Healers

guys dat interview you know dat. Dey knew dat Rastafari get awful treatment fe bringin' dis One Love into a standard. So right now Rastafari just want to show dem an' tell dem an' give dem de vibes. An' wit'out love, it cayn't work. Becuz people try to live wit'out love. Dey live a way dat doan't let de small people deal wit' de happiness of life becuz dey doan't want to deal wit' love de way it supposed to. Dis One Love supposed to go from dis island."

"I think the fact that we had many Rastas at the press conference," I said, "and that we had it at Bob Marley's home and we wrote a book called *Rasta Heart* acknowledges Rastafari's place in all this but I'm really trying to be sure that people see this isn't primarily about Rasta but about One Love."

"Yes. Dat is so," Scram agreed, "but when dey say 'Rasta love,' me feel glad, you know. An' when dey ask, 'How come you believe dat Rasta love is enuf to bring de island to a standstill?' I cayn say, 'Yes, mon. It is.' Becuz love doan't 'ave no wrinkles. An' we make it real. Everyone must make it right wit' de Creator. An' we are just passin' it on becuz I doan't want anyt'ing 'pon my shoulders," he said and we all laughed.

"We are doin' what JAH sent us to do," he continued. "An' you all de way from de States, so far away, an' you bring dis news, dey should run and grab it up."

"But we have to give everyone time," Julia added. "We're asking them to get it real quick. We're probably causing some discomfort because this is a new thought system to many. They may resist it but when they sense our happiness, they will want to join us. It will be a gradual thing. Nothing happens quick in Jamaica. This will be more like a groundswell than a tsunami wave."

"You know after doing these TV and radio shows," I said, "I can tell these interviewers are giving us minimal resistance. They seem to be treating us respectfully, not as naive idealists or opportunists. We haven't gotten the resistance I expected."

"Well, now," Scram said. "Doan't you feel any way down becuz I am 'ere to comfort you. I know you will reach to a stage dat you t'ink dese people are so stiff-headed, you just want to turn back. You know, people were talkin' 'bout what you say on Ronnie's show on de bus dis morning. Dis woman was talkin' about dis One Love. An' if you say somet'ing stupid, everybody call up an' say somet'ing but nobody called after you talked on 'is show. An' after you were on TV de ot'er day and de commercial was over, an dos two guys came back on, dey we're arguing over who would get de book. One guy say, 'Dere only one book 'ere. I t'ink I need to read it first.' An' de o'ter guy say 'e need to read it first," and we all laughed.

"An' when dey ask 'ow are we goin' to do dis," he continued, "you cayn say dat you are relying on people on de island dat know what love is to finish de job. Dat is why I said at de conference dat we are all witness to dis an' we all must meditate alike on dis One Love. An' we know 'ow to make it real becuz I know my heart is smooth about ev'ryt'ing. Becuz I looked in myself fe anyone I had to forgive an' I did dat to clean up myself to do de work. So dem dat know love, it is dere duty to pass it on. An' even though it may not look like your eyes want it to look, our message is gettin' into de heart of de people."

"This is a time to be feeling great fullness," Julia said, "The drumbeat got out there in a very powerful way. I want to bring the Jamaican women into this because they're the strongest peacemakers. The war between men and women, that's the major war, and when you settle that you really will have peace on earth."

"That would be good to link the man-woman thing and the black-white problem with the 'Fires of Forgiveness,' " I said, picking up on Julia's train of thinking, "because that would allow the women to forgive men for millenniums of male dominance and disrespect."

"Though our group is small," Scram said, "it's gwan make a big change becuz you see right now we're workin' on de heart of de people an' we're workin' spiritually. We're working on de hearts of de wrongdoers an' dere minds. If de rest of de people let it stay in dere hearts like we 'ave it, it change in no time."

Months later, in early April, when I was back home writing this book, I got a sort of confirmation for this concept when I got the following e-mail from someone on my broadcast e-mail list:

Gathering of the Healers

"Dear Mr. & Mrs. Roskind,

I have just read your letter dated April 1st, 2002 in the *Jamaican Observer* about the upcoming "Fires of Forgiveness" ceremony. The image you described of Jamaica's shining light of forgiveness being picked up by a satellite, reminded me of an experience I had many years ago in Jamaica. For what its worth, I feel moved to share it with you.

In 1979, a great personality (guru) from India visited Jamaica. His name was Prabhat R. Sarkar also known as Shrii Shrii Anandamurti. I had just started at UWI when I saw his photo in the *Gleaner* announcing his visit. I never had enough interest to find out who he was or why he was there. However, in 1985 soon after I was introduced to yoga and meditation, I went to India. My guru was Shrii Shrii Anandamurti. At that time, I had the interest to ask why he had come to Jamaica.

I was told that he was in Europe on his one and only European tour and he asked to go to Jamaica. Those closest to him argued against this decision saying that Jamaica had nothing to offer the world and it would be better for all if he went to the USA where long lasting links and relationships could be established. Shrii Shrii Anandamurti insisted on going to Jamaica. He said to the organizers at the time (my paraphrasing) 'You cannot see into the future but I can. Now communism is apparently strong but in 10 years time there will be no Berlin Wall and communism as we know it today will be dead. After the collapse of the communist economy, the capitalist economy will begin to unravel and for a while the world will be in total chaos. In the darkest moment people will come to Jamaica for spiritual upliftment. Jamaica will be like a shining light for the world.'

Jamaica was the only country he visited this side of the Atlantic. Over the years I have wondered when will

Gathering of the Healers

this great light begin to appear. Lately, I have come to realize that it has already been turned on by individual selfless acts and events such as yours (Tall Ship & Fires of Forgiveness) help intensify the glow.

Sincere wishes, Jonathan Burke"

By now it was time for Scram and I to head over to the Wyndham. Jaime Delgado, who had set up the presentation, met us there where he had a conference room set up for our talk followed by a film on Bob Marley. Signs had been put out around the hotel inviting people to our free presentation. However, by show time there were only three people in the meeting room. Scram reminded me that the numbers didn't matter, that each person was important. We all chatted for awhile and then everyone left except for one guy, PJ, from England. It turned out that he manages 60 people for Thomas Cook, the worldwide travel agency, and he really got excited about what we were doing. We also got a chance to explain to him that outside the Kingston ghettos, Jamaica was safe for tourists, a fact he said he would pass on to his agents.

The next day, I were scheduled to do three talks at Jaime's store located in the shopping plaza at the Half Moon Bay Resort. The store, which sells Marley paraphernalia, clothing, CDs, videos and DVDs, is a labor of love for Jaime and his wife, Camilla. Julia, Alicia, Scram and I all ate at Marguaritaville on the strip in Mobay, dropped Alicia off down the street at the private Doctor's Cave Beach and arrived early at Jaime's so that Scram and I could do an hour interview on ROOTZ-FM, the radio station that broadcasts into the ghetto areas of Kingston.

After our talks at the Bob Marley Experience, we wandered over to the jazz festival going on next door at the Wyndham. A lot of the national and international press was there so we gave them all a copy of *Rasta Heart*. Once again, I ran into Tony Laing, who had been on the panel with me in Kingston. After leaving the Wyndham, we took Scram to the bus station to catch a bus back to Port Antonio.

"You know, Monday night was almost like a dream," I said as we

Gathering of the Healers

drove to the station, "Like a moment in time that stands out from all others. The energy just kept building. Each speaker was so good but so different. You weren't hearing the same thing being repeated. Everyone had a different slant but when you put it all together, it was a complete picture of One Love. Scram, you looked at love from the point of view of the poor and oppressed. Luciano looked at love from the point of social justice. Dennis looked at it from an herbal and personal view. Antonnette from a political view and Abijah from individual action. And Denroy finished with a Biblical view."

"I will 'ave to live dis love life like your family," Scram said, "so dat you cayn prove somet'ing out of me. Dat is my way of tellin' you t'anks fe our movement an' 'ow you come to my place an' sit down an' go into dat depth wit' me an' dat we cayn explain certain t'ings an' reason to dis level. I am very much grateful. Any t'ing 'appen to you or to Miss Julie or Miss Alicia, anywhere on earth, an' you need my assistance, I pray dat I will be in the position to reach to your assistance. Call me an' I'll be dere."

"And you would be the first person that we would call," I said, moved by his affection.

"Yes. I would even come to plant flowers around your river an' feed de fish," he said. We had told Scram how we had rescued a huge trout that was dying in a lake that was being drained nearby and put him in the pond behind our house.

"What is dat fish's name?" Scram asked.

"We call him Sam," Julia answered.

"You must change dat fish's name," Scram said. "Becuz I am like dat fish an' you pulled me out of my hole. You must call dat fish not Sam but Scram," he said and we all cracked up laughing.

Saying goodbye was easy for us. We knew we would be together again soon. By now, we had become used to flowing in and out of each others lives, lives that were so incredibly different yet so much the same. The last two months had been an amazing chapter in our lives and we would be returning in three more months for the next, the "Fires Of Forgiveness," which promised to be as amazing if not more. We all hugged at the bus terminal and once again went separate ways.

Gathering of the Healers

We had our last Jamaican dinner at The Native, an open-air restaurant on the strip overlooking the water. The food and ambiance was excellent and we had a great talk with the waiter who was very interested in what we were doing. After dinner, we dropped Alicia nearby at the Wexford hotel, where she was getting together with a twenty-something couple for the evening on the strip. She had met them several days earlier at Doctor's Cave Beach and, as she is so likely to do with perfect "strangers," had made quick and lasting friendships.

As Julia and I returned back to the hotel, driving bumper-to-bumper through the downtown area still packed at this late hour with the usual Saturday night crowd, I saw something that almost brought me to tears. Two young girls, maybe seven or eight years old, in their clean school uniforms and wearing small backpacks, hailed a small taxi and climbed in with several other adult passengers. It was a common Jamaican scene, played out everyday on an island where few people owned cars and young children often took taxis alone and almost always without incidence. In the U.S., you could be prosecuted for child endangerment for allowing your child to do that. Seeing those two vulnerable children climb into that cab, laughingly assisted by the passengers and the driver, reminded me how truly loving and decent most Jamaicans are and how glad I was that we had been chosen in some way to bring this singular fact the world's attention.

The next morning we all packed to catch our mid-day flight back to North Carolina and the predictable, somewhat reclusive (at least for Julia and I) life we knew and loved so well. Before checking out of our hotel, we tried to reach everyone to thank them all for speaking. We were only able to reach Denroy and Mortimo and left messages on everyone else's machines.

"Denroy, thanks for joining us," Julia said, "What happened that night was very powerful." .

"JAH Rastafari!" he replied strongly. "I want to put Hyacinth and Taliba on so you can tell that to them." Before handing the phone to me,

255

Gathering of the Healers

Julia talked briefly with them, a real heart connection between these three noble women.

"Denroy, thanks again, " I said, "and thanks for insisting I find Mortimo." I had really come to love this man.

"What happened that night was very mystical," Denroy said, enthusiastically. "It is blessed by JAH. You must get me tapes of the conference and copies of the pictures. I will be on tour this summer when you do the "Fires of Forgiveness" but if I can I will fly back to light the fire in Port Antonio that night in June. Anything I can do to help, I will do."

"Mortimo, I want to say goodbye and I love you," Alicia said after Julia and I had talked with him.

"I receive your love, my child. JAH Rastafari!" Mortimo said, his voicing cracking with emotion.

As we headed to the airport we bought a copy of the *Gleaner* from a street vendor. In it was a large article by Anthea McGibbon on our press conference complete with a picture of Luciano playing his guitar, with me in the background. "American Author Promotes the *"Rasta Heart"* for Jamaica's Healing," the headline read. The article went on as follows:

> At a recent press conference at the Bob Marley Museum, Bob Marley was promoted as a "21st century wise man... describing the essence of Rastafari in a holistic way".
>
> The press conference was held to launch the book *Rasta Heart: A Journey Into One Love*, written by organizer Robert Roskind, author from the United States.
>
> A former hippie, Mr. Roskind has written 10 books including *In the Spirit of Business* and *In the Spirit of Marriage*. He has founded 'Do It Yourself Inc.' which produced the award-winning, record-breaking television series, the 'Do It Yourself Show' which aired in the U.S. on PBS, USA Network and The Learning Channel. He is also founder of Y2K Solutions Group Inc.
>
> In October 2000, Mr. Roskind and his family first vis-

256

Gathering of the Healers

ited Jamaica and were impressed by the "kindness, dignity and calm of the Rastafarians" they met in Ocho Rios. More inspiring were the words of Bob Marley, who for the author is as clear and as divinely-sent a teacher of love and in the league as other world-renowned leaders like Mahatma Gandhi, Kofi Annan, Nelson Mandela, Bishop Desmond Tutu and others. As a result, the book was written to, "highlight the wisdom of the Rastas, Bob Marley and Jamaica." The launch was aimed at identifying whether "humanity (Jamaica) is evolved to a point where Jamaica can heal itself with love".

The conference, "Gathering of the Healer: The Healing of the Nation" was an effort to start an island-wide campaign "One Love, Make It Happen" in Jamaica. For the occasion (God-chosen) healers, according to Mr. Roskind, were invited to speak.

Referring to First Corinthians 13, Mr. Roskind brought to the fore his interpretation of love and forgiveness. The meaning of Rastafari is love, he said while forgiveness is "not pardoning", rather it, "is understanding that every so-called attack is an appeal for healing, help and love, no matter what form the attack takes." With great fervor Mr. Roskind pointed to Rastafarian culture as a good ideal to healing the nation.

Thomas "Ramscram" Anderson said that the book could be used to "teach heads of Government to deal with the lower class of people in a proper way."

Singer Luciano reiterated the "need to forgive to allow the power of God's love to flow." His focus was on the need of the nation to realize where individually we have done wrongs as he added that there "can be no love without justice." Identifying stubbornness as the main block to forgiveness, he further noted that many Jamaicans "had amnesia."

The book which also comprises photographs, reflects

257

Gathering of the Healers

the extensive research by the Roskind family with help from friends such as Mr. Anderson. The team made visits mainly to sections of the island populated by the Maroons.

Dr. Dennis Forsythe, who claimed to have been healed in mind, body and soul (a mental decolonization) has hailed the book as "riveting... the incredible adventure that reveals the true essence of the Rasta!" At the conference he supported Mr. Roskind with "Life involves a movement to a high level.. to the seventh level of consciousness." That consciousness being "one love."

As the "One Love, Make It happen" campaign kicks off, another meeting entitled "The Fires of Forgiveness: The Healing of the Nations" is being slated with island-wide bonfires being planned.

The paper also included other articles on Abijah, Luciano, Morgan Heritage and Antonnette, complete with a picture of Horace from the UPP.

We still had a little time before our flight and one book left to give away, so we headed back to the Wyndham and left the signed copy for singer Harry Bellefonte, who was appearing later that day. Two of his songs are quoted in Chapter One of *Rasta Heart*, sung by Verley Valentine, our raft captain on our Rio Grande River trip where I first got the inspiration to write the book. It seemed like a fitting thing to do before leaving the island ,

Epilogue

September 11, 2002

In the first nine months after "The Gathering of the Healers" press conference, the murder rate, which had been climbing for 14 straight months and was predicted to increase as the country entered its volatile election period, decreased 14% (682 murders as of September 16, 2002 compared to 780 for the same period in 2001.)

On June 12, 2002 Prime Minister Patterson and Opposition Leader Edward Seaga appeared together publicly and signed a "Code of Conduct." The code pledged their parties to a rejection of violence and intimidation as political strategies and, at the same time, formally endorsed a policy committing them to new initiatives to combat crime. Prime Minister Patterson told his country, "We want peace. I want to leave a legacy of the most peaceful and democratic elections that have ever been conducted in the history of Jamaica." On October 16, 2002, Patterson was re-elected. The election, predicted by many to be the most violent since the bloody 1980 elections, was the most peaceful in two decades.

The "Fires of Forgiveness: The Healing of the Nations" ceremony was held in Port Antonio on June 14, 2002 but that's another story and another book (due out in 2003). After "The Gathering of the Healers" and "The Fires of Forgiveness," it became clear to both Julia and I that our role had been to offer Jamaicans a new vision of themselves, individually and as a nation, and to bring together some of their best-known healers to embrace and to publicly put forward this vision.

We plan to return to the island to launch this book with another "Gathering of the Healers" again during Bob Marley's birthday week in 2003. This event will be held at the University of the West Indies in Kingston and the theme will be "One Love--Big Up The Youths," as it is now evident to us that our message is best received by young people.

259

Gathering of the Healers

We also plan to spend a few weeks before this event traveling the island talking to colleges and high schools and giving a copy of this book, along with a cassette of the press conference, to business, social, religious and political leaders islandwide. We are also working with the elders of the Havasupai and Hopi Native American Indian tribes toward a possible "Gathering of the Healers" in the U.S. sometime in the future. Who better to lead the United States into forgiveness than the oldest and most peaceful Native tribes?

Note to our readers

Please consider passing this book on to others. It will make a bigger difference in circulation than on a shelf.

Jamaica
By Alicia Roskind

I don't know why it moves me so
In a way I'll never know
Jamaica has it's luscious mountains
And it's natural water fountains
With it's pearly waters too
The sand sticks to you like glue
The people are kind in so many ways
from the Blue Mountains to the sparkling bays
My parents have put on so many events
And the country hasn't been the same since
My favorite place I need not choose
Anywhere, I could not loose
If I had never known the many glories that Jamaica has shown
I would have been a different person
But things would be much worse then
The people there don't give you much space
Oh but how I love this special place

CONTACT INFO:

PEOPLE:

UNITED STATES:
ROBERT & JULIA ROSKIND
P.O. Box 2142
Blowing Rock, NC 28605
(828) 295-4610 Fax: (828) 295-6901
E-mail: onelovepress@hotmail.com
Website: www.onelovepress.com

JAMAICA:
SCRAM (Thomas Anderson)
9 Nuttall Road
Port Antonio, Jamaica
(876) 424-2109

BONGO ROACH (Joseph Roach)
Darliston
Westmoreland, Jamaica

RED (Maurice Lynch)
(876) 852-2395
Negril Post Office
Westmoreland
Negril, Jamaica

Hotels:

Roundhill Hotel and Villas

PO Box 64, Montego Bay, Jamaica, West Indies
Reservations & Information: (800) 972-2159
Tel (876) 956-7050, Fax (876)956-7505
e-mail: roundhill@cwjamaica.com
Website: www.roundhilljamaica.com

Fern Hill Club Hotel

PO Box 100
Port Antonio, Jamaica, West Indies
Phone: (876) 993-7531-2
Fax: (876) 993-7373
e-mail: info@fernhillclubhotel.com
Website: www.fernhillclubhotel.com

Frenchman's Cove

P.O. Box 101
Port Antonio, Jamaica
(876) 993-7270
Fax: (876) 993-8211
e-mail: cdegagne@istar.ca
Website: www.frenchmanscove.com

The Rockhouse

West End Road
Negril, Jamaica
(876) 957-4373
Fax: (876) 957-0557
e-mail: info@rockhousehotel.com
Website: www.rockhousehotel.com

San San Tropez

San San Bay P.O.
Portland, Jamaica
(876) 993-7213/7713

Fax: (876) 993-7399
e-mail: info@sansantropez
Website: www.sansantropez.com

Jackie's On The Reef
(718) 469-2785
jackiesonthereef@rcn.com

Terra Nova Hotel
17 Waterloo Road
Kingston 10, Jamaica
Telephone: (876) 926-2211/9334
Fax: (876) 929-4933
E-mail: terranova@cwjamaica.com

Richmond Hill Inn
PO Box 362 Montego Bay, Jamaica
(876) 952-3859
E-mail infor@richmond-hill-inn.com
Website: www.richmond-hill-inn.com

CAR RENTALS, ATTRACTIONS, ETC.:

THE BOB MARLEY MUSEUM
56 Hope Road
Kingston
(876) 927-9152 Fax: (876) 978-2991

THE BOB MARLEY EXPERIENCE
Half Moon Bay Shopping's Drive
Montego Bay, Jamaica
(876) 953-3946
FAX: (876) 953-9725
E-mail: jdelgado@infochan.com
Website: www.bobmarleyexperience.com

CHALIS CAR RENTALS
Shop 9c
32 Queen's Drive
White Sands P.O.
Montego Bay, Jamaica
(876) 952-9361
FAX: (876) 952-3793
E-mail: chaliscarrental@yahoo.com

TAXI: MICHAEL
(He lives in Port Antonio but will take you there from Mobay reasonably and dependably.) (876) 361-5546

REACH FALLS
(876) 993-6138
(Check out Renny's craft stall.)

THE ORIGINAL MAYFIELD FALLS
(876) 957-3075 (Negril)
(876) 952-6634 (MoBay)
FAX: (876) 957-3075
E-mail: mayfieldfalls@caribbeannet.com
(Ask for Ras Thomas as a guide.)

CHUKKA-BLUE ADVENTURE TOURS
Blue Hole, Sandy Bay
Hanover, Jamaica WI
(876) 817-3624
E-mail:chukkacove@infochan.com
Website: www.chukkacove.com
(Reliable tour company in Montego Bay and Negril)

RIO GRANDE RIVER TOURS
(876) 913-5434 / 993-5778
FAX: (876) 993-5290

TO ORDER BOOKS

For Credit Card Orders:

visit us at www.onelovepress.com

For Money orders and check:

Send $14.95 per book (for 10 or more books for gifting (not resale):
$5.00/each) plus
$4.95 S&H for 1st book/$1.00 ea. additional book
(International $9.00 S&H 1st book/$3.00 ea. add. book)
Make Checks to: **One Love Press**

For Wholesale Orders:

(828) 295-4610
e-mail: onelovepress@hotmail.com

One Love Press

P.O. Box 2142
Blowing Rock, NC 28605
(828) 295-4610 FAX: (828) 295-6901
e-mail: onelovepress@hotmail.com
Website: www.onelovepress.com

BIOGRAPHY

Robert and Julia Roskind are writers, speakers and the event organizers of **"The Gathering of the Healers: The Healing of the Nation"** and **"The Fires of Forgiveness: The Healing of the Nations."** Their books include *Rasta Heart: A Journey into One Love*, *In The Spirit of Business* and *In the Spirit of Marriage*, all teaching unconditional love. They have produced a record-breaking PBS series, as well as shows for The Learning Channel and USA Network. They live in Blowing Rock, North Carolina with their daughter, Alicia, and their dog, Latte.